"Vitally important."
—David Brooks

"Brad Wilcox is an indispensable asset to those who still believe in traditional virtue. His data on marriage is invaluable; his analysis clear and incisive. This book is a godsend."
—Ben Shapiro

"Finally, a book from academia that tells the truth about the value of marriage. Based on sound research and real-life examples, Brad Wilcox calls for a return to the fundamental building block of a healthy society. I wish every adult in America could read this book."
—Gary Chapman, author of *The Five Love Languages*

"*Get Married* is a compelling read from the first page, showing that marriage, far from the happiness killer the media-verse makes it out to be, is instead consistently and solidly linked to more happiness and better mental health. With marriage and fertility rates falling, there has never been a better time for a convincingly comprehensive yet still eminently readable book like *Get Married*."
—Jean M. Twenge, author of *Generations*

"It's rare that someone offers a simple formula to improve happiness, health, and prosperity, but Brad Wilcox masterfully does just that in *Get Married*. Read this book and share its truths with the people you love."
—Arthur C. Brooks, professor at Harvard University and number one *New York Times* bestselling co-author of *Build the Life You Want*

"Impressive in its scope and staggering in its implications, *Get Married* gives us a new vista from which to view society's ills and, more importantly, how to cure them."
—Drs. Les and Leslie Parrott, number one *New York Times* bestselling authors of *Saving Your Marriage Before It Starts*

"Brad Wilcox is one of the most important public intellectuals in the world today. He also tells the truth, and he does so brilliantly in *Get Married*."
—R. Albert Mohler Jr., president of the Southern Baptist Theological Seminary

"Sociologist Brad Wilcox has devoted an illustrious scholarly career to the study, and defense, of the institution of marriage in America. This impressive, passionate, and persuasive book is the fruit of that labor. It has arrived not a moment too soon, for the stakes are high and the hour is late."

— Glenn Loury, professor of economics at Brown University and Paulson Senior Fellow at the Manhattan Institute

"As Americans increasingly prioritize lifestyle choices that keep them from being 'tied down,' Brad shows how marriage still provides security and happiness for couples and children—and society as a whole—like nothing else can. *Get Married* is a timely exhortation to keep defending this indispensable institution."

— Dr. Greg and Erin Smalley, co-authors of *Reconnected*

"*Get Married* is vital reading for anyone who seeks to understand why our social fabric is decaying—and for anyone who seeks to break the cycle of decline."

— Marco Rubio, United States senator and bestselling author of *Decades of Decadence*

"*Get Married* provides the best presentation of the Conservative approach to strengthening families. It's a valuable read, even for liberals who may disagree with it."

— Andrew Cherlin, sociologist at Johns Hopkins University and author of *The Marriage-Go-Round*

"I have never been convinced by those who argue that marriage is a private matter, something in which neither the civil authorities nor the community at large should interfere, but I have never quite known how to articulate this in the public square. Now I do, because in this book, Brad Wilcox both lays out the philosophical importance of marriage to a healthy society and provides the data to support his claims. This is a wonderful treatment of what marriage is and what attitudes and practices characterize healthy ones, all grounded in actual social realities. Highly recommended for anyone who believes in the importance of marriage but wants these convictions rooted in more than subjective personal intuitions."

— Carl R. Trueman, author of *The Rise and Triumph of the Modern Self* and professor of biblical and religious studies at Grove City College

GET
MARRIED

ALSO BY BRAD WILCOX

Soul Mates: Religion, Sex, Love, and Marriage among African Americans and Latinos

Soft Patriarchs, New Men: How Christianity Shapes Fathers and Husbands

GET
MARRIED

WHY AMERICANS MUST DEFY
THE ELITES, FORGE STRONG FAMILIES,
AND SAVE CIVILIZATION

BRAD WILCOX

BROADSIDE BOOKS

HarperCollins books may be purchased for educational, business, or sales promotional use. For information, please email the Special Markets Department at SPsales@harpercollins.com.

Broadside Books™ and the Broadside logo are trademarks of HarperCollins Publishers.

FIRST EDITION

Library of Congress Cataloging-in-Publication Data

Names: Wilcox, William Bradford, 1970– author.
Title: Get married: why Americans must defy the elites, forge strong families, and save civilization / William B. Wilcox.
Description: First edition. | New York: HarperCollins Publishers, [2024] | Includes index.
Identifiers: LCCN 2023031211 (print) | LCCN 2023031212 (ebook) | ISBN 9780063210851 (hardcover) | ISBN 9780063210868 (ebook)
Subjects: LCSH: Marriage.
Classification: LCC GN480 .W57 2024 (print) | LCC GN480 (ebook) | DDC 306.81—dc23/eng/20230804
LC record available at https://lccn.loc.gov/2023031211
LC ebook record available at https://lccn.loc.gov/2023031212

23 24 25 26 27 LBC 5 4 3 2 1

For Danielle

CONTENTS

PREFACE:
DEVALUING OUR MOST
IMPORTANT INSTITUTION

The biggest voice in the online manosphere today—with more than twelve billion views on TikTok alone—is no fan of marriage. Andrew Tate, a former kickboxer who has been described as the "king of toxic masculinity,"[1] has made it clear that he does not think much of our oldest social institution.

"The problem is, there is zero advantage to marriage in the Western world for a man," said Tate. "There is zero statistical advantage. If you use your mind, if you use your head instead of your heart, and you look at the advantages to getting married, there are absolutely none."

Tate is convinced that men should not invest in a marriage, financially or emotionally, because marital unions often end with "her leaving. And it's very common that women leave, right?"[2] To Tate, it seems, women are objects to be used for sexual gratification and status, not partners in life and love. They cannot be trusted, only controlled.

Consequently, any man in his right mind ought to stay single, make lots of money, play with his toys (Tate is partial to his Bugatti), and use—but not invest in—the opposite sex. Tate exemplifies the ways a growing minority of men on the far right view marriage: as a ball and chain, best avoided if you wish to maximize your money and pleasure, minimize constraints on your lifestyle, and keep your options open.

Andrew Tate's message—marked by his cartoonish definition of masculinity and his dismissal of marriage—seems to be particularly appealing to young men and teenage boys today who are struggling in school, work, life, or love. These are the "West's lost boys," to borrow the evocative phrasing of the Brookings Institution's Richard Reeves.[3] (If you doubt that Tate's message is resonating with a substantial minority of young men, ask a teenage boy in your circle about him.) In a world where so many boys and men are rudderless, devoid of meaning, purpose, and a place in the world, Tate seems to have answers to the questions they are asking about the path that a man should take in life.

Surprisingly, some aspects of Tate's perspective on marriage are echoed from the opposite end of the political spectrum. Consider the following *Bloomberg* headline trending on Twitter one night as I was finishing this book: "Women Who Stay Single and Don't Have Kids Are Getting Richer."

Women "forgoing marriage and parenthood" are doing better financially than women who have embraced marriage and family life, journalist Molly Smith assures us, accumulating more assets than their peers who are married mothers. Leaning into a job for corporate America, rather than into family life, is the pathway to prosperity. Moreover, the women profiled in this story are not just making bank; they are all, to a woman, very happy with the life choices they have made.

"I love my life and feel very fulfilled," says Ashley Marrero, a forty-three-year-old single, childless professional profiled in the article. Ashley is enjoying the "lifestyle and financial freedoms that come with being a single, child-free woman," including splitting her time between high-end properties in New York City and the Jersey Shore and taking "frequent travel for pleasure as well as work." The message the article conveys to women is clear and surprisingly congruent with Andrew Tate's message to men (minus the misogyny): work, money, freedom, and the unencumbered life are the recipe for a meaningful and happy life.[4]

Smith joins a growing list of progressive journalists, professors, and other professionals celebrating singleness, childlessness, and divorce in the pages of other prominent publications, from the *Atlantic* ("The Case against Marriage") to *Time* ("Having It All without Having Children") to the *New York Times* ("Divorce Can Be an Act of Radical Self-Love").[5] Taken together, this elite messaging, largely from the left, leaves the distinct impression that the path to prosperity, a meaningful life, and happiness leads away from family formation and toward singledom, work, and travel. Work hard. Play hard. Stay single. Keep your options open. Above all, make your life about "self-love."

This advice is seductive in our individualistic age, so long as you have never looked at the actual statistics. Let's see what social science has to say about all this.

Let's talk about money first. Guess which group of women is richer: childless singles or married mothers?

Actually, it's married mothers. In 2020, married mothers ages eighteen to fifty-five had a median family income of $108,000, compared to $41,000 for childless single women of the same ages.[6] That's over twice as much for the married mothers—plenty more, even if it's split with a spouse. And as these married mothers head into retirement in their fifties, they've accumulated $322,000 in median assets, compared to $100,000 for their single, childless peers.[7] Contra *Bloomberg*, today's married mothers are getting markedly "richer" than single women with no children.

Much the same story applies to men, as we will see in the pages ahead. Stably married men heading into retirement, for instance, have a staggering ten times more assets than their divorced or never-married male peers.[8] The ostensibly rich Tate is completely nonrepresentative on this score.

But there are some things that money can't buy, like a meaningful life. Guess which group of women reports greater success in this pursuit?

Married mothers. In 2021, 60 percent of married mothers ages eighteen to fifty-five reported that their lives were meaningful "most" or "all" of the time." Only 36 percent of single, childless women of the same ages said their lives were that meaningful.[9]

What about happiness? Guess which group of women is happier, the women with the greatest freedom or the women with the greatest family responsibilities?

Again, married mothers. Looking again at women eighteen to fifty-five, 75 percent of married mothers reported in 2022 that they were either "completely" or "somewhat" satisfied with their lives, compared to 54 percent of single, childless women.[10]

There is no question that married fathers also report the most meaning and greatest happiness in their lives, as we shall see in the pages ahead. So, if you are a man who wishes to be happy, you would be well advised to do the opposite of whatever Andrew Tate tells you to do when it comes to love. May I suggest the M-word?

YES, MANY KIDS ARE RESILIENT, BUT SOME ARE NOT

More importantly, how are kids faring in an America that values marriage much less than it used to? Is it really true, as University of San Francisco professor Lara Bazelon recently told us in the *New York Times*, that divorce is "liberating, pointing the way toward a different life that leaves everyone better off, including the children"?[11]

It turns out that children whose parents get divorced *are* heading "toward a different life"—but not in the direction Bazelon would like us to believe. They are almost twice as likely to be suspended or expelled from school,[12] 75 percent more likely to use drugs,[13] and about half as likely to graduate from college.[14] To be sure, many kids from divorced homes turn out just fine (and there are ways that divorcing parents can help mitigate the risks of these outcomes), but the data certainly don't tell us that children are left "better off" by having their parents call it quits.

These are the kinds of conclusions that I've found in surveying the social science on marriage, family life, and child well-being as a professor of sociology and director of the National Marriage Project at the University of Virginia for the past fifteen years. In addition, I've analyzed data from seven nationally representative surveys in my research for this book.

For adults, the data tell us that living for ourselves or our jobs (our own happiness and success) is not very likely to bring us to a destination filled with meaning and happiness—whether we are men or women.

But giving ourselves to others—especially spouses and families—is *the* path most likely to lead to a meaningful and generally happy life for most of us. And because marriage allows couples to pool income and assets *and* enjoy economies of scale *and* avoid redundant expenses, it also leads to a heck of a lot more prosperity for the average Joe and Jane than staying single or ending your marriage.[15]

The data could not be clearer: women like *Bloomberg*'s Ashley and men like Andrew Tate are outliers.

Likewise, having the benefit of a family headed by stably married parents, where both parents are on hand to love you day in, day out, share life's joys and frustrations, and devote their combined financial resources to your home, your extracurriculars, and your schooling ends up being the ultimate privilege for the millions of today's boys and girls across America who are fortunate enough to grow up in an intact family. If Richard Reeves has found Wendy's "Lost Boys," then Professor Bazelon seems to have found Alice's looking glass—and fallen through it to a place where small is big and down is up.

A DREAM SLIPPING AWAY

Outside of the gentrified urban neighborhoods and gilded suburbs where highly educated and well-heeled Americans make their homes today, we know that the American Dream is out of reach for untold millions. Too many communities in rural and urban America are riddled with violent crime, fentanyl, school failure, and idle men. Divorced and never-married working-class men and women are turning to drink, pills, or the barrel of a gun in record numbers, dying premature "deaths of despair" by the hundreds of thousands.[16] Growing numbers of young men and women are anxious, lonely, and unmoored, devoid of meaning and purpose in their lives.[17] Fertility is falling to unprecedented lows. Not surprisingly, in the recent words of one major media outlet, "American happiness hits record lows," with working-class and poor Americans affected most by the dip in happiness.[18]

Why the downward spiral? From mainstream media outlets, on college campuses, in public schools, and on the floor of Congress, we hear that problems like these are about the economy, or failing schools, or inequality, or race, or inadequate public policies. All the while, *the* factor that often supersedes these other factors cannot be mentioned.[19]

I'm talking about that M-word again. Marriage. So many of the biggest problems across America are rooted in the collapse of marriage and family life in all too many communities and homes across the country. For all of the outcomes mentioned above—from our nation's growing happiness divide to surging deaths of despair to the stagnant state of the American Dream—questions of marriage and family are often *better* predictors of outcomes for people than the topics that currently dominate our public conversation—like race, education, and government spending.[20]

When Harvard economist Raj Chetty and his colleagues looked at the factors driving economic mobility for poor children—i.e., their capacity to go from rags in childhood to riches in adulthood—they compared results from one local community to another, in locations across the United States. They found that "the strongest and most robust predictor [of children's economic mobility] is the fraction of children [in the community] with single parents."[21] In other words, the best community predictor of poor children remaining stuck in poverty as adults was the share of kids in their communities living in a single-parent family. Not income inequality. Not race. Not school quality. Family structure was the biggest factor in predicting poor kids' odds of realizing the American Dream in communities across the country.[22]

Or consider the growing happiness divide in American life. Educated and affluent Americans have seen their happiness levels dip a bit in recent years, but the "happiness of lower-SES people" has decreased dramatically, according to psychologist Jean Twenge. This means there's a growing happiness gap between more privileged and less privileged Americans. Guess what is one of the biggest factors explaining our country's class divide in happiness?

Marriage.

It turns out that the marriage rate is in free fall among our country's poor and working class. This translates into "less happiness among those with lower SES," Twenge observed. By contrast, marriage is in much better shape among affluent Americans. "Although marriage doesn't account for the entire class gap, it does explain about half of it."[23]

Research like this tells us that fixing what ails America starts with renewing marriage and family life, especially in poor and working-class communities where the fabric of family life is weakest. This insight, along with a desire to help ordinary men and women build meaningful and satisfying lives for themselves and their children, compelled me to write this book.

INTRODUCTION:
MARRIAGE SINCE THE
"ME" DECADE

I was born in 1970, the beginning of what came to be known as the "Me" Decade.[1] My closest cultural connection as a kid to the spirit of the seventies—besides wearing bell-bottom jeans and a burnt-orange T-shirt and singing "Kumbaya" around summer campfires—came from listening to the vinyl record by Marlo Thomas, *Free to Be . . . You and Me*, on many a night before I fell asleep as a young boy. The album (and the TV show of the same name), released in 1972, almost perfectly expressed that seventies spirit.[2] The album had many feminist-inspired songs, like "William Wants a Doll," which attempted to instill in little boys new gender norms: "I'd give my bat and ball and glove to have a doll that I could love." There were also plenty of songs celebrating me-ism—like "The Sun and the Moon," with this takeaway: "I think I'd rather be the sun that shines so bold and bright, than be the moon that only glows with someone else's light."[3]

The promise held out in the 1970s was that casting aside the values and virtues of an older era and focusing on your own needs, your own desires, and your own projects would bring you happiness. This was a time when one institution after another was losing its moral standing or abandoning its own traditions, from the presidency (think Watergate) to the military (think Vietnam) to organized religion, as "Do unto others . . ." gave way to the *new* Golden Rule: "If it feels good, do it." Men and women across the nation were abandoning their faith in these institutions to instead follow the "truth they found within."

Amid the tectonic cultural quakes of this era, another institution was crumbling: marriage. Men and women were deciding in record numbers that it could be discarded if it failed to make them "fulfilled" or happy.

As a child, I had a front-row seat to the divorce revolution that upended so many marriages during this era. Two of my close friends—Marina and Toby—had parents who divorced before I met them. I didn't think much of this at the time, in part because I was swimming in a sea of family diversity. My own mother was a single mom, I was surrounded by lots of different family types, and the shows I watched growing up, like *The Brady Bunch*, lent an aura of normalcy to divorce, remarriage, and single parenthood.

But truth be told, I was shocked and unmoored as I moved through adolescence and into young adulthood to learn that the parents of two other close friends from childhood—B.J. and Chris—had also called it quits. That's partly because, as a boy growing up without a father, I gravitated to the fathers of my friends. I had enjoyed the pleasures of camping in the wilds of New England, hearing fascinating tales about running a small business, and discussing the news of the day with them. In their own ways, these men had helped to fill the hole in my soul left by my own absent father (my dad died when I was three).

But, influenced by the spirit of the "Me" Decade, the cultural currents of the Divorce Revolution, the wear and tear of married life, and doubtless other strains unknown to me, these marriages that I had so admired fell apart. Maybe one spouse had dived into a book like *The Courage to Divorce*, a best-selling divorce how-to guide published in 1975, which claimed that after "an initial period of confusion or depression," divorced people would, almost without exception, "look and feel better than ever before. They act warmer, . . . tap sources of strength they never knew they had, enjoy their careers and their children more, and begin to explore new vocations and hobbies."[4] This kind of adult-centered prodivorce messaging that proliferated in the 1970s helps explain why, of the five close friends I had growing up, four ended up with parents who parted ways.

My experience is but one example of the turmoil and tumult that swept through countless Boomer marriages of this era, leaving an indelible mark on their lives—*and* the lives of their kids. This decade witnessed dramatic increases in divorce, childbearing outside of wedlock, and single parenthood. The marriage rate in America fell precipitously.

By the end of the "Me" Decade, in 1980, that famous statistic—"One in two marriages will end in divorce"—had come to accurately describe, perhaps for the first time ever, marriage in America. Family instability climbed to a record high; by the early twenty-first century, about one in two kids in America would spend at least some part of their childhood living apart from their own married parents.[5] In the wake of the family revolution that began in the late 1960s and took off in the 1970s, marriage no longer seemed a safe harbor for American men, women, and children.

SABOTAGING OUR MOST IMPORTANT SOCIAL INSTITUTION

The Harvard anthropologist Joseph Henrich has observed that "marriage represents the keystone institution for most—though not all—societies and may be the most primeval of human institutions."[6] What he is getting at is that in most civilizations, the institution of marriage plays a central role in organizing family life, promoting human flourishing, and maintaining social order. Marriage binds men to the children they father. It stabilizes the romantic relationships of adults and the family lives of children. It bridges the gender divide between men and women; endows the lives of women and especially men with a deeper sense of meaning, direction, and solidarity; and, above all, provides the ideal context for the bearing and rearing of children.

In doing these things, the institution of marriage helps men settle down, work harder and smarter, and steer clear of trouble. It maximizes the prosperity and financial security of men, women, and children. It increases the likelihood that children are raised well, flourish in school, avoid incarceration, and become productive members of our society. It minimizes the odds that men and women are lonely and unsupported as they move through life. And, as Linda Waite and Maggie Gallagher have observed, marriage dramatically increases our chances of realizing our "longing to receive and to be the source of dependable love."[7]

Marriage is certainly the "keystone institution" for our nation. At the civilizational level, this institution has, across the course of American history, promoted prosperity and reduced the risk of widespread poverty at both the state and national levels. It has reinforced the rule of law and minimized the risk of crime and mass disorder. It has boosted the physical health and emotional well-being of the general population. It has maximized the odds that children across the country are happy, healthy, and well prepared to take their place as virtuous citizens in our civilization.[8] For all these reasons, married families maximize the odds that ordinary men, women, and children succeed at that quintessential American quest, "the pursuit of happiness."

But over the last half-century, dominant elites have advanced ideas that devalue and demean marriage, cast aside the normative guardrails that forge strong families, passed laws that penalize marriage for the poor and working class, and superintended the rise of a new economy that benefits them but has put marriage and family life out of reach for millions of their fellow Americans. The irony, as we shall see, is that the very group—our ruling class—that has sabotaged our most fundamental social institution has figured out ways to protect their own families even as marriage flounders in the nation at large. So, strong and stable families remain the norm for the wealthy and well-educated—from McLean, Virginia, to the Upper East Side of Manhattan; from San Mateo, California, to Montgomery County in Maryland. Meanwhile, in all too many poor and working-class communities, marriage is disappearing— from Jackson County, Ohio, to the South Bronx; from Greene County in rural Virginia to downtown Memphis. This unequal retreat from marriage is part and parcel of why, for the first time in our nation's history, less than half of American adults are married.[9]

FAMILY-FIRST MARRIAGES IN TODAY'S AMERICA

The marriage story told in this book is sobering, but not without signs of hope. Some groups of Americans have recovered from the tumult of the 1970s and now *are* forging strong and stable marriages. One group succeeding at marriage today is what I call the "Strivers," those educated and affluent Americans from which our "ruling class" of elites is drawn.

Although many Strivers experimented with the individualistic spirit of the seventies, and paid a familial price for doing so, in recent years they have largely course-corrected and taken a more marriage-minded path that has benefited them and their kids.

Consider a 2011 article from the *New York Times* spotlighting the marital experience of Gen Xers—those who grew up like me at the height of the divorce-as-chic moment. Many are now living in hotbeds of hipness such as Park Slope, Brooklyn, and Seattle. In "How Divorce Lost Its Groove," journalist Pamela Paul chronicles how contemporary mothers in these communities are wrestling with marriage and divorce in ways that indicate many have abandoned the easy come, easy go marital ethic of so many of their parents.[10]

Seattle writer and mother Claire Dederer said of the 1970s family ethic that though "the feminists, the hippies, the protesters, the cultural elite all said, 'It's O.K. to drop out'" of marriage, she was determined to take a very different approach. "We made up our minds, my brother and I, and so many of the grown children of the runaway moms, that we would put our families first and ourselves second," the left-leaning Dederer told Paul. "We would be good, all the time. We would stay married, no matter what, and drink organic milk."

This turning away from the libertinism of their parents' generation has become the norm for college-educated men and women who have married and had children since the 1970s. Marriages among these Strivers are stronger today. College-educated parents' risk of divorce has fallen by about 25 percent since the 1970s, and almost 90 percent of their children are being raised in married, largely intact families today.[11]

Many of these parents are marrying and staying together because they have rediscovered a perennial truth, as Yale sociologist Nicholas Christakis has noted: deep and abiding pair bonds are an "optimal reproductive strategy" for men and women intent on maximizing the welfare of their offspring by also maximizing the "investment in children" of *both* parents.[12] Richard Reeves from Brookings thinks Striver parents are succeeding because they are combining a child-centered approach to family life with a work-family strategy that is "egalitarian about gender roles." In his view, strong and stable marriages are built around a joint commitment to "highly invested parenting" and social liberalism.[13]

But Reeves is only half right. While it is true that Strivers' commitment to their kids helps explain their marital success, the fact that many of them lean left does not. The latter point has been visible to me in my own social circle, which *leans right* and is largely made up of church-going Catholics, like me, or faithful evangelical Protestants, Jews, and Latter-day Saints, along with a few secular conservatives. My circle of right-leaning friends is dominated by strong and stable marriages. Yes, two of my close friends are divorced, but they are the clear exception. My wife and I have been married for twenty-eight years. The vast majority of our millennial and Gen X friends—in their forties and fifties—are stably married. What's especially striking is that many of my friends are themselves children of divorce. But they are determined to reject that dark road they were forced to walk as kids. And they are *not* socially liberal.

My experience parallels trends in the nation at large. The uptick in family stability has been especially pronounced among parents like my

FIGURE I.1: CONSERVATIVE, COLLEGE-EDUCATED PARENTS ESPECIALLY LIKELY TO BE IN FIRST MARRIAGE

Percent in first marriages, by ideology and education

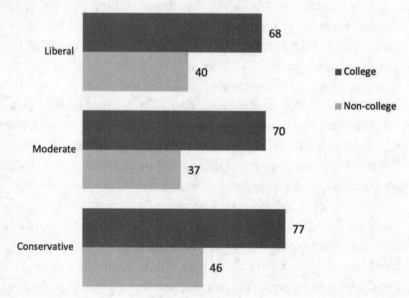

Based on adults aged 18 to 55 with children. Source: General Social Survey, 2014–2018.

friends: conservative, college-educated fathers and mothers. Figure I.1 indicates that no group of parents is as likely to be in their first marriage as this group. More than 75 percent of self-described conservative mothers and fathers with a college degree are in their first marriage, compared to about 70 percent of moderate and liberal college-educated parents, and less than half of parents without a college degree.[14] Right-leaning husbands and wives are also happier than their more left-leaning peers in their marriages, among both the more- and less-educated set, as we will see later.

These patterns hint at an important truth about which groups of Americans are most likely to forge successful, family-first marriages. Who succeeds in marriage today is not only about class—about having money and the right degree on the wall. It's also about culture—religion, ethnicity, and even ideology. We will learn about members of a group I call the Faithful: religious Americans like Joseph and Graciela Baker, a devout fortysomething couple forging a strong and largely traditional family life in the foothills of the Wasatch Mountains. We will learn about Asian Americans like Lisa Lee, a first-generation immigrant from Korea now living in Fairfax, Virginia. This successful professional's rock-solid marriage is influenced by her traditional Confucian values *and* her desire to give her kids the kind of stable family that sets them up for achieving the American Dream. We will meet married Conservatives like Martin and Kimberly Jones, two thirtysomething African Americans living in the suburbs of Washington, DC, who are consciously rejecting the zeitgeist around them to forge an intentionally family-focused life with their three young children.

Get Married is partly the story of how these four groups—the Strivers, the Faithful, Asian Americans, and Conservatives—are building stable and largely satisfying marriages. We will learn how they forge family-first marriages by rejecting three myths that distort our thinking about love, marriage, and family life today: the flying solo myth, the family diversity myth, and the soulmate myth. All of these have gained considerable currency in our culture but are antithetical to good marriages. Then we turn to a set of constructive values and virtues, the five pillars of stable and happy unions in twenty-first-century America. Finally, I describe a public policy agenda that can help revive the fortunes of marriage and family life for all Americans in the years ahead.

In exploring the character and contours of American marriages and family life, I relied upon seven large surveys to paint an empirical portrait of what is happening in homes across the country: the Early Childhood Longitudinal Study; the Education Longitudinal Study of 2002; the National Longitudinal Survey of Youth, 1979 and 1997 cohorts (NLSY79 and NLSY97); the General Social Survey; the American Family Survey; and the State of Our Unions Survey of 2022. The figures in the book illustrate unadjusted, bivariate relationships between key independent and dependent variables of interest drawn from these datasets. Furthermore, the text often reports additional statistical analyses of these variables, net of controls for factors like race, education, and income that might confound the relationship between these independent and dependent variables. I conducted most of these analyses in collaboration with Dr. Wendy Wang, the director of research at the Institute for Family Studies.

My colleagues and I also spoke to more than forty men and women across the United States about their experience of love and marriage to gain additional insights into the state of our unions. Most of those respondents are given pseudonyms to protect their anonymity.[15] Finally, because less than 1 percent of married families with children in America are headed by same-sex parents,[16] which makes it difficult to conduct statistical analyses of such families, this book focuses on heterosexual married men and women ages eighteen to fifty-five, most of whom are married with children.

In writing *Get Married*, my aim is not to argue that everyone should put a ring on it. Not everyone can or should marry. Nor stay married. But for most of us, getting married and forging a strong family is the best way to build a prosperous, meaningful, and happy life—and a way that needs a lot more guidance and support from the culture and law than it is now garnering. Nothing less than the future of our civilization depends on more Americans succeeding in this most fundamental social institution. And in a world where trust is falling, loneliness is soaring, and economic inequality is endemic, nothing may matter more for your future and the sake of your children than forming, feeding, and enjoying your own family-first marriage.

CHAPTER 1

THE CLOSING OF THE
AMERICAN HEART

The State of Our Unions

My students at the University of Virginia (UVA) inspire me every day—they're curious, hardworking to a fault, and friendly, and many of them have big hearts for good causes here in Charlottesville, from tutoring poor children in city schools to visiting the elderly at local nursing homes. But they do suffer from one big blind spot. They are overwhelmingly preoccupied with their education and future careers, to the exclusion of love and marriage. "Résumé virtues" are much more salient to them than "eulogy virtues."[1] Talking and thinking about marriage—or even dating someone seriously—is a rarity among students at UVA.

"UVA students are definitely more focused on their education and getting their career started than getting into a serious relationship," said Holly, a recent graduate. "If it happens, great, but the focus is definitely on building our own brands first. The thought process is, relationships and love are a risk, but you will always have your career and success to fall back on—at least while you are young."

UVA students like Holly are not alone in focusing on education and work. This propensity to believe that education, work, and money matter more than marriage and family life is now common among young adults. One recent poll found that only 32 percent of young adults ages eighteen through forty think that marriage is essential to living a fulfilling life, compared to 64 percent who think education and 75 percent who think making a good living is crucial to fulfillment.[2]

It's no accident that today's young adults are leaning out from marriage. Parents, peers, and pop culture encourage them to put love and marriage on the back burner. In fact, a recent Pew poll found that 88 percent of parents believe that it is important for their kids to be financially independent, and the same share think it important that their kids have "careers they enjoy" when they are adults; *only* 21 percent said it is important their kids get married, and only 20 percent believed it to be important that their kids have children of their own.[3] The legacy of the divorce revolution has also made plenty of young adults gun-shy about marriage, including young women like Holly, whose parents split up when she was young. And growing up in the wake of the economic turbulence associated with the Great Recession and COVID-19 has made countless young adults keen on nailing down a good job and a steady income before they even let their minds and hearts drift toward thoughts of love and marriage.

These young people, without knowing it, have soaked up a set of pervasive modern assumptions about the purpose of life. Many have bought into the belief that anything good about marriage comes with various unpleasant side effects: boredom, forgone job opportunities, the burdens of parenthood, oppressive gender roles, being tied down. Others are under the impression that the responsibilities of marriage and family life are best postponed to their thirties, when they have their career well in hand. By contrast, they imagine, steering clear of marriage maximizes your freedom, wealth, and fulfillment—especially when you are in your twenties.

But Taylor's life experience suggests that it's a big mistake to prioritize education, work, and money to the detriment of love and marriage as you move through young adulthood. Taylor, who at thirty-three is about ten years older than Holly, was told, "Oh, don't get married too early, make sure you . . . finish college, don't get married too young, go out and see the world and do all these other things, and don't get too attached to anyone too quickly." She took this advice seriously and focused on a career in digital marketing in her twenties rather than on dating with an eye to getting married in that decade.

Now, this single professional woman living in Denver is less confident about her prospects for starting a family. "I look back on that [advice] and I'm like, you know, if I could do it again . . . I would actually focus on finding a husband a little bit earlier," she said. Her single state is especially hard for her because she feels like she "doesn't have a ton of meaning" in her life right now. By contrast, the time she spends babysitting for her nieces and nephews—which she loves—has left her thinking that she would be more fulfilled if she were married with children.

The notion that life is all about work "bugs me the older I get, because I'm like, I spent so much time believing that and I'm like, you know, is there a chance that I could have a family of my own right now? You know, do fun things with them? Finger paint, whatever. I don't know what kids do."

Taylor is onto something. We are social animals, as Aristotle taught us. For most of us, the ties we forge with family and friends, including the opportunities we have to love and be loved, to care for and be cared for by others, end up being more important to us than the markers of achievement or status—or the ability to keep our options open—that our culture prioritizes today. The modern dream of success is measured merely in dollar signs and "free" time. It does nothing to measure things like meaning. Marriage and family life are often more important for our sense of meaning, direction, and happiness than the degree on our wall, the place we punch a clock, or our ability to maximize our autonomy.[4]

Social science tells us that your marital status—whether you are married or not—is a crucial predictor of a whole host of important economic, emotional, and health outcomes for men and women throughout their adult lives.[5] In fact, as figure 1.1 shows, the odds that men and women are "very happy" with their lives are 151 percent higher for those who are married, compared to those who are unmarried, according to the General Social Survey. What's more, being married is a better predictor of happiness than other factors that get more attention in today's culture, like education, work, money, race, and gender. And marital quality is, far and away, the top predictor I have run across of

FIGURE 1.1: MARRIAGE PREDICTS HAPPINESS BETTER THAN EDUCATION, WORK, AND MONEY

Odds of being "very happy" increase by . . .

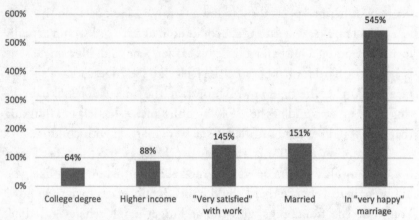

Based on adults aged 18 to 55. Higher income refers to family income of equal to or more than $60,000 a year. Those in "very happy" marriages compared with those who are unmarried or in less than "very happy" marriages. Each model controls for race, gender, and age. Source: General Social Survey, 2014–2018.

life satisfaction in America. Specifically, the odds that men and women say they are "very happy" with their lives are a staggering 545 percent higher for those who are very happily married, compared to their peers who are not married or who are less than very happy in their marriages. When it comes to predicting overall happiness, a good marriage is far more important than how much education you get, how much money you make, how often you have sex, and, yes, even how satisfied you are with your work.[6] Findings like these suggest that today's young adults are mistaken to prioritize life goals related to work and money over marriage and family life.

One famous study, the Harvard Study of Adult Development, spotlighted in a new book, *The Good Life: Lessons from the World's Longest Scientific Study of Happiness*,[7] points us in a similar direction. It found that good relationships, including marriage, are especially important to us in the final chapters of our lives. In the study, older people who had good marriages back in their fifties also had the best physical and emotional outcomes in their seventies and eighties—being the most protected against problems like memory loss, chronic disease, and mental illness.[8] "Just like the millennials in the recent survey, many of our men when they were starting out as young adults really believed that fame and wealth and high achievement were what they needed to go after to have a good life," said Robert Waldinger, director of this Harvard study. "But over and over, our study has shown that the people who fared best were the people who leaned into relationships with family, with friends, with community."[9]

Research like this suggests that we should pay more attention to the state of our unions.

THE GOOD NEWS: THE KIDS ARE ... ALL RIGHT?

You could be forgiven for thinking—after the divorce revolution, and so much family turbulence over the last fifty years—that the state of marriage in America today is a disaster for kids.

You might come to this conclusion from consulting your own recent family history, or that of your childhood friends, as my own experience suggests.

You might come to this conclusion after scanning the covers of *People*, *Us*, and *In Touch* in the checkout line at your local grocery store. From chronicling the Kardashians' latest family drama to spotlighting the aftermath of the Bezoses' breakup to catching up on the latest episode of MTV's *Teen Mom*, the cover stories on these magazines often paint a pretty bleak picture of the state of our unions in America.

You might come to this conclusion from taking in the latest movies and books, like the Oscar-winning *Marriage Story*, starring Adam Driver and Scarlett Johansson, or Taffy Brodesser-Akner's critically acclaimed *Fleishman Is in Trouble*, which was turned into a hit series on Hulu. Both of these offerings serve up dispiriting depictions of twenty-first-century marriages spiraling downward to divorce over work-family conflicts, unmet emotional needs, and sundry disappointments with spousal failures.

Or you might come to this conclusion from reading an article in the *Atlantic* titled "How to Live in a World Where Marriage Is in Decline," where sociologist Philip Cohen wrote that we just need to face "the reality that fewer and fewer children are being raised in homes with two married parents."[10] Meanwhile, in his 1994 book *Why Marriages Succeed or Fail*, psychologist John Gottman wrote, "There is no denying that this is a frightening time for American couples," adding, "More than half of all first marriages end in divorce."[11]

These offerings from pop culture, psychologists, and professors paint a dark picture of the state of our unions, one that suggests, among other things, that marriage is fast fading as the preferred venue for bearing and rearing children.

However, the divorce revolution seems to have done something no one expected. It spawned a counterrevolution. Many millennials and Gen Xers, as we saw in the introduction, are rejecting the divorce revolution of their parents. Steven Spielberg has spent his entire career working through the ramifications of his parents' divorce, finally addressing the topic head-on in his 2022 *The Fabelmans*, in which his childhood devastation shines through strongly. This same type of regret has shaped the way that Gen X and millennial parents have approached marriage and family life—at least for those who got married

FIGURE 1.2: US DIVORCE RATE DOWN SINCE 1980

Number of newly divorced people per 1,000 married Americans

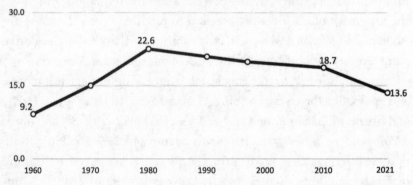

Source: Institute for Family Studies, "New Census Data: Key Takeaways on Divorce, Marriage, and Fertility in the U.S.," September 22, 2022.

before they had children. Many children of the divorce revolution seem to have decided they really don't want to inflict this situation on kids of their own.

Perhaps that's why there is some good news to report when it comes to the state of our unions, at least when it comes to our kids. Contra Cohen, the share of children being "raised in homes with two married parents" is not falling. In fact, what we are seeing is that the share of children being raised in an intact, married family has ticked up a bit in recent years.

This is largely because, surprisingly, the divorce rate has fallen since 1980. As figure 1.2 indicates, the divorce rate fell about 40 percent, from 22.6 divorces per one thousand married adults in 1980 to 13.6 divorces per one thousand married adults in 2021.[12] This statistic is a bit more complicated than it appears—more on that later—but the most important thing that this means is that most children born to married parents will *not* see their parents get a divorce, at least during their childhood—unlike so many of the kids born in the 1970s. Marriage, then, is a safer harbor today for kids than it was in the 1970s.

Since the Great Recession, the share of babies born out of wedlock has also stabilized. This is also a surprise, because from 1960 to 2009, the nonmarital childbearing rate went up, and up, and up, from 5 percent in 1960 to 18 percent in 1980 to 41 percent in 2009. But since 2009, the rate has hovered just under 41 percent.[13] This means that marriage precedes the baby carriage for about six in ten children today.

So, less divorce and no increase in children born outside of marriage equals . . . more stable, married families for our kids. In fact, figure 1.3 indicates that the share of children being raised by their own married biological parents has ticked up from 57.8 percent in 2012 to 58.9 percent in 2022. To be sure, the nation witnessed a dramatic decline in the share of children raised in an intact, married family across their entire childhood from about three-quarters in 1960 to about 51 percent today.[14] Still, what we are now seeing is that a slim majority of children today are reaching adulthood in a home headed by their two married biological parents.[15] This matters because those kids are much more likely to flourish than their peers raised outside of intact homes.

At least from the perspective of kids, marriage is more likely to

FIGURE 1.3: SHARE OF CHILDREN IN INTACT, MARRIED FAMILIES TICKING UP

Percent of children aged 0 to 17 living with married biological parents

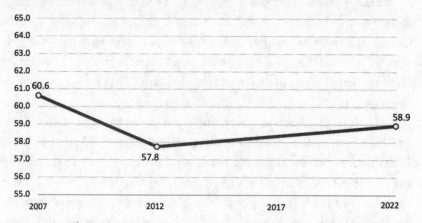

Source: US Census Bureau, Current Population Surveys, ASEC, 2007, 2012, 2022 (IPUMS).

FIGURE 1.4: US MARRIAGE RATE CLOSE TO ALL-TIME LOW IN 2021

Number of newly married people per 1,000 unmarried Americans aged 15 and up

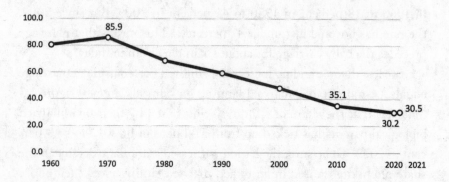

Source: Institute for Family Studies, "New Census Data: Key Takeaways on Divorce, Marriage, and Fertility in the U.S.," September 22, 2022.

ground and guide children's lives today than it was a decade ago—in 2012. That's the good news.

THE BAD NEWS

But when we turn our attention away from the kids, and toward the adults, the news is darker. The American heart is closing before our very eyes. Our civilization is in the midst of an epochal shift, a shift away from marriage and all the fruits that follow from this most fundamental social institution: children, kin, financial stability, and innumerable opportunities to love and be loved by another. Too many young men and women are closing their hearts to marriage and family life—or are unable to find a partner with whom to forge a family in the first place.

Let's begin with marriage. The marriage rate has fallen about 65 percent in the last half century, from a recent peak of almost eighty-six marriages per one thousand unmarried people in 1970 to fewer than thirty-one marriages per one thousand unmarried people in 2021, close to its lowest level in our nation's history (see figure 1.4). *Declines in marriage and increases in divorce mean that slightly less than one in two adults are currently married, down from about 75 percent in 1960.*[16]

Part of this decline can be attributed to men and women just marrying at older ages. Today, the median age at first marriage is close to thirty. But even when we look at those in midlife, the share of Americans who are currently married at ages thirty-five through fifty-five has fallen from 84 percent in 1960 to 62 percent in 2021.[17] In place of marriage, many Americans are remaining single or simply living together without wedding rings. And to be clear, it's more of the former than the latter.[18] In recent years, as marriage has lost ground as the anchor of American adulthood, the share of Americans who are flying solo has risen swiftly. The share of "unpartnered" men and women ages twenty-five through fifty-four rose from 29 percent in 1990 to 38 percent in 2019, according to the Pew Research Center.[19]

Looking to the future, demographers predict that the share of Americans who marry by age forty will fall from more than 80 percent of Gen Xers to less than 70 percent of today's young adults.[20] This is important because few Americans marry for the first time after forty, which means that a large minority of contemporary young men and women, perhaps as many as one-third, will never marry. This is a bad omen for our civilization, because although not every person wants to or should get married, ordinary men and women are most likely to flourish when they are married, and most unmarried American men and women report that they would prefer to marry.[21] This closing of the American heart *is* a problem, then; many never-married men and women will end up as unwilling bachelors and bachelorettes, confronting midlife and late life without the benefit of a partner to love and be loved by.

What about the quality and stability of marriages for those men and women who do manage to tie the knot nowadays? Here the news is better for the shrinking share of men and women who are married.

Marital happiness is high for a stable majority. While reports of marital happiness fell in the 1970s and early 1980s, they have stabilized since the mid-1980s. A majority of American husbands and wives ages eighteen through fifty-five, about 60 percent, report they are "very happy" in their marriages, according to the General Social Survey, one of the best barometers of Americans' attitudes and experiences. Another 36 percent say they are "pretty happy" in their marriages, and 4 percent report that are "not too happy" in their marriages.[22] Still, this also means that a large minority are not indicating that they are "very happy" in their marriages. This is important because it's married men and women who are "very happy" in their unions who are also most likely to report they are happy with life in general.

When we turn toward the adult divorce story, the news is good but not great. John Gottman's prediction that about "half of all first marriages end in divorce" now seems too pessimistic. Analyses of recent census data suggest that slightly more than 40 percent of first marriages will end in divorce.[23] This means that less than half of today's marriages are headed for a breakup, but still, a large minority of couples will see their marriages end. Given the toll that divorce takes on men, women, and the intergenerational family fabric, from holiday celebrations to weddings, from retirement savings to grandparents' assistance with college tuition for grandchildren, this is still sobering news.

The other big story darkening the horizon of American family life is our falling fertility rate. The number of empty cradles across the land is growing. After a sharp decline in the 1970s, the total fertility rate hovered until 2009 around 2.1 children per woman—the replacement level needed to keep our population size relatively constant (without immigration). But since the Great Recession, the fertility rate has fallen well below this replacement level, and COVID has pushed it even lower. It fell from 2.1 babies per woman in 2007 to 1.6 in 2020, a record-setting low. About one-third of American women ages forty to forty-four have no children (17 percent) or just one child (18 percent). That's up from just 20 percent in 1976, when 10 percent of women at this age had never given birth and 10 percent had one child.[24] The birth rate has never been so low in America.

What this means, practically, is that our country has forgone more than seven million babies since the Great Recession. In other words, if the fertility rate had remained close to 2.1 children per woman since 2009, the country would have welcomed an extra seven million baby boys and girls. It also means that a rising share of American men and women will be childless—about 25 percent, according to demographer Lyman Stone.[25]

The problems with so many empty cradles are threefold. First, dramatic declines in fertility translate into declining dynamism for the United States economy in the coming years, as the number of workers making and buying things falls. Second, it means that millions of men and especially women will not have the kids they hoped to have—we're already seeing many more middle-aged women report this.[26] Finally, and most importantly, ours will be a nation populated by millions of men and women without any kin. This is the other profound way in which young people have closed their hearts to family life, either wittingly or unwittingly.

If you put these two trends together, less marriage and fewer babies, what you see is that a growing share of prime-aged adults (eighteen to fifty-five) do not have immediate kin—defined here as a spouse or children. In fact, as figure 1.5 indicates, starting in 2019, *the share of prime-aged adults who do not have immediate kin exceeded the share of Americans who are married with children for the first time in our nation's history.*

This demographic shift also means family life is an increasingly

**FIGURE 1.5: SHARE MARRIED WITH CHILDREN
VS. SINGLE, NO CHILDREN 1970–2022**

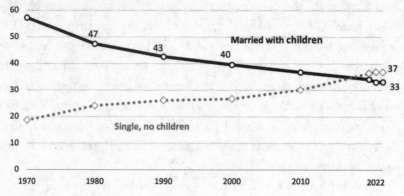

Percent of adults aged 18 to 55

Source: Current Population Survey (IPUMS).

selective phenomenon in America today. In other words, a smaller share of men and women will marry, just as a smaller share of men and women will end up having children. This also helps explain the good news for children noted above: because the kinds of people who are marrying and having families now are also the groups that tend to enjoy more family stability—relatively more educated and affluent, as well as more conservative and religious—US children are slightly more likely (than not) to be born and raised in stable homes.

But as our elites downplay or denigrate the value of marriage and childbearing, our churchgoing has grown less common, our electronic opiates have become more enticing, our emotional and financial expectations for marriage have soared, our men have become less likely to hold down a full-time job, and our public policies continue to penalize working-class marriages, we are pairing off and welcoming new life into our homes less and less.

So, the bad news about family life in America is that *a large and growing minority of men and women will not marry or have children, leaving them without any immediate kin as they head into midlife and later life.* In China, there is a term for men without such kin: "bare branches."[27] In our country, in coming years there will be millions of men *and* women who could also be described as "bare branches" as they push past fifty. One portent of this coming reality can be seen in a recent survey, which found that the share of retiring adults with adult children within ten miles has fallen from 68 percent in 1994 to 51 percent in 2016—and this number is poised to head much lower.[28]

Another portent is that more and more older Americans are living without a spouse. Today, the share of Americans age sixty and older who are divorced or never married has more than doubled, up from 12 percent in 1970 to 25 percent in 2021, and this number will only climb in the coming years.[29]

This is sobering because so many of the growing number of family-less Americans will wish they could have married or had children, but failed to realize their dreams for a family while they were still possible. This is sobering because so many of these bare branches will sway to the siren songs of social media influencers, talking heads, and political demagogues now holding out the false promise of meaning and community to them. This is sobering because many of them will end up aging and dying essentially alone, largely unvisited and uncared for in their final years by anyone but a nursing-home attendant, home-health-care aide, or care robot.[30]

Looking across the Pacific, we can see what lies ahead for the United States if we do not succeed in reviving marriage and childbearing here at home. The "bare branches" phenomenon is already well underway in East Asian countries like Japan, South Korea, and Taiwan—all places where sex, marriage, and childbearing are in free fall. In Japan, for instance, fertility hit our current rate in 1988 before falling much lower—it now sits at 1.26 children per woman—and it's not pretty.[31] Lots of old people and comparatively few young people equal population decline (by about eight hundred thousand per year),[32] economic stagnation, and the largest public debt of any nation in the world.[33]

Most importantly, the closing of the Japanese heart has meant that sex and marriage have plummeted even as loneliness has surged, among both the young and the old. The share of young men without full-time employment, called "freeters," is rising in Japan. So is the amount of time and attention these men devote to Japan's thriving virtual world, from anime to Line, the nation's leading social network. Dating and having sex have dropped off their radar. Ano Matsui, a twenty-six-year-old man recently profiled on BBC, confessed, "I don't have any self-confidence" about asking women out, adding he's not alone on this score: "There are a lot of men like me who find women scary." In fact, a staggering share—about one-quarter—of young Japanese adults ages eighteen to thirty-four report that they are virgins, more than 60 percent of unmarried young adults say they have no relationship with a member of the opposite sex, and the rates of the never-married young men and women in the island nation keep climbing.[34]

For older adults, Japanese family trends mean that millions of older people are experiencing unprecedented levels of loneliness.[35] A harrowing *New York Times* story recently explained how the decline of Japanese families now means that a "generation of elderly Japanese is dying alone," living in "extreme isolation," often left to themselves for weeks on end, even in death. In fact, the "extreme isolation of elderly Japanese is so common that an entire industry has emerged around it, specializing in cleaning out apartments where decomposing remains are found."[36]

The United States is not yet close to reaching the familial nadir unfolding in Japan, a nation that might be better described today as the land of the setting sun. But given that fertility is only holding steady among married couples in America, and marriage rates keep hitting historic lows, we are in danger of taking a similar path.[37] So many of our broader unfolding crises can be seen in the context of this core social unraveling. Collapsing rates of marriage and parenthood drop as we see surges in antisocial political extremism, a loneliness crisis, addiction to technology, and economic inequality. Meanwhile, elites who have the money to insulate themselves from these crises continue to promote anti-nuptial and anti-natalist ideas that make them worse.

Our elites will push nearly any other solution besides marriage and family life. They'll argue that we need to deepen our dedication to work, have the government fund childcare, spend more on education, expand access to contraception, or spend more on cash welfare programs, including a universal basic income. The default assumption underlying many of these proposals is that people are autonomous, isolated individuals. So, the state and the market should step in to reinforce our independence and reduce the value and power of family ties. In reality, however, the counterintuitive truth is that flourishing families—bound together by healthy, mutual dependencies—are essential for our civilization. Married people are happier and more prosperous than unmarried people. The responsibilities and commitments of marriage and family life provide meaning and direction for young men and women, along with comfort and security in later life.

For the sake of our civilization, and especially for the sake of the rising generation, the Hollys and Taylors of the world, we must find, spotlight, and explain who is *succeeding* at marriage in America today. Today's young women and men need to know that there are still viable paths toward opening their hearts to a strong and stable marriage and family life in the twenty-first century, especially because so much of our elite culture is intent on sending them down pathways that lead ultimately to spending the last chapter of life as "bare branches," lonely and devoid of a family of their own. We turn to this task in the next chapter.

CHAPTER 2

THE MASTERS OF MARRIAGE

Asian Americans, Conservatives, the Faithful, and Strivers

Everyone wants to know the surefire secret to success at love and marriage. Supermarket checkout lines are laden with magazines advertising lists of guaranteed romantic tips. It's not just the readers of these magazines, though, who are on the hunt for the magic formula. Psychologists have been hard at work looking for the answer as well, investigating the relational skills possessed by spouses for the keys to success. Meanwhile, public intellectuals tend to see everything in terms of big structures—economic class and government policy. So, which is it? The personal skills, or the big structures? As we'll see, it's worth considering more than just these two popular narratives about why marriages succeed or fail. Looking at the ways in which marriages are more likely to flourish in particular types of communities can show us how culture impacts marital success in ways that individual choices and economic conditions don't.

Let's consider the psychological approach first. In search of the secrets of marital success, psychologist John Gottman opened what came to be known as the "Love Lab" at the University of Washington (UW) in Seattle in 1986. The Love Lab was a well-appointed apartment on the UW campus overlooking the canal that connects Portage Bay to Lake Washington on the eastern edge of the city.[1] Gottman and his colleagues would get married couples to come for a getaway in the lab—to enjoy some fun time together in one of the more picturesque parts of Seattle, but also to tackle some relationship homework.

Gottman described the Love Lab this way: "It [had] a beautiful picture window there, boats going by, and people just sort of listened to the music they wanted to listen to, watched television, brought newspapers to read, and did whatever they wanted to do." He added, "The only difference between [the Love Lab] and an ordinary bed and breakfast was we had four cameras bolted to the wall and they wore monitors that measured two channels of electrocardiogram. And when they urinated, we took a urine sample to measure stress hormones."[2]

A couple's time in the Love Lab was measured, charted, and analyzed to understand their married life. By monitoring his face's response to her bid for attention, the play of her lips when he told a story, and how much his blood pressure spiked when she raised concerns about his on-again-off-again displays of bad temper with the kids, Gottman and his team were able to determine which kinds of marriages looked strong and which ones looked like they were headed for trouble. By tracking hundreds of couples over time in the Love Lab, Gottman reported he was able to figure out which couples were likely to divorce with over 90 percent accuracy.[3]

The couples in trouble, for instance, had distinctive physical responses to conflict. "What we saw is that when [couples in distress] were having a conflict discussion, their bodies went into flight-or-fight mode," says Dr. Julie Schwartz Gottman, John's wife and research collaborator. Blood flow quickened, heart rates rose, and they started sweating profusely. This kind of dramatic physical response to conflict meant that the husband or wife was unable to deal constructively with conflict and was in great danger of ending up divorced. In fact, the Gottmans had a name for couples who responded like this to ordinary conflict: "disasters."[4]

By contrast, the word for those couples who handled conflict gracefully, without dramatic physical responses, and who directed lots of positive attention to one another over the course of their time in the Love Lab, was "masters." The masters of marriage that the Gottman team tracked over time typically enjoyed high-quality marriages and did not divorce.

After Gottman and his team had tracked the films and physiological responses of hundreds of couples in the Love Lab, five sets of behaviors stood out. These behaviors predicted whether couples were more likely to be masters or disasters in marriage. On the negative side, there were four behaviors that Gottman came to describe as the "Four Horsemen of the Apocalypse," that is, harbingers of marital failure: stonewalling, defensiveness, criticism, and contempt.[5]

STONEWALLING, more common among men, is when a spouse just shuts down in the face of conflict, difficult conversations, or requests for change because they feel physiologically flooded or overwhelmed. Maybe he "folds [his] arms, looks down and away, there's no facial movement, there's no vocalization, maybe an occasional glance at the speaker just to see if the ogre [has] magically disappeared," reports Gottman. "That's stonewalling."[6]

DEFENSIVENESS, also more common among men, is when husbands or wives respond to a concern or criticism from their spouse by defending themselves without acknowledging any of the merits of their partner's concerns, or just by going on the attack, pointing out their partner's flaws without acknowledging the legitimacy of their complaints.

CRITICISM, more common among women, is when one spouse ties a complaint or concern to an attack on the very character or personality of the other spouse. Criticism is often marked by adding words like "you always" or "you never" when expressing a concern.

CONTEMPT, found among both men and women, turned out to be the biggest relationship killer in Gottman's research. Contempt is when one spouse displays disgust or an utterly dismissive attitude toward the other spouse, saying things like, "You're such a jerk." Contempt is "sulfuric acid for love," according to Gottman.[7] This kind of contemptuous approach to marriage is toxic.

Couples with marriages marked by frequent displays of these "Four Horsemen of the Apocalypse" are usually headed for divorce. By contrast, the masters of marriage engage in these negative behaviors much less often and are more successful at cultivating a positive culture of mutual appreciation, affection, and gift-giving in their marriages.[8]

The masters of marriage are also known for trading at least five positive interactions for every one negative interaction with their spouse.

In Gottman's writings, this five-to-one rule is one mark of a strong marriage. In the best relationships, you're looking out for what your partner does right, not wrong; expressing appreciation for the person's strengths; and being empathetic, attentive, and the like. The Gottman model suggests that behavioral techniques—a kind word here, a humble request for forgiveness there—paired with a generally positive orientation toward your spouse, hold the key to forging a strong and stable marriage.

When it comes to understanding the microclimate of marriage, I do not doubt the Gottmans are onto something. At some level, we all know these things are right, even if we forget them in the heat of the moment—or when we feel trapped in a difficult and dark place in our marriage.

But what Gottman's model and many, many popular relationship advice books do *not* explain is why, today, the masters of marriages are more likely to be found in some communities, places, and groups of people than others. In other words, why are some macroclimates much more likely to foster successful marriages? Why is it, for instance, that a neighborhood adjacent to Gottman's Love Lab, the picture-perfect Laurelhurst community alongside Lake Washington in Seattle, has some of the strongest families in the nation, with nearly 90 percent headed by two parents? By contrast, why is it that a Seattle neighborhood just several miles south of the Love Lab, South Park, is dominated by single parents?

Surely it isn't because one neighborhood has read and internally digested Gottman's bestselling book *The Relationship Cure: A 5-Step Guide to Strengthening Your Marriage, Family, and Friendships*, and the other has not. Perhaps it has something to do with the fact that household income is almost five times as high, and poverty three times less common, in Laurelhurst, compared to South Park?[9]

These are more sociological questions, ones that move us in a different direction than the kinds of topics addressed by Gottman and the countless pop psychology books on relationships. They suggest that we need to move beyond the psychological conceit that a successful marriage is just about two people mastering the perfect set of relationship techniques to maximize their sense of compatibility, communication, fulfillment, romance, or self-actualization. A good marriage may not just be about becoming an amateur relationship guru; it may have something to do with the kind of community you join, the kind of cash flow coming into your household, and the culture of family you embrace.

WHERE IS MARRIAGE STRONGEST?

If becoming a master of marriage is not just about a set of techniques, but also about other, more sociological factors, how do we discover what else determines who become masters rather than disasters? One way to answer this question is to look at family trends through the lens of another kind of "love lab," the neighborhoods in which men, women, and children live.

Across the country from Seattle, Ian Rowe, the former CEO of Public Prep, a public charter–school network in New York City, has seen the divergent character of family life in different neighborhoods up close and personal. He recently moved Public Prep's headquarters to a neighborhood in the South Bronx. The first week he and his staff were settling into their new digs, they went out to explore the neighborhood and score a chile relleno. On the way to lunch, they saw something that left him speechless.

"Along the way, we encountered a twenty-seven-foot, baby blue Winnebago truck, that—judging by the cheery reaction of the people standing nearby—was a familiar and welcome fixture in the neighborhood," Rowe recalls. "On the side of the truck, vividly inscribed in graffiti lettering, was the phrase, 'Who's Your Daddy?' The truck turned out to be a mobile DNA testing center"[10] that charged several hundred dollars for each test to help children, moms, and fathers figure out if they were related to one another.[11]

"I was surprised that such a truck and its on-demand services even existed," Rowe observed. "But what astonished me more was the absolute normalcy and acceptance of its existence. The 'Who's Your Daddy?' truck was clearly providing a needed function to the community." The business's owner told Rowe that people are "carrying around a huge burden—sometimes for decades." They are seeking answers to questions like "Who is my father?," "Who is my brother?" "Am I really who I think I am?"

These questions emerge from a neighborhood context where family instability is common, marriage is rare, and single parenthood is the norm. Indeed, in the South Bronx neighborhood where Public Prep is headquartered, 65 percent of the families with children are headed by single parents.[12] "A lot of our families are struggling," says Rowe. "There are a lot of single parents, a lot of unemployment, and a lot of poverty." His comments suggest a clear link between lower income and higher family instability.

Rowe's daily commute only reinforces this connection between class and marriage in America's neighborhoods. After work, the Black married father of two drives home to the prosperous bedroom community of Pelham, New York. His home is just about ten miles north of his office in the South Bronx, but it might as well be on a different planet, family-wise. In his own community, devoted dads, not absent or mysterious fathers, are the norm.

"A 'Who's Your Daddy?' truck would be met with an instantaneously negative response in my neighborhood," notes Rowe. "We wouldn't want our kids to see that. Pelham is a tight-knit, family-centered place where most families are married and dads are hands-on. The fathers around here take their kids to Boy Scouts or tutoring. Most weekends they can be found ferrying their children to soccer, baseball, or swimming."

Indeed, in his neighborhood, over 80 percent of the families are headed by two parents—and the median household income is $160,000, more than seven times the amount in the South Bronx neighborhood where Rowe works, which is $21,000.[13] "My work and my home remind me how much of a class divide has emerged in this country around marriage," observes Rowe, who is trying to bridge that divide by giving the students in his school a shot at a better education and a better life—one that he hopes will include not only a decent job but also a stable family.

Ian Rowe's daily commute offers a clue about how closely the structure of our families is now tied to class—measured in terms of income and education—in neighborhoods across America. Raj Chetty, the Harvard economist, has been mapping out neighborhood trends with a number of other scholars in a project called the Opportunity Atlas. When my colleague Wendy Wang and I looked at data from Chetty's atlas, we found there's a very clear connection between income at the neighborhood level and the share of single-parent families in the community. This pattern was consistent across America, from Seattle to Silicon Valley, from Falls Church to Fort Wayne, and from New Orleans to New York. Higher-income neighborhoods are dominated by two-parent families—with about 80 percent of the families with children in these communities headed by such couples. Lower-income neighborhoods, by contrast, are places where almost 50 percent of families are headed by single parents.[14]

Indeed, across the country, segregation by class—by income and education—is increasing.[15] This means that today's college-educated Americans, and Americans with family incomes greater than $100,000, are much more likely to live not only in neighborhoods with lots of other educated and affluent people but also in *neighborhoods that are dominated by married adults and two-parent families.*

If we treat these neighborhood trends as one kind of "love lab," they suggest that socioeconomic class is driving who succeeds and who fails at marriage. In fact, these trends are consistent with a view that is popular among many public intellectuals writing about marriage and family life in America today.

Writing from the left in the *Atlantic*, psychologist Eli Finkel contends that "a major reason why the marriages of poorer, less-educated Americans are struggling is that economic realities make it difficult to live up to the new cultural ideal" of marriage as a vehicle for emotional connection and personal growth.[16] And from the right, Charles Murray has also underlined the class divide in American family life in his recent book, *Coming Apart*: "Over the last half century, marriage has become the fault line dividing American classes."[17] As a conservative, of course, Murray has a rather different explanation for this state of affairs than Finkel, but the bigger point here is that the most popular accounts of marriage and divorce in America often leave us thinking that class is *the* primary factor determining who is a master of marriage.

Which American Counties Are Winning at Marriage?

I do not dispute the importance of income and education in understanding what's happening to marriage and family life in America. Class clearly matters. But class isn't the whole story. When we shift our gaze from neighborhoods and look instead at a different set of "love labs," counties across the United States, another more cultural factor shaping family life zooms into focus: faith.

Consider, for instance, Provo, the county seat of Utah County, Utah. It sits in the heart of the state, about 730 miles southeast of Gottman's Seattle. When first visiting Provo, you might initially think it is just like any other Western city. A saloon anchors one corner of the downtown, mountains loom on the eastern edge of town, and the climate is arid. But on closer inspection, Provo is not your average Western city. The "saloon" is a hair salon, the large building that sits just north of downtown is the biggest local recreation center I have ever seen, and the church just south of downtown is constantly buzzing with activity, even on the hot Tuesday in August when I visited the city.

Provo, of course, is deep in the heart of Mormon country. Utah County has the highest proportion of married families of any midsize-to-large county (more than fifty thousand people) in America. In recent years, Utah County has prospered in part because it has attracted a number of California companies—from Adobe to Intel—and midwifed a number of startups seeking out its highly motivated workforce and markedly lower tax burden than that found in the Golden State. But still, Provo is not in the upper echelons of America when it comes to income: the median household income in Utah County was around $77,000 in 2021, which positions the county in a solidly middle-class bracket.[18] What really makes Provo and the entire county stand out is the faith factor.

Take Joseph, forty-four, and Graciela Baker, forty-three, who live in a comfortable middle-class Provo neighborhood in the foothills of the Wasatch Mountains. They have been married for twenty-one years and have three children, ranging in age from six to eighteen. Joseph is an insurance salesman from Utah, and Graciela is a stay-at-home mother from Argentina who also helps Joseph at his business. But what really stands out about them is not their socioeconomic status—which is middle-class—but their faith and family outlook.

"Our faith impacts our perspective on our marriage," said Joseph, reflecting on the role of the Latter-day Saint faith in his relationship—

including overcoming disappointments and disagreements in his marriage. "I think [we] both kind of look at the long game in [ways that]
present problems [in perspective] and that has definitely been a help to
us in our marriage. . . . We believe that we marry for eternity." To be
sure, he recognizes that "marriages have their ups and downs," and he
thinks divorce is merited in some cases. But his faith gives him a *very*
long-term perspective that has helped him forge a stable and generally
happy union.

Graciela, meanwhile, contrasts their mindset on marriage and family life with that of her sister, a nominal Catholic who does not attend
church regularly and took a very different approach to married life. "My
sister divorced," she said, noting that her sister navigated marriage more
individualistically, for instance, keeping separate checking accounts.
The sisters' approaches to marriage could not be more divergent. "We
are family, it is very important . . . It's [the] main focus, I think, of our
church. . . . I love that." One expression of this approach is that Graciela
and Joseph have a joint checking account, which she manages.

The Bakers' marriage is a quintessentially family-first marriage in a
county dominated by a quintessentially family-first religion.

The Bakers are not outliers. It's no accident that when we look at
the midsize-to-large counties with the most children living in a married
family (table 2.1), the most religious counties in the country—measured
here by the share of adults who report a religious affiliation—are disproportionately likely to make the list. Utah County is number one on
this family indicator, and the second most religious county in America.

But this is not just a Mormon story. Outside of Utah, places like
Williamson County in Tennessee, which has lots of churchgoing evangelical Protestants, and Geauga County in Ohio, which is 20 percent
Amish, also land on this list. Of these top ten counties, half are among
the most religious places in the nation (in the top quartile—the top
25 percent—for religious affiliation in the nation). Clearly, then, religion
is one factor at the regional level when it comes to family stability.

But class matters, as well. As table 2.1 shows, counties in the top
quartile for education and family income dominate the ranks. Take,
for instance, Loudoun County in Virginia. Located just outside of
Washington, DC, Loudoun ranks in the top 25 percent for education

TABLE 2.1 THE TOP 10 COUNTIES FOR CHILDREN IN MARRIED FAMILIES

Ranking based on 983 counties with a population > 50,000

	Percent of children under 18 in married-couple families	Percent college educated	Median family income	Percent Asian American	Percent religious
1. Utah County, UT	89	40[T]	$76,626	1	89[T]
2. Williamson County, TN	87	59[T]	$122,501[T]	4[T]	56[T]
3. Forsyth County, GA	86	52[T]	$112,835[T]	12[T]	42
4. Loudoun County, VA	86	61[T]	$153,521[T]	18[T]	29
5. Geauga County, OH	86	38[T]	$94,654[T]	1	73[T]
6. Hunterdon County, NJ	86	52[T]	$140,904[T]	4[T]	39
7. Davis County, UT	85	38[T]	$88,027[T]	2	76[T]
8. Cache County, UT	85	38[T]	$66,241	2	82[T]
9. Dallas County, IA	85	49[T]	$109,051[T]	4[T]	47
10. Broomfield County, CO	85	55[T]	$111,341[T]	7[T]	28
US (all counties > 50,000)	67	28	$72,882	3	24

Note: [T] = top 25 percent of all US counties with a population of more than 50,000 for this category. Sources: American Community Survey (2021), US Religion Census (2020).

and family income; indeed, it is the richest county in America, with the highest median family income of any midsize-to-large county. It has 86 percent of its children living with married parents.

Table 2.1 also reveals that Asian Americans are disproportionately common in these counties, particularly in the more affluent ones. The Atlanta suburb of Forsyth County, Georgia, for instance, has a large number of Indian American families. Indeed, the share of Asian

Americans in a county is also a significant predictor of family stability in midsize-to-large counties across the United States.[19]

When we look more broadly at counties in the top quartile for two-parent families, we see a similar story. Figure 2.1 shows that these counties overwhelmingly hail from the Rocky Mountain West, the Midwest, and the wealthy suburbs of major metropolitan cities like New York, San Francisco, and Washington.

Observant readers may pick up on three other things from figure 2.1 about this discussion of region and family life: stable families are rarer in the South, in Appalachia, and in communities with more African Americans. Recall from chapter 1 the well-established links between a more stable family life and having more money, more education, and/or stronger religious ties. Scotch-Irish culture and less education help explain why Appalachian and Southern family life is less stable. The

FIGURE 2.1: COUNTIES WITH THE MOST TWO-PARENT FAMILIES

Darker regions have more two-parent families.

Percent of children in two-parent families

0–19%   20–39%   40–59%   60–79%   80–100%

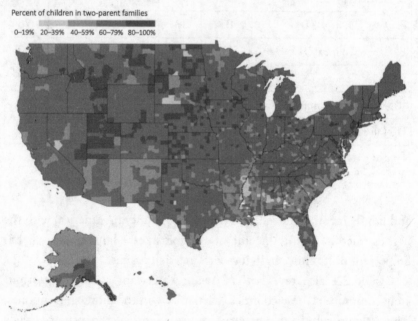

Source: The Opportunity Atlas, by Raj Chetty et al. Data obtained from the 2012–2016 American Community Survey. Courtesy of American Enterprise Institute.

Scotch-Irish were accurately described as "Born Fighting" by former senator James Webb, one reason why they are disproportionately more likely to be members of the US military *and* less likely to be heading up stable families.[20] Meanwhile, the cumulative effects of slavery and Jim Crow help explain why counties with more Black Americans have higher rates of single parenthood.[21]

THE MASTERS OF MARRIAGE

If we look above and beyond neighborhoods and counties to consider the nation as a whole as a kind of "love lab," we can finalize our effort to understand where and among whom our marital unions are strongest. When looking at nationally representative surveys, four groups stand out for being masters of marriage—those fortunate Americans who are especially likely to get married, steer clear of divorce court, *and* forge reasonably happy unions.

The first group is the Faithful. I use the term loosely to refer to those Americans who identify as churchgoing Christians—from evangelical Protestants to Catholics to mainline Protestants—as well as members of other religious traditions, including Jews. I do not have the space here to deal with the theological differences that divide these religious groups. My focus is on all religious believers who regularly attend church (or synagogue, mosque, temple, and so on); that is, several times a month or more. Their ties to their local religious communities, and their faith, endow their marriages and family lives with deep spiritual significance. And fellow adherents can provide practical, social, emotional, and even financial support when it comes to handling the ups and downs of modern family life. They are also the Americans most likely to believe, on principle, that the institution of marriage is good for the well-being of kids, communities, and the country.[22]

The second group is the Conservatives. This group embraces classic American middle-class, or what scholars call "bourgeois," values—like hard work and personal responsibility—as well as "traditional" values like the importance of marriage, sexual fidelity in marriage, the idea that men and women are inherently different, and the value of religion.[23] Today, for Conservatives who are and are not religious, their commitments to more

traditional beliefs about family, sex, and gender are also shaped by conservative media, public intellectuals, and friends. And since the "Great
Awokening" of 2014,[24] the period when many Americans embraced extremely progressive ideas about race, sex, and gender, Conservatives have
been the people most likely to reject "woke" ideas about family, sex, and
gender. All this helps explain why Americans identifying as "conservative" or "Republican" are more likely than others to be married today.[25]

The third group is Strivers. This group also embraces "bourgeois"
values—education, hard work, and financial success. They tend to be
more likely to take the long-term view of things and embrace delayed
gratification. They are, in the words of Chris Arnade, "front-row kids,"
those who as children were "always eager to learn and make sure the
teacher knew they were learning" and have now grown up to be the men
and women who wish "to get ahead." It is at least in part because of their
efforts that these Strivers largely dominate the professions, the business
world, the universities, and the media.[26] Even though many hold fash-
ionably liberal views about family matters—including politically correct
attitudes about family diversity, single motherhood, and so on—they do
not put these views into practice in their own private lives.[27] Wouldn't
be prudent.

The fourth group is Asian Americans. In recent decades, immigrants
from Asia—especially China, India, the Philippines, and South Korea—
have flocked to America in large numbers, to the point where more than
twenty million Americans are of Asian heritage.[28] These immigrants
and their children also tend to embrace Striver-style values—education,
hard work, delayed gratification, and financial success. In fact, today
"they are the highest-income, best-educated, and fastest-growing racial
group in the United States," as Bruce Drake from the Pew Research
Center recently pointed out.[29]

Asian Americans' devotion to Eastern-style traditional family values is also a big part of their American success story. Take Lisa Lee, a
Korean American living in Fairfax, Virginia. When she was growing up
as a first-generation immigrant in Pennsylvania, "family relationships
were incredibly important to the fabric of the entire Korean immigrant
culture." Now, as a wife and mother, she says, "We teach our kids that
there's no one more important than your family."

This family-first orientation shapes how she thinks about marriage, too. Romance is not her first priority in her marriage: "It may sound really cold to say that it's an economic partnership, but in some ways it is. And the project of raising our children is, at the moment, the overwhelming priority for [me and my husband] until they are out of the house and financially independent." Lee's mindset is consistent with my research showing that Asian Americans are more likely than Whites, Hispanics, and Blacks to believe that couples with children should make every effort to stay married, even if they are not happy.[30] Their orientation to marriage is rooted in a combination of principle and prudence: their traditions—be they Confucian, Hindu, or Muslim—push them in a family-first direction. *And* they recognize that stable families give their kids a big head start in their pursuit of the American Dream.

Of course, husbands and wives who hail from three or four of these groups—the Faithful, Conservatives, Strivers, and Asian Americans—tend to do especially well. But for the sake of simplicity, let's explore how religion, conservatism, education, and ethnicity are independently related to entrance into, the stability of, and the quality of marriage in America today.

Getting Married and Avoiding Divorce Court

Although one fault line in the American family, class, has gotten most of the attention in our public conversation when we look at trends in marriage, divorce, and children's family structure, we see that America is divided not just by class but also by religion, ideology, and race/ethnicity. It's not just the educated and wealthy who are masters of marriage, it's also the Faithful, the Conservatives, and Asian Americans.

When it comes to putting a ring on it, if we use a college degree as a proxy for being a Striver, fully 58 percent of Strivers ages eighteen to fifty-five are currently married, compared to 39 percent of adults this age without a college degree. Conservatives are also most likely to be married, with 57 percent of them married, compared to 40 percent of liberals and 43 percent of moderates. Those who regularly attend church are also most likely to be married (56 percent), compared to those who attend only occasionally (44 percent) and those who rarely or never attend (39 percent). There are also differences by ethnicity and race among Americans ages eighteen to fifty-five: Asian Americans are the most likely to be married (57 percent), followed by Whites (50 percent), Hispanics (43 percent), and Blacks (27 percent).[31]

Strivers are also more likely to go the distance when it comes to marriage. Figure 2.2 shows that only 22 percent of men and women ages eighteen to fifty-five with a college degree who have ever married have gotten divorced, compared to 37 percent of those without such a degree on their wall. In fact, a college diploma is the *top predictor* of avoiding divorce in the General Social Survey (GSS). But what about divorce and religion?

FIGURE 2.2: ASIAN AMERICANS, FAITHFUL, AND STRIVERS LEAST LIKELY TO BE DIVORCED

Percent ever divorced among ever-married adults aged 18 to 55

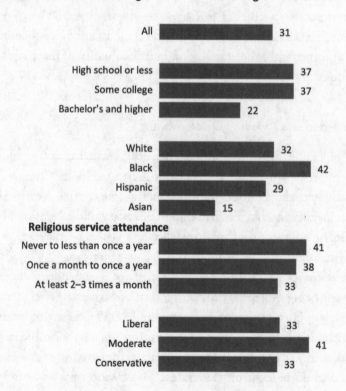

Source: American Community Survey, 2021 (IPUMS). Religion and ideology data from General Social Survey, 2014–2018.

Today, Americans who are regulars at their church, like the Bakers, are clearly more likely to marry for life. Data from the GSS tell us that only 33 percent of ever-married Americans (eighteen to fifty-five) who regularly attend church have divorced, compared to 38 percent of those known as "Christeasters," those who go to church infrequently—like on Christmas and Easter. Of those who rarely or never attend, 41 percent have divorced. Other studies that track husbands and wives over time using longitudinal data indicate that regular churchgoers are between 30 and 50 percent less likely than others to get divorced.[32] Regular religious attendance is the third most powerful predictor of marital stability in the GSS.

When it comes to the Conservatives, however, ideology is not clearly linked to a lower risk of divorce. Reporting a conservative worldview increases your odds of getting married in the first place, but after you've tied the knot, it does not much reduce your odds of getting divorced.[33]

When it comes to marital stability, no group compares to Asian Americans. The most stably married group in America is Indian Americans, according to the US Census. And when you look at Asian Americans as a whole, what you see is that only 15 percent of ever-married Asian Americans ages eighteen to fifty-five have divorced, compared to 32 percent of Whites, 29 percent of Hispanics, and 42 percent of African Americans. GSS data tell us that Asian Americans are 64 percent less likely to divorce than other Americans are—and that ethnicity is the second-best predictor of marital stability, following education.[34] Similarly, a study by sociologists Yuanting Zhang and Jennifer Van Hook found that Asian American couples are 86 percent less likely than White couples to divorce.[35] In other words, the familism found in Asian culture translates, in America, as in Asia, to markedly greater marital stability.

These family trends have obvious and important implications for children. Children from Conservative, Faithful, Striver, or Asian homes are disproportionately likely to grow up in stable families. In fact, when we look at intact, married families with children, we see that the majority are headed by parents who are either college educated, conservative, religious, Asian, or some combination of these. Specifically, 44 percent have a four-year degree, 42 percent attend church regularly, 38 percent are conservative, and 5 percent are Asian Americans. Together, parents who are in at least one of these groups make up 78 percent of adults ages eighteen to fifty-five who are stably married with children.[36] In other words, a clear majority of the most stable families in America hail from the ranks of the Faithful, the Strivers, Conservatives, or Asian Americans.

Wedded Bliss

Family stability is one thing, but the quality of married life also matters a great deal when it comes to determining who are the masters of marriage. After all, a stable marriage is not as valuable for the children or for the adults if the parents are miserable. So, how do these four groups fare when it comes not just to the stability of their marriages but also to the quality of their unions?

Strivers are happier husbands and wives. Figure 2.3 indicates that college-educated husbands and wives are about 5 percentage points more likely to report that they are "very happy" in their marriages, compared to married adults without a college degree. In fact, higher education is the second most powerful predictor of marital quality when we account for key sociodemographic factors in our analyses.[37] Strivers manage not just to stay married but—more often than not—to be happily married.

For the Faithful, meanwhile, the data are especially clear. Couples like the Bakers are markedly happier husbands and wives, especially if they are "equally yoked"—that is, if they share a common faith—with their spouse. Husbands and wives who attend religious services frequently are about 6 percentage points more likely to report they are "very happy" in their marriages, compared to those who attend sporadically or not at all.[38] In fact, faith is the *strongest* predictor of marital quality—when compared to other factors like ideology, education, race, and income—in the GSS. For reasons we will explore in the second half of this book, the Faithful are the group most likely to enjoy wedded bliss.

Conservatives are also happier in their marriages. As figure 2.3 indicates, they enjoy a 6-percentage-point advantage over moderates and a 5-percentage-point advantage over liberals. More fine-grained analyses indicate that the happiest husbands and wives hail from the "very conservative" camp.[39] They also tell us that some of the Conservative

FIGURE 2.3: FAITHFUL, CONSERVATIVES, STRIVERS, WHITES, AND ASIANS MOST LIKELY TO BE HAPPILY MARRIED

Percentage of husbands and wives who are "very happy" in marriage

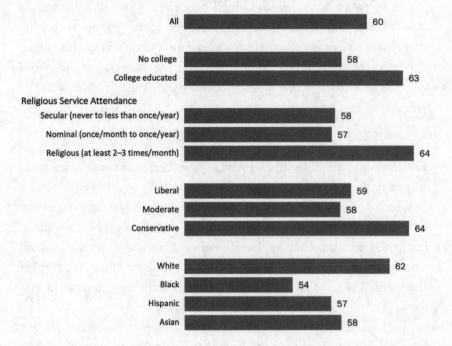

Based on married adults aged 18 to 55. Source: General Social Survey, 2014–2018.

advantages when it comes to marital happiness are limited to the conservatives who are also more religious.

The Asian advantage is more modest when it comes to marital quality. Indians, Chinese, Koreans, and other Asian Americans do enjoy markedly more stable unions, but only a minor marital-quality advantage, at least as Americans. They are only a few percentage points more likely to be in the happiest wives and husbands club, as figure 2.3 indicates, compared to married African Americans and Hispanics, and they are *not* happier than married Whites. Their principled and prudential commitment to family stability and marital permanence may not always translate into markedly higher levels of marital satisfaction, a fact hinted at by Lisa Lee's insistence that her primary focus is on her kids' welfare and not romance. In fact, it is precisely because Asian Americans are more likely to pursue family stability that they are more willing than other Americans to put up with a difficult marriage. More on that later.

If we think of the entire United States as a "love lab," the family stability and marital quality statistics tell a clear and perhaps surprising story. At least for those men and women who are marrying and having children, the state of our unions is generally strongest for these four groups: Asian Americans, Conservatives, the Faithful, and Strivers.

HOW DO THEY DO IT?

Relationship gurus like John Gottman have taught us the psychological secrets of a good marriage. They have revealed the microclimate that husbands and wives should seek to cultivate in their own marriages, the techniques and mindsets that boost the odds of marital bliss. Trade at least five positive comments for each critical comment you make about your husband. Preface your expression of concern about your wife's spending with a positive comment about her dedication to making sure the kids have nice outfits for school. And so on.

This is all helpful, so far as it goes. But this psychological approach doesn't tell us about the larger forces—cultural, communal, and economic—that put us on the path to better or worse unions. It does not tell us which communities are more likely to produce masters of marriage in contemporary America, and why. It does not tell us which values and virtues are better to pursue, and which vices are better to avoid. It does not tell us which kinds of people we should surround ourselves with when we desire marital support, and which kinds of people we should steer clear of.

So far, then, we have learned that the Faithful, Conservatives, Strivers, and Asian Americans have the most stable and satisfying marriages. But we have not yet learned *how* they do it.

One key attribute that they share is a tendency, as groups, to reject the anti-marriage messaging promoted by our ruling class. Conservatives and the Faithful tend to have ideological hedges that prevent them from falling prey to elite myths. Asian Americans' strong familist ethic helps them resist the individualistic siren songs in the culture. As for

Strivers, they tend to enter the ranks of the elites themselves . . . at which point, they copy that class's family-first habits, even as they parrot its lip service to family diversity and individual choice.

In the next few chapters, we'll walk through the various myths our elites promote and answer some key questions about those myths, for example: Why do so many people believe the false narrative that it's better to fly solo, despite the data? Why is it trendy to prop up myths like the value of "family diversity"? And above all, why do people who *privately* benefit from the value of marriage work so hard in *public* to deny or downplay the truth about our most fundamental institution?

CHAPTER 3

THE FLYING SOLO MYTH

Marriage Is of No Benefit to Men and Women Today

Marriage is not worth it. It's not worth the practical and financial sacrifices, the forgone romantic and sexual opportunities, and the lack of freedom." The benefits of marriage do little to "counteract the massive cost men pay to be married."

So wrote a young man named Craig, in response to a 2016 video of mine on marriage and men that went viral on the internet, garnering more than two million views.[1] The video, which made the case that marriage was good for men, generated lots of online pushback from men's rights activists, with thousands of negative comments posted online or emailed to me—including the email I got from twenty-nine-year-old Craig in Florida. He went on to write, "I would much rather buy a 75k condo by the beach in Florida working 10–20 hours a week with plenty of time and money to relax at the beach, sail, play golf and tennis as well as hang out with friends than marry a 30-year-old woman and take care of her into old age by working 50 hours a week at a job I don't like."

Craig also stressed that he was in excellent physical condition because he is not tied down to a regular nine-to-five job like most married men: "The fact is, my six-pack abs have gotten me far more sex with high-quality women in their prime than a man's six-figure income ever will. The sex is passionate and did not require begging like married men often have to do as the women are physically attracted to me rather than just interested in my ability to provide."

Craig's bill of particulars with marriage is long, and disappointingly narcissistic. But he does an excellent job of summarizing a view that I've encountered among a lot of young men lately: marriage is a ball and chain, of little benefit to the average guy.[2]

Voices from the female side of the argument, in major media outlets and online forums, often express an equal measure of skepticism about marriage. Women also worry about the price that marriage exacts from their own independence, albeit from a more progressive perspective. Consider reporter Amisha Padnani, who recently addressed the topic of marriage and women in a *New York Times* article entitled "Is Marriage a Prize?"[3] Her answer, as one might predict, was no. After all, "fewer and fewer women are letting [traditional] messages" about the importance of marriage "dictate how they live their adult lives, including when—or whether—to marry."

No, it's not a prize, because work is actually more important than marriage for today's women. After all, a Pew Research Center survey found that today's women are more likely to consider "career enjoyment," not marriage, as the "key to living a fulfilling life."[4] Finally, marriage is not a prize, because you can be just as happy flying solo as you can be flying with a copilot. Padnani reports that actress Tracee Ellis Ross said as much to her: "I am choicefully single, happily, gloriously single."[5]

Padnani represents a view that is popular among many young adults, and even more so among the rising generation of journalists, academics, and thought leaders who dominate the commanding cultural heights and generally lean left. The message is that marriage is at best unimportant, and at worst an obstacle to women's progress.[6] Similar messages are reinforced in pop culture, where the message is that your twenties are for career and fun, not marriage and family, and after that, marriage is optional, not necessary, and certainly not crucial to your own welfare or the good of society.

These messages have penetrated the minds of ordinary men and women, especially young adults, which helps explain why so many people now judge work, education, and money as better predictors of "fulfillment" than marriage and family life.[7]

What we are seeing emerge, often articulated by men and women from opposite ends of the ideological spectrum, is what I call the flying solo myth. This first great myth against marriage that I address in this book holds that marriage is of little or no importance today. People can find fulfillment in a variety of relationships, from friendships to cohabiting relationships, from living apart together (LAT) to polyamorous relationships; we need not privilege marriage. Oh, yes, and the meaning, direction, purpose, and community found at work can more than make up for the absence of marriage's emotional intimacy and family life. Likewise, the path toward financial stability and success is supposed to run through education and work, not wedlock. "Freedom" is found and maintained by avoiding marriage—or at least putting it off as long as possible.

One of the most remarkable things about the flying solo myth is that it crosses gender and political lines. It's a true unifying belief in our culture. The objections are partly economic in nature. Many of the young men and women I speak with nowadays are convinced that marriage is "just a piece of paper" that offers no financial value to them. This view has gained popularity in part because many elite journalists, scholars, and public intellectuals—like *Bloomberg* journalist Molly Smith, introduced in the preface—advance it confidently. Some specifically argue that marriage per se offers no material benefit to people beyond perhaps its propensity to bring together men and women who are already flourishing financially.

"Married people are less impoverished because people who are not impoverished are more likely to get married," wrote Matt Bruenig, the president of the People's Policy Project, for the *American Prospect*. "With marriage, you have an institution that attracts and retains more economically secure and stable people, not an institution that creates them."[8] In his view, marriage today unites prosperous men and women, but it doesn't increase the odds that ordinary men and women become prosperous.

Doug would beg to differ. This forty-four-year-old man from Maineville, Ohio, started his career at age eighteen, operating a press at a factory in Indiana for $16,000 a year while living in his parents' basement. "I really didn't have a care in the world," Doug said. "I didn't really have any bills." Later, after marrying and having kids, his perspective shifted: "I had to step up and think about something besides myself and start taking care of them."

So, as I noted in the *Washington Post*, Doug left his factory job and joined the US Army—which raised his salary to $24,000 and provided housing and health care for his new family. He sought regular opportunities for promotion in the service to boost his income. After more than a decade in the army, out of a desire to give his family a stronger financial footing, he left the service to work as a finance manager at a car dealership, where he is now earning six figures. Even though he never got a college degree.[9]

Doug's story is suggestive of the ways in which marriage can be good for men, financially. Married men—men like Doug—work harder, smarter, and more successfully than their peers who are not married. That is because, even today, men still associate marriage with growing up and providing for their own family. The providership "norm," as the late sociologist Steven Nock observed, is still alive and well in contemporary America, and it still engenders a "responsibility ethic" among men today. This marriage-induced responsibility ethic means married men work more hours, seek out higher-paying jobs, and are generally more reliable employees than their unmarried peers.[10] One Harvard study found, for instance, that married men are markedly less likely to be fired than their single peers, with only 7 percent of married men having experienced termination, compared to 17 percent of single men.[11]

The transformative power of marriage for men translates into a "marriage premium," where married men earn about 10 to 20 percent more than their peers with roughly similar backgrounds. One study of identical twins from Minnesota found that married twins made 18 to 26 percent more than their identical twins who were not married.[12] Another study from Penn State pegged the premium at 12 percent for married men in their late twenties.[13] Still another study found that marriage boosts "hours worked and wage rates," generating "an 18 percent–19 percent increase in earnings, with about one-third to one-half of the marriage earnings premium attributable to higher work effort."[14]

Scholars debate how much this premium is "causal"—that is, attributable specifically to the effect marriage has upon men's lives—and

TABLE 3.1: BY THEIR THIRTIES, MARRIED MEN AND WOMEN HAVE THE LARGEST INCOMES

Median household income by relationship status

	Men	Women
Married	$95,000	$90,000
Cohabiting	$68,000	$67,500
Single	$42,000	$38,000

Based on adults aged 32–38, surveyed 2017–2018. Source: National Longitudinal Survey of Youth, 1997.

how much it rather demonstrates a *selection effect*, where more industrious or responsible men select into marriage.[15] But given all the ways in which marriage changes men's approach to work and life, there is no doubt that some share of this marriage premium can be attributed to how marriage changes a man.

Marriage also benefits men financially in two big ways other than personal earning levels.

First, partly because most wives work today, married men generally enjoy a markedly larger household income than their single peers. And even when their wife does not work, having a partner at home often helps and motivates men, including some of the most financially successful men in America, to work harder and smarter. One San Francisco homemaker wife I spoke with noted that the intense travel required by her husband's seven-figure job in finance was only possible because she kept the trains running on time on the home front. It's no accident that the share of home-focused wives like her is largest among households where the man makes more than $250,000.[16]

Table 3.1 shows the difference in household income for married men in their thirties versus their cohabiting and single peers. There is no comparison, obviously, with the median married thirtysomething man taking in a household income of approximately $95,000, compared to $68,000 for the cohabiting man and $42,000 for the single man.[17] Even when we control for household size, age, education, race, ethnicity, and the presence of children, married men have 40 percent more household income than their unmarried peers.[18] Married men ages eighteen to fifty-five are also 55 percent less likely to be living in poverty, compared to their single peers, even controlling for factors like race and education.[19]

Second, in addition to the financial benefits of marriage, there are often serious financial penalties for men who disregard the institution. Men who do not get and stay married are more likely to find themselves in situations that torpedo their income and assets. Unlike Doug, who has remained stably married and managed to acquire a home and a nice nest egg, David Martin, a thirty-five-year-old man living in Tennessee, has very little to show for the fifteen years he has spent pulling down a salary. David has moved in and out of a series of romantic relationships, fathered three children with different partners, and only recently married. All that instability has proved costly.

"Financially it impacted me a lot," notes David. He started off as a grocery-store clerk making just $8 an hour but kept moving up the job ladder to the point where he is now a customer service representative for an insurance company, pulling in about $40,000 per year. Every two weeks his net pay is $1,400, but $600 of that, or about 40 percent of his take-home pay, goes to child support. "Every time I would find a better opportunity, it seems like I got knocked three steps back." Right now, David would like to put more money into the new home he just purchased with his wife, but so much of it goes right out the door: "It is frustrating because when you see your paycheck and you see, well, geez, I . . . still have child support coming out." David has learned the hard way that family instability is expensive.

Doug and David are no outliers. Men who marry *before* having children are three times more likely to move into the middle class or higher and four times more likely to avoid poverty by the time they hit their thirties, compared to their peers who put parenthood before marriage, even after factoring in socioeconomic differences between these groups of men.[20] Following the script of that classic nursery-school rhyme—"First comes love, then comes marriage, then comes baby in the baby carriage"—actually pays off financially for men.

Family stability also has big long-term benefits. Stably married men

FIGURE 3.1: MARRIED MEN IN THEIR FIFTIES HAVE MORE ASSETS

Median financial assets in 2016 dollars

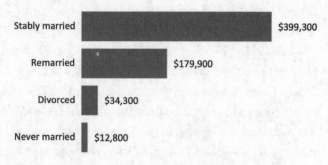

Based on adults aged 51 to 60, surveyed in 2016. "Divorced" includes those who are separated or widowed. Source: National Longitudinal Survey of Youth, 1979.

are more likely to invest in purchasing a home and to plow money into a retirement fund, compared to their unmarried peers from roughly similar backgrounds.[21] And they are less likely to incur costs related to family breakups.[22] Over time, these financial advantages really add up.

Today, stably married men heading into their golden years are in a much better position than their peers who have not followed that same path. They have more than ten times the median assets of their unmarried peers.[23] Even after factoring in differences in education level, race, and employment, the average marriage *premium* in household assets amounts to more than $290,000 for stably married men, compared to never-married, divorced, or remarried men.[24]

Much of this same story, a story where marriage engenders financial security and stability, also applies to women. Taylor, the thirty-three-year-old living in Denver, thinks she has lost out, financially, because she has not yet married. "I would be better off if I were married," she said, adding, "I mean, yeah, when you're married, you're paying for two people . . . but at the same time, you either have one or more paychecks, and that money is being used a lot more efficiently around more people."

Taylor's reasoning is sound. Although the marriage premium for women today is modest when it comes to their personal income (one new study finds that married twentysomething women earn about 6 percent more than their unmarried female peers),[25] it's very large when it comes to their family income. Table 3.1 indicates that married women in their thirties enjoy about $22,000 more in family income, compared to cohabiting women, and $52,000 compared to single women. Even after factoring in a range of control variables, including the presence of children, education, and race, married women have household incomes that are 45 percent larger than their unmarried peers.[26]

More income plus fewer redundant expenses, as Taylor observed, means that married women are usually much better off financially than their single peers. This explains why married women ages eighteen to fifty-five are about 80 percent less likely to be poor, compared to single women, even after controlling for other factors that lead to poverty, like low education and unemployment.[27] It's also no accident that single mothers are six times more likely to be poor, compared to married mothers.[28] Married women—and their kids, if they have them—typically live in nicer homes and safer neighborhoods, with access to better schools. Taylor, for instance, has noticed that "every married couple that I know that's about my age owns a home right now," even as she rents a condo owned by her parents.

And married women heading into retirement are in a much better position than their never-married or divorced peers, as figure 3.2 indicates. Stably married women typically have about $357,000 in assets in their fifties, compared to $243,000 for remarried women, $28,000 for divorced women, and $13,000 for never-married women. Even after controlling for factors that influence these differences, married women in their fifties enjoy a marriage premium that ranges from $42,000 (compared to remarried women) to more than $300,000 (compared to divorced and never-married women).[29]

Contrary to the messaging of left-leaning think tankers and right-leaning men's rights activists, marriage still matters financially. In a world where the cost of housing in our major metro areas keeps spiraling upward, where income inequality has soared over the last fifty years, where financial turmoil seems to upend the American economy every ten years, and where the cost of raising and educating children continues its relentless rise,[30] marriage is a financial safe harbor like none other.

FIGURE 3.2: MARRIED WOMEN IN THEIR FIFTIES HAVE MORE ASSETS

Median financial assets in 2016 dollars

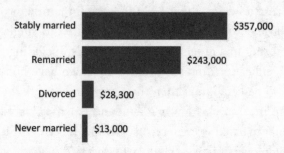

Stably married — $357,000
Remarried — $243,000
Divorced — $28,300
Never married — $13,000

Based on adults aged 51 to 60, surveyed in 2016. "Divorced" includes those who are separated or widowed. Source: National Longitudinal Survey of Youth, 1979.

With access to two potential incomes, two kinship networks, and a life partner for domestic tasks and expenses—and, let's not forget, the ability to steer clear of the thousands of dollars in expenses that arise from the relationship carousel that takes so many men and women for a turn or two or three these days—married men and women are generally in much better financial shape. Today, flying without a marital copilot can be especially challenging, as the world becomes ever more difficult to navigate, moneywise.

The benefits of marriage transcend mere economic advantages, however. There are important emotional effects of marriage. Let's consider its effect on a particularly extreme expression of societal despair.

BONDING AND BELIEVING

Why do people kill themselves? This was one of the big questions that captured the imagination of Emile Durkheim, the great nineteenth-century French sociologist, in his classic book *On Suicide*. And the answers he came up with were not psychological—tailored to the unique afflictions, inner dramas, or psychoses of particular individuals—they were sociological. In studying suicide, he discerned profoundly *social* patterns in determining who killed themselves.

Durkheim came to the conclusion that in Europe (at that time),

Protestants were more likely to kill themselves than Catholics were. Those with more education were more likely to kill themselves than those with less education. And the unmarried were more likely to kill themselves than married people were.[31]

These social patterns in suicide led him inexorably to the conclusion that the quality and character of our social ties have a significant impact on how much we are flourishing or floundering, and in this particular case, falling into a pit of deadly despair.

In *On Suicide*, Durkheim described two patterns of suicide that are particularly relevant for our day. First, he noted how much we depend on regular social interaction with others—what he termed "integration." Men and women who are not sufficiently integrated into the social fabric—who are not the regular recipients of care and concern, nor the givers of such care—are more likely to succumb to "egoistic suicide" as an expression of profound loneliness or lack of connection to others.[32]

Second, we also depend on clear norms and values to give direction and meaning to our lives—what sociologists call a "nomos" (the Greek word for the spiritual law governing human behavior), which orders our days in this world. Men and women who lack clear norms and values in their lives are more likely to succumb to "anomic suicide" when their lives lack rhythms and routines, direction, and purpose.[33]

In all this, the importance of living for something or someone else is paramount. In Durkheim's words, "man cannot live unless he attaches himself to an object that is greater than himself and outlives him." The storms of life are much easier to navigate when a person has a North Star in sight: "Life, they say, is only tolerable if one can see some purpose in it, if it has a goal and one that is worth pursuing."[34]

Marriage and other family ties are key vehicles for the kind of bonding and believing that protect against the two forms of suicide Durkheim observed. Marriage binds us to another person and to the children that the union creates. These connections allow us to receive the care and concern of others. They also force us to come out of ourselves, to live for someone else—day in and day out. These family ties bind us to the broader society, be it schools, sports leagues, or Sunday school. Having these ties protects us from feeling too alone in this world, from the kind of "egoism" that can tempt us to consider ending it all.

Marriage and family life also play a key role in supplying routines and meaning to our daily lives, thereby protecting us from anomic suicide. Work is endowed with new meaning, especially for men, as a vehicle to provide for one's family. Seemingly quotidian household matters—from cooking to cleaning to taking out the trash—shape the warp and woof of one's days. The responsibilities that flow from parenthood—from helping with homework to celebrating holiday traditions for Christmas, Passover, or Ramadan—guide and ground the ebb and flow of fathers' and mothers' lives.[35] Living for the good of one's family endows life with an extra layer of meaning not found in virtually any other domain of social life.[36]

Today, ordinary Americans are much more likely to succumb not just to suicide but also to a whole host of related maladies—like loneliness, meaninglessness, despair, and drug use—if they are living as "bare branches." Scott O'Sullivan is one such bare branch, his life marked by the absence of marriage and family. By the standards of success in today's culture, nothing should bother Scott, thirty-four, who is unmarried. He's got a college degree from Clemson University, an engaging career as a military contractor, a house of his own, and a good-sized bank account, as he pulls in more than $100,000 annually. But these educational and professional accomplishments are not enough.

"You know, I've got degrees on my wall, I've got accomplishments and certificates, but it doesn't mean anything in the end," he told me. "It's not like I can take any of that with me after [I die]."

Scott feels alone and adrift on many a day: "I have to get up every day and look in the mirror and realize I'm alone. I have nobody." And he worries about the kind of fate that might await him if he should ever fall sick, later in life: "I have no help, you know, if something happened to me tomorrow, there'd be no one for me."

As he talks about his days living in a Washington, DC, suburb, the meaninglessness is palpable: "I mean, I come home. I take my dog out, eat dinner, and I go to bed—[and I] repeat this five days a week. I've nothing to look forward to. Nope. I don't feel [like] anybody is cheering me on." Without the rhythms and routines of marriage and family life and the care and concern of a spouse and children, Scott struggles with a toxic mix of loneliness, meaninglessness, and sadness.

Scott is not the only single person who feels this way. Taylor also reports that she has struggled with loneliness and anxiety related to living alone. She also worries about her personal safety. "I was actually having regular nightmares, and I was really anxious, and I was always checking all the closets when I got home because I was alone," she said. Taylor's anxiety only subsided after she got a dog.

But do their experiences correspond to the lives of single men and women across America in general? In *Going Solo: The Extraordinary Rise and Surprising Appeal of Living Alone*, NYU sociologist Eric Klinenberg argues that the growing ranks of single men and women ages eighteen to fifty-five (who numbered seventy-one million in 2020, up from nineteen million in 1970) are generally doing just fine, by his reckoning.[37] After all, there are other forms of social integration besides marriage. Compared with marrieds, for instance, he contends, "single people are more likely to spend time with friends and neighbors, go to restaurants and attend art classes and lectures."[38]

In "The Case against Marriage," which ran in the *Atlantic*, journalist Mandy Len Catron echoed this view, arguing that "marriage actually weakens other social ties" that are integral to our lives. Sure, in marriage you gain the company of a spouse, but that comes at the cost of weaker ties to extended family members, members of your local community, and friends.[39]

Of course, some single adults are flourishing socially. As the median age for first marriage has risen from twenty-two in 1970 to twenty-nine today,[40] and as slightly more than half of the adult population is unmarried, plenty of people do appreciate the opportunities associated with flying solo.

Consider Mark, an investment banker mentioned in *Going Solo*. He has parlayed his singledom into international travel and a rich professional life. Mark's life is described this way: "Staying single through his thirties allowed him to experience things that his friends who married and had children could only dream about: Living in different countries. Taking adventurous vacations. Dating lots of women and figuring out what kind of partner he wants . . . spending so much time and effort building a professional network early in his career."[41]

Mark's story sounds pretty good, right? It would seem to lend plausibility to the bottom line suggested by the likes of Klinenberg and Catron when it comes to assessing the "extraordinary rise and surprising appeal of living alone": there is nothing to worry about here, folks. Unmarried Americans are finding new ways to forge strong and meaningful social ties with others, and there is no big psychological or social downside to America's retreat from marriage and the rising numbers of men and women flying solo.

But, in truth, they could not be more wrong in describing how things are actually playing out for *average* men and women, rather than affluent professionals like Mark.

First, when it comes to social ties, as the sociologist Nicholas Wolfinger has pointed out, it is not true that married men and women are uniformly more socially withdrawn than their unmarried peers. Drawing on data from the General Social Survey, he finds that "married adults are more likely to do volunteer work than are single people. They also attend religious services more frequently, and often share their places of worship with their friends. The only measure of outside engagement they fare less well on is how often they hang out with friends—and it only feels natural that people hang out less with other friends when they're living with the person presumed to be their best friend."[42]

But marriage and family life do much more than connect you to your local church or youth soccer league. They dramatically increase your odds of giving and receiving care and concern in daily life. This is one reason Lisa O'Neill is glad she is married: "I feel so cared for by my husband," adding, "I need lots of hugs and snuggling." Being married to her husband, Sean, "has made me a lot less lonely—having someone to share every day and all the kind of good and bad challenges that come with life." Lisa feels like her life has a firmer foundation, a "foundation that is so important because that is what's gonna be there to get you through when the storm comes, when the plague comes, when all the other hard things in life" hit.

Speaking of plagues, the presence of Sean and their children was crucial for thirty-two-year-old Lisa during COVID time. The conversations with Sean, and the opportunities to care for and be with her children, were an emotional lifeline at a time when she could not hug family and friends outside her household. "I don't think I would be doing really well. The idea of being by myself, kind of trapped in my house" without her young family would have been unbearable. Sean and the kids were "really necessary for my mental health" amid all the isolation and alienation unleashed by the pandemic.

Family ties like these translate into higher reports of meaning and lower reports of loneliness for married Americans. In Lisa's words, "I think having kids completely changed my entire life," adding that to an important extent "they are my purpose and my meaning now." The 2021 IFS/Wheatley Institute Family Survey indicates that married Americans like Lisa are markedly more likely to report their lives are meaningful. Sixty percent of married parents say their lives are meaningful "most of or all of the time," compared to just 38 percent of single, childless adults. Men and women married with children most commonly report high levels of meaning in their lives: 59 percent of married fathers and 60 percent of married mothers.[43]

The differences between married and unmarried Americans when it comes to loneliness are also striking. Single, childless adults are about twice as likely to feel lonely than their married peers, with or without children, as figure 3.3 indicates. Marriage clearly helps to protect men and women from loneliness in America today.

Many of these dynamics are reflected in the research on suicide.

FIGURE 3.3: LIFE FOR MARRIED PARENTS IS LESS LONELY

Percentage of Americans who say their life is lonely most or all of the time

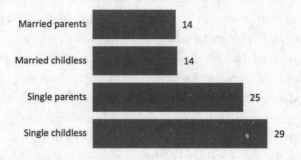

Based on adults aged 18 to 55. Source: IFS/Wheatley Institute Family Survey (2021).

In the words of one study: "In general, married persons have lower suicide rates than persons who have never married or persons who are divorced or widowed."[44] As Durkheim would predict, suicide is lowest for Americans who are married with children, with another study finding that, compared to single adults living alone, those who are married with no children have a 33 percent decreased risk, and those who are married with children experience a 48 percent decreased risk.[45] And, as Durkheim would have predicted, the research indicates that marriage is especially protective against suicide for men.[46]

In fact, declines in marriage also appear to be powering the surge in "deaths of despair"—death by suicide, drugs, or alcohol—now afflicting the White working class, especially White working-class men.[47] In 2015 Princeton economists Anne Case and Angus Deaton discovered that White, working-class people were killing themselves in record numbers, usually by shooting or hanging themselves, overdosing on opioids and other drugs, or drinking themselves to death.[48] After studying the trend, sociologist Philip Cohen, no booster for marriage, nevertheless concluded that rising deaths of despair for this group are connected to the decline of working-class marriage. In his words, "The overall rise in White mortality is limited almost exclusively to those who are not married, for men and women."[49] The ebbing fortunes of marriage among poor and working-class Americans, especially men, appear to have opened the way to a toxic tidal wave of pill-popping, alcohol-induced cirrhosis, and deaths by firearm, a wave that has torn through all too many working-class communities across the country.

So the idea that the dramatic increase in single living in America is no cause for concern for our civilization could not be further from the truth. Today, married men and women report a greater sense of meaning and less loneliness than their unmarried peers. By contrast, unmarried Americans are much more likely to be living lives marked by boredom, isolation, and meaninglessness. This loneliness is especially felt by unmarried working-class men and women, who don't have the benefits of high-flying professional jobs and strong community ties (as is often the case for the more affluent and educated).[50] The truth is that women and especially men flying solo in America today are significantly more likely than their married fellow citizens to crash and burn—

even to the point of ending up in an early grave. Durkheim would not be surprised.

HAPPILY EVER AFTER?

From the halls of academe to the red carpets of Hollywood, we are often told that marriage is unnecessary, undesirable, or, if you have your heart set upon tying the knot, best done later in life, after you have had time for career and fun in your twenties. In the *New York Times*, Eric Klinenberg celebrated the rise in people living alone for promoting "freedom, personal control and self-realization—all prized aspects of contemporary life."[51] Movies like *How to Be Single* tell us that the twenty-something single years are the "Best Time of Your Life."[52]

The anti-nuptial message Americans get from our ruling class comes through in polling. The very group that dominates elite America, college-educated liberals, for instance, is the group *least* likely to say that marriage is good for society. Twenty-five percent of college-educated liberals say society is better off when more people are married, versus 49 percent of other Americans.[53] And these messages from the media, academy, and pop culture have had their impact on our young adults, who, as noted earlier, polls tell us now believe that work and money matter more for their fulfillment than do marriage and parenthood.[54]

But the truth is that married men and women are markedly happier

FIGURE 3.4: MARRIED MEN AND WOMEN ARE HAPPIER

Percent "very happy," by marital status and gender

Based on men and women aged 18 to 55. Source: General Social Survey, 2014–2018.

than their unmarried peers. Figure 3.4 shows that, among Americans ages eighteen to fifty-five, about 40 percent of married men and women are very happy with their lives, compared to about 21 percent of those who are not married. Even after factoring in differences in income, education, and other demographic factors, married men and women are twice as likely to be happy with their lives, compared to their unmarried peers. What's more, and contrary to the narrative arc of what seems like a thousand popular television shows, even twentysomething married Americans are about 80 percent more likely to be happy than their unmarried fellow twentysomethings.[55]

Lisa is one of those women who counts herself a happier person now that she is married. She is somewhat wistful about having less time for friends and music festivals now that she is married, but she describes her current life, marked as it is by caring for two young children, as more "substantial" than her life before marriage and parenthood: "I think that my marriage and my family are like absolutely the number one source of my happiness."

"I feel a little bit spoiled because I have somebody to share [parenting] with," Lisa says, including the hard things but also "the joy in it." She appreciates having "somebody who is just as excited to see my child smile for the first time or roll over—you know, somebody who loves these children in the same way that I do." Lisa is getting at something profound. *Sharing* meaningful experiences—like raising a child—is often a lot more happiness-inducing than experiencing them on your own.

This helps explain why science reveals marriage as a much more powerful predictor of happiness than two other factors that many young adults think will bring them happiness: work and money. Having a job only boosts your odds of being happy by 50 percent. An above-average income only boosts them by 88 percent. Marriage is associated with a 151 percent increase in your odds of being happy, compared to being never married.[56] In fact, two economists found that a stable marriage was estimated to be worth approximately $100,000 per year of extra happiness, compared to being widowed or separated.[57]

The marriage premium in happiness also helps account for the growing class divide in happiness noted in the preface.[58] "Although marriage doesn't account for the entire class gap, it does explain about half of it," psychologist Jean Twenge wrote, adding, although the "data can't answer the question of whether marriage causes happiness or happiness causes marriage . . . it does suggest that one reason for the growing class gap in happiness is the growing marriage gap by class."[59] A big reason, then, so many working-class and poor Americans may have succumbed to deaths of despair is that the prospect of finding happiness through a good, stable marriage now seems out of reach.

There are plenty of skeptics regarding the idea that marriage causes happiness. Chief among them is the psychologist Bella DePaulo, the author of *Singled Out: How Singles Are Stereotyped, Stigmatized, and Ignored, and Still Live Happily Ever After*.[60] Her argument is threefold. First, plenty of singles are doing just fine. "Many single people savor solitude, they don't dread it," DePaulo said, adding, "Remember that Supreme Court Justice who said marriage responds to the universal fear that a lonely person might call out and find no one there. Well, my fear is that I wake up in the middle of night and find someone else is there—hogging the blankets, snoring, and farting."[61]

Second, single people make up for the lack of having that one person to turn to for emotional and social support by having lots of people to rely upon—friends, kin, neighbors, and many others. "The story we are told is that married people have 'the one.' The untold, more revealing story is that single people have 'the ones.'"[62] Here, she echoes the argument of Catron and Klinenberg.

And third, insofar as we do see that married men and women are happier, which we do, it is because the types of people who get and stay married are different from others, not because marriage as an institution confers any unique benefits. "So it was not marriage that 'made' them happier than single people; they were already happier," DePaulo contends, arguing also that any happiness advantage peters out shortly after the honeymoon.[63] This is a good example of the selection-effect argument, the idea that marriage per se does not cause happiness but, rather, happy people are more likely to get and stay married.

She is right that some people really do prefer living alone and that marriage is not for them. However, these men and women are the *exceptions*. Because we are social animals, most of us do better together, not alone. This helps explain why her second argument—about singles relying on the "ones" rather than the "one"—is not compelling, given that loneliness is *still* markedly higher among the unmarried today than it is among married men and women.

What about her third argument? No doubt part of the link between marriage and happiness is about selection effects.[64] People who are more socially adept, take the long-term view, and are more religious, for instance, are more likely to be stably married and also more likely to be happy.

But marriage is not simply an institution that collects relatively hardworking, socially adept, and happy people. It is also an institution that transforms people, bonding men and women to a particular person, to a whole way of life. In doing so, as we have seen, it endows their lives, day in and day out, with more meaning, prosperity, stability, and solidarity, all of which typically boost the sense of satisfaction that men and women take from their lives *after* they enter our civilization's most fundamental institution. In other words, the effect of marriage on the human happiness of people like Lisa O'Neill is also causal.

Consider one study tracking happiness in two groups of adults—some who married and some who did not—over time, by economists Shawn Grover and John Helliwell. They controlled for happiness prior to marriage and still found "a causal effect [on happiness] at all stages of the marriage, from pre-nuptial bliss to marriages of long duration."[65] In fact, they found the happiness-boosting power of marriage was largest in midlife, when people were in their late forties and fifties and adult happiness is at its nadir, thereby knocking down arguments made by scholars like DePaulo that any marriage effects on happiness are just "honeymoon" effects, limited to the first bloom of marital love.[66]

Reviewing this study and other research on marriage and wellbeing, Harvard's Tyler VanderWeele, a professor of biostatistics in the university's school of public health, is convinced that the effects of marriage on men and women cannot be attributed only to selection. In his words, "The effects of marriage on health, happiness and life satisfaction, meaning and purpose, character and virtue, close social relationships, and financial stability are thus profound."[67] There's no question in the mind of this Harvard professor that marriage advances the common good—and maximizes the odds that ordinary men and women have a shot at succeeding in the pursuit of happiness.

FLYING WITH A COPILOT IS USUALLY BETTER

Many voices in our culture—from men's groups on the right to progressive-minded female journalists on the left—discount the value of marriage. For different reasons, they think flying solo is fine, sometimes even better than navigating life with a copilot.

But contrary to the flying solo myth, social science tells us that men and women who get married in America typically reap large returns from the investments they make in wedlock. Those who get and stay married today are much more likely to be prospering, flourishing socially, and happy. To be sure, things are not always "happily ever after" in wedlock. Anyone who has been married knows that there are days, months, and even seasons of married life that can leave you angry, disappointed, or dispirited. Most of the time, however, flying with a copilot in life is better than going it alone.

But there are two exceptions to this general rule.

The first exception is divorce. When I talk up the benefits of marriage, one of the biggest concerns that I hear men articulate about marriage is that it leaves them vulnerable to divorce. "I have seen so many divorces," said Scott O'Sullivan, adding that both he and many of his friends have become gun-shy about marriage because they have seen so many people fail at marriage: "It's like taking an airplane when you see the airplanes crashing so many times; eventually, you're not going to get on board."

Given that about two-thirds of divorces today are initiated by women,[68] some for good reasons and some for not-so-good reasons, Scott O'Sullivan's fears about flying with a copilot are understandable. Marriage is *not* a good investment—financially, socially, or emotionally— if the flight crashes and burns. And while the divorce rate is falling, slightly more than 40 percent of marriages are still currently projected to end in divorce. So divorce is one of the primary exceptions to the rule that having a copilot makes the journey better.

The other major exception applies to marriages scarred by violence, drug abuse, or infidelity—in other words, highly conflicted or toxic marriages. Men and women in such marriages are much less likely to flourish physically and emotionally.[69] There is some evidence that the quality of married life is especially salient for women. The late sociologist Steven Nock observed, "When women benefit from marriage, it is because they are in a satisfying relationship."[70] So, especially for women, it is not just marriage, but a good marriage that brings the benefits.[71]

Fortunately, as we have seen, most marriages are happy—not all, but most of the time. But toxic marriages spell trouble for everyone. In chapter 6, we will begin to review the ingredients that go into marriages that are not toxic, but stable and satisfying. And, as will become clear, one reason that Striver, religious, Asian American, and Conservative husbands and wives are more likely to be in satisfying marriages—or married in the first place—may well be that they are more likely than the population at large to recognize and reject the flying solo myth.[72]

CHAPTER 4

THE FAMILY DIVERSITY MYTH

Love and Money, Not Marriage, Make a Family

After bouncing through seven foster families in California, eight-year-old Rob finally landed with his forever family. At last, the dizzying turns around the family-go-round seemed over, as did much of the misbehavior that had followed in the wake of his constant moves. Prior to moving in with the Hendersons, his new adoptive parents, Rob had learned pickpocketing from foster siblings, tried to steal his second-grade teacher's wallet right out of her purse at school, and gotten into all sorts of other trouble.

But after he moved in with his new adoptive parents, things took a turn for the better. "I had, you know, a mom and a dad and a sister now," he recalls, adding that he appreciated the stability, love, and attention they gave him. They were also more forbearing when he acted up than his foster parents had been. "I still remember getting in trouble, but they were much more understanding of me and what I was, where I had come from." This was a "fairly happy part of my childhood."

But two years later, around Christmastime, Rob's world was turned upside down again. "My mom and dad sat my sister and me down and said, 'We're getting divorced,'" Rob recalled. At the news, his five-year-old sister got up to give a comforting hug to their parents, who were both clearly upset.

But Rob stayed where he was across the room. He remembers thinking at the time, *Does this mean I have to leave yet another home?* And he also remembers feeling "just emotionally cold" at the prospect of taking another turn on the family-go-round.

Sure enough, after the divorce, Rob had to move out of the family's single-family home into a smaller duplex with just his mom. The physical and emotional instability occasioned by the divorce also ushered in a return of previous bad behavior: "I got in a lot of trouble at school and was sort of backsliding into older habits." He ignored school assignments, got into fights at recess, and was pulled over for driving drunk. Even though he is exceedingly bright, Rob graduated from high school with a subpar GPA, assumed college was not in his future, and headed off to the Air Force to get a new start in life.

The Air Force gave him the structure, stability, and success his tumultuous family life had denied him. It also gave him the confidence to rethink the prospect of attending college. In fact, as he finished up his tour, he applied to a few colleges—including what he considered a long shot, Yale University. Much to his surprise, he got in, on the strength of his unusual life story and top-tier SAT scores.

Yale was like nothing he had experienced in his life. The collegiate Gothic halls graced by ivy and the intense academic and social opportunities afforded by one of the nation's premier universities wowed him. But as someone who grew up in a turbulent, working-class home, Rob also felt out of place.

One day, for instance, one of his professors asked the students how many of them had been raised by their birth parents. The vast majority raised their hands. "This was a shock to me—[finding out] twenty-three out of twenty-five students had been raised by their birth parents," Rob said. And as he talked to other Yale students about their lives, he discovered "the typical student at this place, they had both of their parents."

This disparity between the Yale family pattern and the patterns he witnessed growing up got Rob thinking. "I started reflecting more on what are those sorts of steps that lead to success. Why is it that these people are studying at this great university, while [my] friends back home are either in jail or working at a batting cage or strung out on drugs?" This question was especially striking because almost none of his friends from back in California had even gone to a four-year college, not to mention a school like Yale. The family pattern he encountered in that sociology class, and Yale more generally, led him to conclude that family structure was a big part of why some young adults had a shot at success and others did not.

However, he discovered that talking about this family pattern in class at Yale was not easy. "I remember discussing my life in this class and there being this weird silence. And I think part of it was because a lot of these students had never met anybody like me," Rob said. "My sense of it was that no one, no one wants to talk about family."

When the idea of family structure ever "came up in any way, there was always an effort to bring it back to poverty." That's because most of his fellow students at Yale didn't want to make "normative value judgments about the family, so they retreated into ideas like 'we just need to give people more money' or 'economic opportunities.'" Both the awkward silences around these issues and the move to pin all family troubles on economics were driven partly by a pervasive "nonjudgmental attitude" surrounding and superintending public discussions of family life. But they were also driven by the notion, dominant in elite circles, that today's family diversity is a mark of moral progress in society.[1]

This brings us to the second great myth, the family diversity myth: that love and money, not marriage, make a family. The family diversity myth is the idea that all types of families are equally safe and beneficial for children, because family is about the affection and attention that adults and children exchange with one another, provided that families have enough money to support themselves. The marital status of the adults in a family is irrelevant. Shaped by commitments to inclusion, individual choice, and progress, this myth requires silence when it comes to publicly acknowledging any advantages that marriage might afford kids.

CELEBRATING FAMILY DIVERSITY

Nowadays, the family diversity myth is propagated across a variety of cultural platforms, including those controlled by big business. Consider the 2018 "Holiday" ad from Heineken, the second-largest beer company in the world. The ad opened with a seemingly old-school domestic tableau: with Dean Martin's "You're Nobody till Somebody Loves You" playing in the background, the camera slowly pans to a happy family hosting a festive holiday party in an elegant old home. "Dad" (all the ad's characters are helpfully captioned) is reading a newspaper next to a roaring fire with a grin on his face and a Heineken at his side. Seated adjacent to him in a drawing room with richly paneled walls are "Mom" and "Sister," grinning and offering playful waves to the camera. So far, so traditional.

But then the quaint scene gets more complicated and much more contemporary. As the camera pans across the drawing room, it alights upon "Mom's New Boyfriend," who is painting, also beaming at the camera, and then upon "His Stepdaughter," who offers a wan smile and wave of her own. The camera continues through different rooms in the richly appointed home, introducing us to "Dad's New Family"—a young man dancing blissfully by himself with closed eyes to music on headphones and a pair of blond twins chatting and smiling. Heineken's ad concludes by presenting one big, happy blended family portrait marked by this caption: "Tradition doesn't always have to be traditional."[2]

This offering from Madison Avenue, with its upbeat gloss on contemporary family complexity, is just one example of the family diversity myth being pushed out by much of pop culture, the media, schools and universities, and now even the business world. Out of a desire to appear inclusive, sensitive, or in step with the times, many of our culture's leaders give voice to the myth that for kids, all family structures are equal. Or—out of a desire to not run afoul of progressive sensibilities—they subtly minimize the impact of alternative family structures on children in their public language, sometimes avoiding the subject entirely. The truth about the ways that single parenthood, divorce, nonmarital childbearing, and family instability affect children is rarely spoken of in public by our elites.

The mainstream media insists, in the words of one *Huffington Post* article, that we should be "Embracing a More Realistic and Inclusive Definition of Family." The descriptive reality that many "households in the U.S. depart from the 'nuclear family' model of a married husband and wife and their children" is taken as proof of the need to affirm "that families come in all shapes and sizes."[3] The merits of family diversity are assumed rather than argued.

The message we get from the ivory tower about family diversity and child outcomes is somewhat less rose-colored—especially from serious family scholars who actually crunch the data and know how family structures affect kids. But plenty of academics—both in and outside of the classroom—still celebrate family diversity or downplay the impact that different family structures can have on children's lives. In an article titled "Good Riddance to 'The Family,'" sociologist Judith Stacey writes, "Family sociologists should take the lead in burying the ideology of 'the family' and in rebuilding a social environment in which diverse family forms can sustain themselves with dignity and mutual respect."[4]

Other scholars minimize the importance of family structure in favor of family process. "All of our research points to the fact that it's the quality of the relationship that matters, and the handling of communication and conflict, and the number of people in the household is not really the key," says Pamela Braboy Jackson, a professor of sociology at Indiana University. "Just because family structure is different doesn't mean that family operates any differently."[5] The takeaway: it's the love, not the structure, that matters for healthy families.

Philip Cohen, a sociologist at the University of Maryland and the author of a popular college textbook, *The Family: Diversity, Inequality, and Social Change*, does what he can to celebrate contemporary family diversity and minimize its downsides in his writing and public commentary on family matters. From his perspective, money is much more important for families and children than marriage.[6]

This approach was on full display in an exchange Cohen had on *Fox & Friends* about the diversity of American family life today. Asked point-blank if children from intact married families do better than other children, Cohen discounted the importance of family structure "per se," stressed the importance of money over marital status for children's well-being, and affirmed family diversity by talking about the "pros and cons and the challenges that people face in all different arrangements": "Well, people with married parents have the benefit of two incomes for one thing. If people grow up with single mothers who have adequate income, [they] do fine on average. What we find is they do have a lot of challenges from the lack of resources but family structure per se is not as big a factor."[7]

Cohen's goal here was to push the idea that money matters more than marriage for children.

Other scholars and journalists do not explicitly give voice to the family diversity myth, but they tend to sweep the issue of family structure under the rug in covering major issues—from education to crime to poverty—that have a marriage angle.

"Poor Kids Who Do Everything Right Don't Do Better than Rich Kids Who Do Everything Wrong" read the headline of a *Washington Post* article detailing the way in which children from rich families who drop out of high school do about as well financially as adults as children from poor families who graduate from college. This *Post* story was based on a Brookings Institution study by Isabel Sawhill and Richard Reeves that found that these two groups of children are about equally likely to land on the bottom income rung when they reach adulthood.[8] The implication? Money gives rich kids a big advantage when it comes to realizing the American Dream as adults, an advantage that can outweigh their lack of education.

This is true enough, but guess what the story left out? The same Brookings report also found that being "raised by continuously married parents . . . appears to provide a strong defense against falling behind and a strong foundation for moving ahead" for rich and poor kids, respectively, when it comes to their financial position as adults.[9] In other words, marriage matters, too. But money, not marriage, got the spotlight in the *Washington Post* article.

Beyond this particular study, however, what does the broader evidence say about marriage, family structure, and the educational, social, emotional, and economic well-being of our kids? Is it really true that money matters more than marriage for kids today? Is there any evidence for this theory? We turn now to answering these questions.

BEST IN CLASS: THE EDUCATIONAL AND SOCIAL ADVANTAGES OF INTACT FAMILIES

The Jefferson Scholarship at the University of Virginia is one of the most competitive merit-based programs in America. The program aims "to attract to the University the most promising leaders, scholars, and citizens in the world."[10] It does this by offering at least thirty exceptionally talented high-school seniors a full ride—tuition plus room and board for four years at UVA, worth more than $150,000. Students are nominated from over five thousand schools as well as forty-two countries worldwide, and 120 of these nominees make it to a final selection event in Charlottesville, where the scholars are chosen.

The finalists are markedly diverse in most respects, representing every major continent of the world; a range of political, religious, and ideological views; and interests that span the intellectual and extracurricular spectrum, from a young scientist studying "The Effect of Hydrocarbon Contamination on the Root" to an all-Ireland Irish Dance champion to high-school football captains.[11] The finalists are also a racially and ethnically diverse group.

But this group is not diverse in one respect: family structure. As a regular faculty reviewer for the Jefferson Scholars Program, I have found that more than 80 percent of the nominees that I end up evaluating for the scholarship list *both* of their parents at the same address. This is striking, because only about half of American high-school seniors can do the same. Nominees for the Jefferson Scholarship are *much* more likely than the average high school senior to hail from a home with both their married parents.

The family life of John, twenty-seven, a Jefferson Scholar and recent UVA graduate, is indicative of the ways in which a strong and stable family can give high-school students a leg up in climbing the ladder of the American meritocracy. "I always felt like I had people who were in my corner, who were on my team," said John, reflecting on the support he got from his parents and close, extended family growing up in suburban Richmond, Virginia. Many of his brothers and cousins attended the same Classical Christian school he did—and his parents, grandparents, uncles, and aunts were regulars at school events and athletic contests.

"My family provided me with a lot of support and pushed me academically, extracurricularly, and professionally," said John, who is the oldest of four boys. His dad, a lawyer, would read his essays and listen to him prepare for in-class presentations, giving him feedback on "how to present and communicate in a very effective manner." Likewise, his mom, a pharmacist, "was always there checking all of our math homework."

Besides the academic encouragement, his parents offered what psychologists call an "authoritative" style of parenting, mixing involvement and affection with clear expectations about good behavior.[12] His dad would share his own life philosophy with him on the morning commute to school and on the playing field, as he coached many of John's soccer and baseball teams growing up. "He imparted the value of hard work and not making any excuses or taking anything for granted," he recalls.

His mom was the family's "organizational engine," making sure that John and his brothers ate dinner at home most nights, got to and from extracurricular activities successfully, got their homework done, and went to church as a family on Sundays.

The strong and secure home base John had growing up helped him excel in the classroom (with a weighted 4.4 GPA), on the athletic field (in varsity baseball), and as a volunteer in Richmond, where he headed up a teen mentoring program. All of these achievements, in turn, paved the way for his selection as a Jefferson Scholar at the University of Virginia.

John's experience is emblematic not just of the Jefferson Scholars Program but also of what we see more generally among students at elite colleges like Duke, Harvard, Michigan, Princeton, Stanford, UCLA, and UVA.[13] While not all of these students come from a family exactly like John's, the vast majority of them come from families where both parents are at home, "in their corner" and "on their team."

In fact, 20 percent of children from intact families like John's end up graduating from an elite college, compared to just 8 percent of those from other types of families, according to the Education Longitudinal Study.[14] This also means—as Rob from Yale discovered—that young men and women from intact families dominate the campuses of America's elite colleges, with nearly three-quarters of the students on these campuses coming from families headed by their own married mother and father.[15]

This pattern does not just apply to our most elite colleges; it also applies to graduating from college in general. When we break down the graduation rate at colleges across America by family structure, as figure 4.1 does, we see that young adults from intact families are more than twice as likely to earn a four-year college degree than those from other family types, even after controlling for factors that we know affect the

FIGURE 4.1: CHILDREN FROM INTACT FAMILIES MOST LIKELY TO GRADUATE COLLEGE

Percent with bachelor's degree by age 28

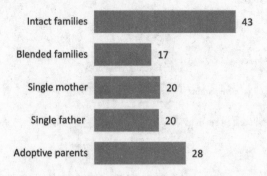

Based on adults aged 28 to 34, surveyed 2013–2014. Source: National Longitudinal Survey of Youth, 1997.

odds of graduation—like parents' race or education level.[16] Moreover, the link between family structure and college graduation is clear for both men and women: 38 percent of young men from intact families graduate from college, versus just 14 percent of their peers from non-intact families; for young women, the share graduating is 49 percent for those from intact families and 23 percent for those from non-intact families. And when it comes to predicting college graduation for young men and women combined, money is about as important as marriage, insofar as your family income as you are growing up is almost as predictive of college graduation as your family structure in adolescence.[17] *Almost.*

Not surprisingly, this stable-family stronger academic performance pattern locks in well before college. Children in elementary, middle, and high schools from intact families get more As and are much less likely to land in the principal's office. By contrast, kids raised in other types of families are more likely to struggle in school. These conclusions were abundantly clear to me after analyzing a number of education surveys with psychologist Nicholas Zill.[18]

Let's look at misbehavior. Girls and boys are more likely to be sent to the principal's office and to be suspended from school when mom and dad don't live together at home. Figure 4.2 shows how this pattern

FIGURE 4.2: CHILDREN FROM NON-INTACT FAMILIES MORE LIKELY TO HAVE PROBLEMS AT SCHOOL

Percentage of parents contacted by school for children's behavior problems

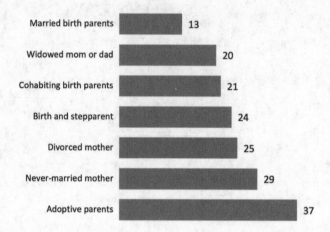

Source: US Department of Education, National Household Education Survey, 2016.

varies by family structure, with children from intact, biological married families getting the fewest emails, texts, and calls from principals and teachers, and children from never-married and adoptive homes garnering the most contacts from schools regarding problems like fighting or talking back. In other words, students like Rob tend to end up in the principal's office, whereas students like John tend to end up on the honor roll. Even after adjusting for other factors, like parental education, race, ethnicity, and the child's sex and age, we find that parents heading up non-intact families are almost twice as likely to be contacted by the school in reference to a child's misbehavior. And on this outcome, kids' family structure matters quite a lot more than how much money their families have.[19]

When it comes to problems at school and with the law, boys from broken homes are especially vulnerable. Research using data from the Early Childhood Longitudinal Study found that the suspension gender gap in eighth grade was only 10 percentage points for kids from intact families (6 percent of girls and 16 percent of boys from intact families were suspended), whereas it was a staggering 26 percentage points for kids from single-mother families (15 percent of girls and 41 percent of boys).[20]

Figure 4.3 depicts the odds of young men and young women ending up in jail or prison depending on their family structure growing up. We can see that young men from non-intact families are at much greater risk, with 21 percent of them spending some time incarcerated, compared to 9 percent of young men from intact families, an effect that is more pronounced for young men than for their female peers. The data also indicate that young men from families without both of their parents, are, incredibly, *more likely to go to prison (21 percent) than they are to graduate from college (14 percent).*

Even after controlling for factors like family income and race, the National Longitudinal Survey of Youth (NLSY97) indicates that young men from non-intact families are twice as likely to end up spending time in jail or prison, compared to young men from families headed by their

FIGURE 4.3: YOUNG MEN AND WOMEN FROM NON-INTACT FAMILIES MORE LIKELY TO GO TO PRISON

Percent ever incarcerated by age 28

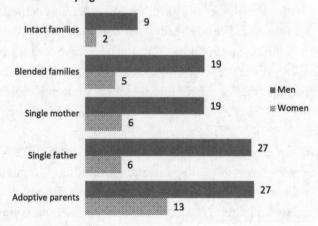

Based on adults aged 28 to 34, surveyed 2013–2014. Source: National Longitudinal Survey of Youth, 1997.

own two biological parents. Oh, and family structure, again, is a better predictor than family income of which boys end up behind bars.[21] The results here, of course, also dovetail with research telling us that violent crime and homicide are much more common in communities where marriage is weak and fathers are largely absent.[22] Family instability does not just exact an individual cost on scores of young men across the United States; it exacts a civilizational price on the communities they harm.

When it comes to educational and social outcomes, the evidence could not be clearer: family structure matters, especially for boys. "Boys particularly seem to benefit more from being in a married household or committed household—with the time, attention and income that brings," economist David Autor told the *New York Times*. "It's quite possible that daughters are drawing the lesson that I'm going [to] be the sole provider and the head of the family and take care of everything," he added. "Sons could be drawing the lesson that the men I see around me are not working or committed fathers."[23]

UNHAPPY AND ABUSED: THE EMOTIONAL AND PHYSICAL RISKS OF FAMILY INSTABILITY

When marital bonds collapse, it is often a painful experience for all parties involved, especially the children. When suffering, boys are more likely to express their pain by doing what psychologists call "externalizing." That's a social scientific term for being defiant, delinquent, impulsive, or aggressive. We've already seen that such externalizing behavior is more common among boys from unstable homes. This is not to say that girls don't engage in externalizing behavior. Anyone who has raised a teenage daughter or taught middle school knows that girls can externalize! It's just that boys are more likely to resort to this behavior under pressure.[24]

Girls in emotional pain are more likely to "internalize." That's a social scientific term for turning inward with feelings like anxiety, depression, or loneliness. Again, boys can experience internalizing feelings like anxiety and depression. It's just that this is more common among girls.[25]

Consider Annabelle ("Anna") in Rockville, Maryland. Anna was doing pretty well until she turned twelve. She had As and Bs in school, enjoyed playing soccer as a striker in the local soccer league, was involved in her church youth group, and had her share of good friends from her neighborhood middle school. But that all changed one March afternoon in 2016.

Anna was outside doing yard work with her family, and her mother was not happy with the job her dad was doing edging the bushes. "I'm fed up with this," said her mom. "You never do what you're supposed to do, what I want you to do. I'm done." Anna knew there had been tension between her parents, but this was the first time her mother had made a comment this definitive. She was flabbergasted when her mom just packed up her belongings and left the family home that evening.

After her mom left, Anna's world collapsed. Her grades cratered; the school counselor explained to her dad that she was smart but "just doesn't do any work" and "doesn't focus." Anna suffered from severe anxiety at school. Her mood darkened, and so did her clothes, as she began to dress "emo." This meant wearing dark hoodies, dark makeup, dyed hair combed to partially cover her face, tons of piercings, and some tattoos for good measure.

Before this change in appearance, Anna had resembled her mom. But after she adopted the emo style, Anna looked nothing like her, and that was the point. "I hate my mom," said Anna. "She left me."

Anna's experience is no outlier. When we look at adolescents more generally, we see that anxiety and depression are more common, and happiness is harder to be had, among teens growing up in non-intact families. To be sure, most teens are *not* anxious or depressed, nor are they unhappy, regardless of family background. But girls like Anna and boys like Rob are more likely to report that they are depressed than are their peers from stable homes. Just 22 percent of adolescents raised by their own married parents report that they are sad a lot of the time, compared to 34 percent from non-intact families. That makes depression 50 percent more likely for the teens from non-intact families, even after taking into account a range of socioeconomic factors. Here (can you guess?), family structure is more predictive of depression than is family income.[26]

This deep sadness—as an internalizing response—is more likely to manifest itself among girls than boys. The gap between boys and girls from intact families when it comes to sadness is only 5 percentage points, whereas the gender gap is 13 points for adolescents from non-intact families. Thus turmoil on the home front is especially likely to be seen in boys as externalizing (misbehavior) and in girls as internalizing (depression, etc.).

Broken homes hurt kids, but abuse on top of that can be even more devastating. Intact homes provide many kids with a buffer against abuse and neglect. The research tells us that children who are exposed to high levels of family instability—and especially to unrelated males in the household—are more likely to end up physically, sexually, or emotionally abused[27] and/or neglected.[28] A recent federal report found that children in any kind of non-intact family were more likely to be abused.[29] And while many stepparents do a great job, there is no question that kids in homes with a stepparent are at greater risk, in general. In fact, psychologists Martin Daly and Margo Wilson observed that living "with a stepparent has turned out to be the most powerful predictor of severe child abuse yet."[30]

As figure 4.4 shows, one type of family form has proven especially risky for kids: unmarried households with one biological parent and an unrelated adult—typically mom cohabiting with a boyfriend. Kids in these homes are about ten times more likely to be sexually, physically, or emotionally abused, compared to children being raised by their own married mother and father.[31] Needless to say, this is a dramatic difference.

When cases of child abuse surface in the public eye, we often come to learn that a boyfriend cohabiting with mom is involved. Consider Nate Feuerstein's story. Nate is now a global superstar known as NF, a rapper with numerous top-ten hits and bestselling albums under his belt. He's also the victim of abuse. His parents divorced when he was a child, his mother went on to have a series of relationships, and, by his account, he ended up being abused.

Nate's emotionally charged, evocative music touches on the abuse and the psychological fallout for him. In his hit song "Mansion," he describes his treatment at the hands of one of his mother's boyfriends:

FIGURE 4.4: CHILD ABUSE MORE COMMON
IN NON-INTACT FAMILIES

Number of children who experienced the incidence of harm per 1,000 children

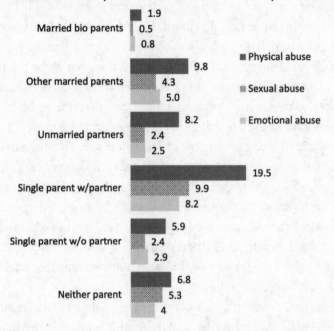

Source: Fourth National Incidence Study of Child Abuse and Neglect (2010).

"Physically abused, now that's the room I don't wanna be in. . . . You used to put me in the corner, so you could see the fear in my eyes / Then took me downstairs and beat me till I screamed and I cried." In his eponymous hit "Nate," he goes on to chronicle the emotional fallout of his abuse and tumultuous family life: "You know how we've always struggled with abandonment? (Yeah)." NF's story reminds us that putting kids in the path of men who have no biological, legal, or cultural tie to them can be risky.

Put more positively, the data on child abuse—brought to life here by NF's heartfelt and heartbreaking music—tell us, then, that the safest place for kids on average is the intact, married family.[32]

LIVING THE DREAM: HOW FAMILY STRUCTURE
HELPS KIDS LAUNCH WELL AND LAND WELL

Divorce isn't really a big deal—if your parents are rich. This was the takeaway from an article by journalist Matthew Yglesias in 2013. Yglesias criticized *New York Times* columnist David Brooks for falling afoul of Brooks's own moral code: he had just gotten divorced, despite being a long-standing proponent of the two-parent family. Yglesias took the view that divorce does not pose a long-term threat to a child's future success, so long as the divorcing parents are educated and wealthy. "My anecdotal experience growing up in affluent circles in Manhattan was that parental marriage disruption is very hard on kids, even on rich kids," he wrote for *Slate*. "But that's hard meaning that it's *sad*, not meaning that it's a substantial barrier to the kids going to college and maintaining a high socioeconomic status. My guess is that Brooks's kids will find their parents' breakup to be pretty upsetting but that they'll also get along fine in life, possessing all the various advantages that come from being David Brooks's children."[33]

Like many on the left, Yglesias's thinking here was that money and education—which help define socioeconomic status—are what *really* matter for kids to "get along fine in life." The kind of family instability Brooks had worried about in his writings would ultimately prove inconsequential for his own children.

But as it turns out, not even rich kids completely escape the long-term effects of divorce.[34] Students from wealthy families whose parents are stably married are almost twice as likely to graduate college, compared to their peers who are not from stably married homes.[35] And when the Pew Charitable Trusts studied the adult financial success of rich kids, it found that 54 percent of them were still rich in their thirties, *if* they grew up in a stably married home with both their biological parents. But only 37 percent of rich kids whose parents had divorced were wealthy by their thirties. In fact, rich kids whose parents divorced were about 33 percent more likely to end up *poor* as thirtysomething adults, compared to rich kids whose parents had not divorced.[36]

Of course, it is not just rich kids who are affected financially by family breakdown—all kids are. Following a divorce, parents are more likely to lose their homes, see a drop in family income, and suffer an increased risk of poverty.[37] So when divorce strikes or families fail to form in the first place, that means parents have less money for the necessities of life, not to mention the challenges of navigating subpar schools or dangerous neighborhoods.[38]

It's no accident, then, that children raised in single-parent families are more than four times as likely to be poor than their peers raised in stably married homes.[39] Or that children whose parents don't stay together are much more likely to experience hunger and financial hardship—and much less likely to be able to afford extras like youth soccer, tutoring, or the tuition bill for a good college.[40] In fact, a study that I led with the economists Joseph Price and Robert Lerman found that one of the top predictors of child poverty in states across America was the share of married parents in a state. This measure surpassed race, education, and even state spending as a predictor.[41] This is an example of the civilizational price we pay for family instability today.

Breaking the cycle of poverty often requires a successful launch for young women and men into the workplace. Family breakdown makes this less likely. Young adults are more likely to end up idle, to work less, and to earn less money if they came from a non-intact family.[42] In fact, these young men are 36 percent less likely to hold down a full-time job by the time they hit their mid-twenties, and the young women are 30 percent less likely to do so.[43]

On the other hand, poor kids are much more likely to *break out* of poverty (and realize the American Dream of reaching the middle or upper class) when they have the benefit of being raised in a stable two-parent family. What's more, in looking at which communities are most likely to promote rags-to-riches economic mobility for poor children, as noted in the preface, Harvard economist Raj Chetty and his colleagues found that "the strongest and most robust predictor [of this mobility] is the fraction of children with single parents."[44] By the time they reach their thirties, men and women who were raised by both their married parents are about 60 percent more likely to have landed in the middle and upper classes. And here, family structure is about as important as family income when growing up in predicting which girls and boys go on to succeed this way as adults.[45]

WHY DOES MARRIAGE MATTER SO MUCH?

In America today, our scholars, journalists, educators, pop-culture creators, and policymakers generally propagate the family diversity myth as a story where kids from all kinds of families are about equally likely to flourish. But the truth, evident here in so many ways, is that kids are most likely to flourish when they are raised by their own married parents. But why is this? Why does marriage matter so much for kids?

If you have had kids, taught kids, coached kids, or mentored kids, you know that they thrive on stable routines with stable caregivers.[46] Because marriage remains the gold standard for commitment in America, children born and raised in a married home are much more likely to enjoy a stable, day-in-day-out relationship with both parents, to wake up in the morning and go to bed in the evening in the presence of their mother and father.[47]

And when it comes to the quality of the caregiving relationship, there is no question that two biological parents are more likely to have the history, the primordial sense of connection, and the time to devote attention and affection to their kids than are single, step, and adoptive parents.[48] Studies show that married parents spend significantly more time talking, reading, and playing with their children than do single parents.[49] Married couples are also more likely to keep an eye on the quality of one another's parenting, and to step in when their spouse is tired or stressed out. This helps to explain why two biological parents provide more consistent discipline to children and are less likely to end up being abusive.[50]

And of course, two stably married parents also enjoy a major financial advantage. Nowadays, both parents generally bring income into the family, which makes it easier to afford a decent home, good schools, and the right extracurriculars, as well as to avoid the financial problems that can derail family life. Intact families avoid the immense expenses associated with family breakup—from divorce lawyers to child support to separate dwellings.[51] Intact families can instead accumulate many more assets to share with their children, compared to non-intact families.[52]

NO DEATH SENTENCE

I can still vividly remember the anguish I was feeling when I threw my metal lunchbox across the dining hall at summer camp when I was six. Thankfully, no one was hit or hurt by my outburst. But clearly, all was not well for me at that point. My father had died, and I could not find a constructive way to express my inchoate sense of rage and loss.

But the story doesn't end there. I was fortunate enough to have a mom who always kept cheering me on, connecting me to counselors, coaches, and other male role models who could help me forge a successful path forward in life. I also was fortunate to have grandparents who loved me, my family, and one another beyond measure, as well as some great teachers and professors over the years. With their help, I pulled out of my childhood emotional tailspin and went on to do well in high school, and then—later in life—marry up and hold down a job as a sociologist at the University of Virginia.

My life—not to mention the lives of people like Jeff Bezos, Angelina Jolie, and Barack Obama—tells us that coming from a nontraditional family is no death sentence to a great future. Plenty of successful people have been raised by single mothers, stepparents, grandparents, or foster parents. In fact, the data tell us that most children raised outside of an intact married family turn out just fine. We have already seen, for instance, that the majority of children growing up in families without their married parents are *not* sad, suspended, or incarcerated.

At the same time, as a sociologist who has studied family life for twenty years, I can't ignore the facts: children's odds of thriving are markedly higher if they have the privilege of being raised by married parents, just as their odds of struggling are significantly larger if their parents did not get and stay married.

To be sure, the discerning reader will know that these findings are not entirely causal. We've all heard the phrase "correlation is not causation." And some of the findings discussed here may be explained by factors not measured in the research—from structural factors like the quality of a child's neighborhood school growing up to biological factors like a genetic propensity to depression passed from parent to child. But the newest and best research—from twin studies being done by psychologists to research on families being done by some of our top economists[53]—confirms that many family-structure effects are indeed causal.

After reviewing more than forty rigorous studies designed to tease out the causal effects of family structure on children, the late Princeton sociologist Sara McLanahan and her colleagues concluded that family structure has a modest or minimal effect on cognitive outcomes for kids. Getting divorced is not likely to tank your kids' SAT scores. But the story is different for social and emotional outcomes like depression, delinquency, and dropping out of high school. In McLanahan's estimation, family instability has a noteworthy causal effect on these sorts of outcomes: "We find strong evidence that father absence [and family instability] negatively affects children's social-emotional development . . . and [these effects] may be more pronounced for boys than for girls."[54] Her review clearly parallels the findings in this chapter.

In reflecting on the role of family structure in children's lives, McLanahan and her colleague Gary Sandefur drew the following conclusions in their award-winning book *Growing Up with a Single Parent*:

> If we were asked to design a system for making sure that children's basic needs were met, we would probably come up with something quite similar to the two-parent ideal. Such a design, in theory, would not only ensure that children had access to the time and money of two adults, it also would provide a system of checks and balances that promoted quality parenting. The fact that both parents have a biological connection to the child would increase the likelihood that the parents would identify with the child and be willing to sacrifice for that child, and it would reduce the likelihood that either parent would abuse the child.[55]

In other words, contra the family diversity myth, it's not that love and money matter more than marriage for kids; it's that, on average, marriage maximizes the odds that children get more of their parents' love and money. Unfortunately, since the 1970s, too few American parents have known and taken to heart the ancient truth that children are most likely to flourish when they are raised by their own married parents. This is one reason why family breakdown has been so prevalent since the "Me" Decade.[56]

On a more encouraging note, as we shall see, the very Americans most likely to reject the family diversity myth—Asian Americans, Conservatives, Strivers, and the Faithful—are also the same men and women enjoying some of the greatest success in forging strong and stable marriages today.[57] And that's partly because they appreciate how much their marriage matters for the sake of their children. More on that later.

CHAPTER 5

THE SOULMATE MYTH

Love, for as Long as It Makes *Me* Feel Happy

At the beginning of her runaway bestseller autobiography, *Eat, Pray, Love*, we find Elizabeth (Liz) Gilbert sobbing at 3:00 a.m. on the bathroom floor of the upscale home in the New York suburbs that she shared with her first husband. Tired of the humdrum realities and responsibilities of married life, impatient with "weekends spent roaming the aisles of some box-shaped superstore of our choice,"[1] and terrified of moving forward with their joint plan to have a child after she turned thirty, Liz has a revelation on the floor of her bathroom in the middle of the night: *"I don't want to be married anymore. I don't want to live in this big house. I don't want to have a baby."*[2] So she abandons her first husband to journey halfway across the world to discover what it is she *does* want.

Her journey—in search of sensuality, spirituality, and a soulmate—takes her to Italy, where she indulges her senses ("eat"), to India, where she seeks spiritual enlightenment ("pray"), and to Indonesia, where she finally meets her soulmate ("love"). Gilbert makes it clear to her reader that she is rejecting an older model of life and love—a model that assumed "your life belongs to everyone else . . . your father, your husband, your children, your community"—in favor of a newer model of life and love that puts the desires of the self in the driver's seat. "What if," she asks, "your life belongs to *you*?"[3]

And what is it that Liz desires for herself? Happiness. And she seems to have believed this happiness could only be attained, both in life and in love, by pursuing it directly. In her words, "Happiness is the consequence of personal effort. You fight for it, strive for it, insist upon it, and sometimes even travel around the world looking for it. And once you have achieved a state of happiness, you must never become lax about maintaining it. You must make a mighty effort to keep swimming upward into that happiness forever to stay afloat on top of it."[4]

Gilbert's life, as chronicled in *Eat, Pray, Love*, is a concise illustration of the choices and consequences occasioned by the romantic philosophy of "soulmates." While Gilbert's book looks and sounds like a fantasy, her basic philosophy is now so ubiquitous that many modern people don't even realize that this wasn't always the normal way of thinking about marriage. It's yet another articulation of expressive individualism, the belief, according to Carl Trueman, "that human beings are defined by their individual psychological core, and that the purpose of life is allowing that core to find social expression in relationships. Anything that challenges [the self's desires] is deemed oppressive."[5]

In matters of the heart, Gilbert seems to think that an intense emotional and erotic connection with a soulmate who understands and meets her needs will bring her happiness. And as *Eat, Pray, Love* draws to its conclusion on the lovely island of Bali, Liz indeed seems to have found a soulmate capable of bringing her such happiness. Her new love is José Nunes, a fifty-two-year-old Brazilian divorcé running a gem-importing business in Indonesia. He is described by her as kind, a delectable cook, well-proportioned, a good lover, and enticingly exotic.

She also likes that José is a "good feminist" and an unusually warm man, characterized by "Brazilian over-the-top displays of affection." About her soulmate in Bali, Liz says, "I have never been loved and adored like this before by anyone, never with such pleasure and single-minded concentration."[6] And so, as the book ends, as they are frolicking in the impossibly romantic waters of tropical Indonesia, Liz responds to José's proposal to build a life together between America and Bali with this word drawn from her time in Italy: "*Attraversiamo.*" Let's cross over.

And cross over they did, marrying in 2007, after she came back home to the United States. By her account in the tenth-anniversary edition of *Eat, Pray, Love*, her marriage to José was "a delight, a comfort, a compass, a refuge."[7]

In her tenth year of marriage to José, however, something happened. Or perhaps some*one* happened. Liz left José for a new soulmate, and so their marriage fell apart. Of course, that's fine, because "these days," she writes, "I don't think marriage is supposed to be an endurance contest."[8] Indeed.

There's much that could be said about Elizabeth Gilbert's story and her approach to love and marriage. But if nothing else, it suggests to us that the underlying assumptions in the soulmate love philosophy are not conducive to a permanent commitment. After all, no one person, no one relationship, can give us great pleasure and great happiness all (or even most) of the time. And so men and women who embrace the soulmate model are often left disappointed by the real-world realities of love and marriage. It's probably no accident that Gilbert, who has had four "soulmates" since she left her first husband in 2002, is by last count a single fiftysomething.[9]

Now you may be wondering here if *Eat, Pray, Love* is an unrepresentative outlier in our culture. It's not. The soulmate model of love and marriage is the subject of not just bestselling books like Gilbert's but also countless movies, shows, and songs in our contemporary pop culture. Just check out the Billboard Hot 100 if you are skeptical of this claim.

The idea of a soulmate is a faux-humble philosophy. On the surface, belief in a soulmate seems like an endorsement of a higher power . . . some other person is the perfect fit for you, shaped by fate or God or the universe. What it means in practice is that people assume that marital love is determined by their own personal, romantic feelings, with no other considerations to consult. This makes the transition from a self-regarding romantic love to an other-regarding marital love much more difficult.

This brings us to the third great myth, the myth of the soulmate—the idea that marriage is primarily about feeling an intensely emotional or romantic connection with "the one" that makes you happy and fulfilled.[10] This is a model of marriage deeply shaped by the expressive individualism that took off in the 1970s. This is a model that puts the self's needs, desires, and feelings—for happiness-inducing passion and intimacy—front and center. This is a model that assumes the fit between you and your beloved is almost seamless: after all, a soulmate is supposed to accept us as we are, right? And this is a model that assumes that, if your marital connection frays, loses its romantic spark, or becomes difficult to maintain, it's okay to move on in search of a better soulmate. Marriage, after all, is not "an endurance contest."

FEELINGS ARE A FRAGILE FOUNDATION

The soulmate model of marriage looms large in the hearts and minds of many young adults today. One survey found that more than 90 percent of single young adults believe that when you marry, you want your spouse to be your soulmate "first and foremost."[11] In today's culture, what many young men and women are looking for is a soulmate who is "the one," that unique person on the planet who connects with you by meeting your deepest longings, desires, and needs. And because you are supposed to enjoy such a powerful emotional bond with this person, as psychologist Scott Stanley observes, a "soulmate is someone for whom you would not have to make major compromises."[12] Above all, the expectation is that your soulmate will make you feel happy. And your soulmate will be easy to love.

This view of love is indebted to a romanticized way of thinking. Romantic understandings of love go way back in history—think of the "courtly love" celebrated by troubadours in twelfth-century France or, a few centuries later, in Shakespeare's *Romeo and Juliet*—but this approach to love got a big boost in the United States in the 1970s. The decade's embrace of a more feelings-centered individualism, along with the fact that the young adults who came of age in the 1960s and 1970s had grown up amid unprecedented affluence, meant that many young men and women felt free to abandon a more traditional approach to marriage in favor of a model more attuned to their felt needs.[13]

"A soul mate is someone who has the locks to fit our keys, and the keys to fit our locks," wrote Richard Bach in *Jonathan Livingston Seagull*, a touchstone for this kind of thinking published in 1970, just as the soulmate model was taking off in the culture. "Our soul mate is someone who shares our deepest longings, our sense of direction."[14] The model was a perfect fit for a decade that elevated the search for "self-fulfillment" in and outside of marriage, and expected marriage to be a vehicle for "growth," "staying-in-touch with your own feelings," and "staying true to one's self."[15]

Similar hopes about the emotional nature and possibilities of married life continue to shape the views of many young unmarried adults today. Of those surveyed in one National Marriage Project poll, 88 percent of young unmarried adults agreed there was a "special person, a soul mate, waiting for you somewhere out there." This same poll found that for 80 percent of the women polled, a husband who could articulate his deepest feelings was a better catch than one who earned a good living.[16] The soulmate model, then, tells us that these emotional skills and the ability to spark romantic or sexual chemistry are what matter. These skills are supposed to put men and women on the path to realizing the primary goods of marriage: intimacy, self-expression, and fulfillment. A soulmate marriage is about the intense, pleasure-inducing feeling of being "in love."

"In the happiness-based model, individuals look to their marriage to promote their hedonic well-being (a high pleasure-to-pain ratio) and to feel good about themselves (high self-esteem)," observed psychologist Eli Finkel in his book *The All-or-Nothing Marriage: How the Best Marriages Work*. Devotees of this kind of soulmate model also "believe that sustaining a happy marriage shouldn't require extensive endurance or forbearance."[17]

In fact, if the connection between you and your husband is proving difficult to maintain, conflict is common with your wife, or you are feeling unhappy, maybe you're no longer "in love." These high expectations open the door to thoughts of divorce when the going gets tough. "Soul-mate-ism conveys an expectation of heavenly connection that makes earthbound relationships more difficult," observes Stanley, the psychologist quoted earlier. This dynamic helps explain why the divorce rate rose by more than 50 percent in the 1970s, as the initial appeal of the soulmate model took off.

But the abiding connection between believing in soulmate love and ending up divorced is still present today. Consider Tanya, a thirty-five-year-old working-class mother of two, who left her husband of nine years for their neighbor. Tanya, who was interviewed for the Love and

Marriage in Middle America Project, is calling it quits because she no longer has the intense emotional connection she once had with her husband. Bear in mind, he did not breach the marriage contract; he was not abusive, unfaithful, or addicted to meth. His presence just does not summon up the same feelings in Tanya that it once did.

"I love him, but I'm not 'in love' with him," this Ohio mom said. "I love him as a friend, as the father, but I don't feel that connection as I used to . . . like, not at all."

"There's just a big huge difference between loving somebody and being 'in love' with somebody," Tanya told Amber Lapp, a research fellow at the Institute for Family Studies. Marriage depends on being "in love," where "you can't wait to be around them, you still get the butterflies—when they're at work you can't wait to see 'em, can't wait till they come walking through the door."

Many men and women today, observes Lapp, are enamored of "the idea that love should arise effortlessly, should switch on like a light bulb. And more or less it should stay that way, without additional effort, they thought."[18] It's *these* men and women who are especially vulnerable to ending up in divorce court.

This was apparent in the 2019 California Family Survey, fielded by YouGov, which asked 918 husbands and wives in the Golden State to clarify their approach to marriage and family life. They had to pick whether they saw marriage as "mostly about an intense, emotion/romantic connection" with someone, or if they believed that marriage is "about romance but also about kids, money, [and] raising a family together." The latter approach, the family-first model of marriage, still recognizes the importance of an emotional connection between husband and wife. But it goes beyond that connection by also stressing some of the classic goods of marriage, like having and raising kids, forging a strong financial foundation for your family, and giving support to and receiving it from kin.

The survey found that married men and women who embraced the "soulmate" model were more likely to report that their marriage might not last, compared to those who took the family-first view. After controlling for education, race, ethnicity, and gender, the survey found that husbands and wives who took the soulmate view were about 90 percent more likely to report doubts about the future of their marriage.[19]

Likewise, the 2022 State of Our Unions Survey found that husbands and wives across America following the soulmate model were twice as likely to report that they were divorcing or were likely to divorce in the near future, compared to those following the family-first model.[20] So in the twenty-first century, husbands and wives who hold onto a soulmate model of marriage after they tie the knot appear to be at a greater risk of ending up in divorce court.

People "expect marriage to satisfy more of their psychological and social needs than ever before," says family historian Stephanie Coontz, feminist author of *Marriage, A History: How Love Conquered Marriage*. "Never before in history have societies thought that such a high set of expectations about marriage was either realistic or desirable."[21] Coontz's reflections are especially applicable to the soulmate model of marriage. But as we can see, taking this view of marriage, assuming your marriage will deliver this feeling of being "in love" on an almost constant basis, also appears to increase your risk of divorce. That's because feelings are a fragile foundation for marriage.

THE PARADOX OF MARITAL HAPPINESS

It's no surprise that husbands and wives who maximize their expectations for feeling "in love" in their marriages are more likely to end up divorced. After all, the core ambition of the devotees of the soulmate model is not to be stably married; it's to be happily married. The paradox of marital happiness is that those who prioritize it the most are least likely to find it. It's not that looking for happiness in marriage is bad, it's that placing happy feelings front and center is usually a sign of unrealistic expectations and emotional immaturity. The happiness that devotees of the soulmate model are pursuing is usually not the same as contentment or stability. More often it's a highly transient state of euphoria.

Recall that Liz Gilbert made it her aim in life and love to directly pursue happiness, to "fight for it, strive for it, insist upon it, and sometimes even travel around the world looking for it," committed as she was to making "a mighty effort to keep swimming upward into that happiness forever to stay afloat on top of it."

Fifty-two-year-old Joel Stevenson had taken a similar view of marriage in his union with now ex-wife Stacey. "I believed in it [the soulmate idea]," he recalled, adding, "It's something to strive for. You may not achieve it. It's something to work toward."

Some family scholars believe that this more expressive and individualistic approach to marriage, while less stable, has actually made marriages that survive better off. "Marriage has become more joyful, more loving, and more satisfying for many couples than ever before in history," argues Coontz. "At the same time, it has become more brittle. These two strands of change cannot be disentangled."[22]

But this was certainly not Joel's experience. He was in for a rude awakening after marrying Stacey under the influence of the soulmate ideal. Marriage was harder than he thought it would be and often didn't generate the special feelings he had been led to expect. Partly because they took a romanticized view of love, ongoing disagreements about how best to balance work and family and how to handle his in-laws left Joel and Stacey disillusioned. How could this be "love" if it was so much hard work? And so their relationship spiraled downward into conflict, unhappiness, and eventually divorce court.

The life experiences of men and women like Joel Stevenson and Liz Gilbert suggest that there are two things that adherents of the soulmate model do not know about love and marriage. The first is that the intense passion and happiness we experience in romantic love fades to an extent, even physically, with time—for almost everyone. The feelings we experience at the beginning of a romantic relationship are shaped by hormones, acting like drugs coursing through our veins. In that early phase, the brain makes and releases hormones like dopamine, norepinephrine, and oxytocin that give us a relationship-induced high. These hormones make us feel happy, energetic, and connected to our beloved.[23]

But this hormonal high does not last forever. As every married couple discovers, the "butterflies" we feel early on in a relationship eventually fly away—at least for a time. "If passionate love is a drug—literally a drug—it has to wear off eventually," observes psychologist Jonathan Haidt. "The beloved falls off the pedestal, and then, because our minds are so sensitive to changes, her change in feeling can take on exaggerated importance. 'Oh, my God,' she thinks, 'the magic has worn off. I'm not in love with him anymore.' If she subscribes to the myth of true love, she might even consider breaking up with him. After all, if the magic ended, it can't be true love."[24]

You discover the adorable spouse you married has a weakness for credit card clothing purchases, a temper when dealing with a surly teen, or different plans for the religious upbringing of your children than you do. Your husband leaves dirty dishes in the kitchen sink. Your wife isn't all that impressed with your minor triumphs at work. Flaws and failings like these become more evident each year. Marriage entails more than its fair share of disappointments, compromises, and conflicts, and the shock of this realization hits hardest for those who hold unrealistically high expectations for emotional connection and happiness in marriage.

These high expectations, then, leave women and men like Liz Gilbert and Joel Stevenson in an especially difficult place when the butterflies fly away. The inevitable tensions, difficulties, and offenses of married life are more likely to cause a crushing disappointment for devotees of the soulmate model than for couples who have a more realistic model of married life.

The second thing that adherents of the soulmate model do not understand is that happiness—both in life and in love—is less likely to be found when pursued directly. If you set a course that aims squarely for your own happiness, as Gilbert did, you will often end up sorely disappointed. That's because pursuing your own happiness is like walking toward the water you *think* you see on a desert horizon. As you head toward it, this "water" remains constantly out of reach, never to be actually reached and consumed, leaving you thirsty and exasperated.

In fact, as many of the great religious and philosophical traditions of the world instruct us, happiness is more likely to appear when we set our compass on greater destinations *beyond our limited view*. Aristotle described the "activity of soul in accordance with virtue" as the path to happiness.[25] The New Testament promises us that "whoever would save his life will lose it, and whoever loses his life for my sake will find it."[26] And two thousand years ago, the Jewish sage Hillel noted that the path to genuine fulfillment must involve a cause bigger than the self: "To begin with oneself, but not to end with oneself; to start with oneself, but not to aim at oneself; to comprehend oneself, but not to be preoccupied with oneself."[27] In other words, if you're headed through the desert with a real destination in mind beyond your own self-satisfaction, you will often come across more than a few oases that refresh you along your journey.

This ancient wisdom is confirmed by contemporary psychology. "Doing good makes us feel good," observes psychologist David Myers, adding, "Altruism enhances our self-esteem. It gets our eyes off ourselves, makes us less self-preoccupied, gets us closer to the unself-consciousness" and often leads to happiness.[28]

When it comes to marriage, those who seek not so much to feel good as to *do* good, by loving their spouse and family members in various ways—for instance, being an attentive parent or a reliable breadwinner or a devoted son-in-law—are actually more likely to end up happy in their marriages. The husband and father who sets aside his work, smartphone, and ESPN in the evenings to help with homework, shoot hoops, and tuck the kids in bed will likely take greater satisfaction from his family life than if he had pursued his own pleasures of the moment. And he will likely elicit more admiration, affection, and ardor from his wife, as a natural response. Family first, me second. *This* is the paradoxical route to happiness in marriage.

Consider, for instance, Angela Franklin, a thirty-eight-year-old African American woman from the Atlanta area. Her aim in her marriage is to continuously "work on it"—trying to figure out how best to keep things strong between her husband and herself. She makes a point of regularly kissing her husband, Rusty, and showing other small expressions of love: "Whatever it takes to make the other person feel good, that's what you have to continue, as opposed to being selfish and thinking that I have that person, and that's it." Her approach is reciprocated by Rusty, and they enjoy a marriage where a cycle of mutual devotion and intentional intimacy make for a very satisfying union.[29] But the underlying reason they are flourishing is that Angela has decided to *love* Rusty rather than expecting she will always be "in love" with him.

Angela is not alone. Husbands and wives who embrace the family-first model of marriage—which is more other-centered—report not just more stable marriages but more satisfying ones than those who identify with the soulmate model. The California Family Survey found that husbands and wives who embrace the range of goods associated with the family-first approach to marriage were 58 percent more likely to be satisfied with their marriages, compared to husbands and wives who were adherents of the soulmate model, net of controls for factors like education, race, and income.[30]

Today, husbands and wives who embrace the family-first model enjoy a richer and more realistic view of marriage, one that pushes them to look beyond themselves and their own feelings to prioritize the welfare of their spouse and other family members. They understand that marital love is not about always being "in love"; rather, love is a decision to will the good of the others in your family—starting with your husband or wife.[31] Willing the good of your spouse and family means, practically, adopting a "selfless attitude" where you seek to be humble, forgiving, and positive in relating to them, as family scholar Jason Carroll has observed; it is also about "selfless action" where you aim to serve and emotionally engage them. "The more you seek to serve [them], the more you will feel your love for them grow," adds Carroll, commenting on the way in which a more generous posture toward family members typically (but now always) fuels greater marital and family harmony.[32]

This isn't to minimize the importance of keeping the emotional communion strong in your marriage (which is very important!), but rather to recognize that it is not the only basis or focus of a rich married life. And consistent with Carroll's perspective, we see in this survey that taking an other-centered approach is associated with a modest increase in the chances of being happily married—especially for men. This advantage, of course, is especially striking because the pool of husbands and wives in family-first marriages also includes those who are struggling in their marriages but *not* heading for the exits.

MORE THAN A SOULMATE

Belief in soulmate love in the early days of a relationship isn't necessarily going to lead to disaster . . . as long as that love matures into a more other-centered marital commitment. The first summer that Michelle Robinson got to know Barack Obama, working together in a Chicago law firm, she was in the soulmate phase of their relationship. "As soon as I allowed myself to feel anything for Barack, the feelings came rushing—a toppling blast of lust, gratitude, fulfillment, wonder," she recalls. "Any worries I'd been harboring about my life and career and even about Barack himself seemed to fall away with that first kiss, replaced by a driving need to know him better, to explore and experience everything about him as fast as I could."[33]

But a few years later, by the time they "had two kids, three jobs, two cars, one condo, and what felt like no free time," Michelle's butterflies had flown away. Barack's independent spirit and his cavalier attitude toward punctuality, which had once charmed her, now aggravated her. He was spending days away from her and the kids down in Springfield, serving as a senator in the Illinois legislature. And on many a Thursday night, when he returned from Springfield, he'd arrive much later than she anticipated, even though he'd called to say "I'm on my way" or "Almost home!" Dinners that she'd prepared for him went cold, and their daughters were often disappointed that Dad did not arrive home early enough to kiss them goodnight.

"[As] a working full-time mother with a half-time spouse and a predawn wake-up time, I felt my patience slipping away until finally, at some point, it just fell off a cliff," Michelle recalls. "When Barack made it home, he'd either find me raging or unavailable, having flipped off every light in the house and gone sullenly to sleep."[34]

This was a low moment in the Obamas' marriage, one brought on by the conflicts, miscommunications, and tensions inherent in juggling work and family that can emerge in any marriage. But after seeing a marriage counselor at Michelle's insistence, they were able to recalibrate their expectations about their schedules, improve their communication, and focus on the big picture: they loved one another, Barack was a good father, and the couple had big dreams. Michelle, who grew up in a tight-knit family, which Barack jokingly referred to as the "black version of *Leave it to Beaver*,"[35] was determined to give her kids the "normalcy and stability" that her own parents had given her and her brother. So Barack and Michelle Obama found a way, around the turn of the century, to keep their marriage together. The rest is history.

The Obamas' experience is but one example of the ways in which marriage is more stable nowadays than it was in the 1970s, when a couple facing the kinds of tensions Michelle and Barack faced in their first decade of married life were much more likely to call it quits. Today, insofar as a majority of married couples with children in the home do not divorce, the real "happily ever after"—as opposed to the mythic one so often depicted in popular media—is that most married mothers and fathers find a way to make it through the tough times.

The Obamas' experience also shows how, at least now, the soulmate model ceases to become the controlling expectation for most couples *after* they tie the knot. Once the wedding day has come and gone, and especially after the kids come along, the perspective of many of today's husbands and wives changes, as it did for Michelle Obama. Most realize that a good marriage is not some eat-pray-love experience where people are insisting upon their own individual happiness.

If you come to my house, for instance, on a Wednesday night in the middle of the school year, you'd be quickly disabused of the idea that marriage for me and Danielle is all about candlelight dinners, lingering kisses, heartfelt conversations, or finding our best selves. There's not much of that on Wednesday night. What usually happens is that Nana (my mother-in-law) brings the kids home from school. Then there's a mad dash to get dinner on the table, help kids with homework, get one daughter to volleyball practice, clean up the kitchen, superintend kids' screen usage, do nighttime prayers, pay the bills, and then collapse in front of Amazon Prime. Many a weekday, we're more like soldiers in arms, fighting in the trenches for our family, than we are like Romeo and Juliet, enjoying the burning passion of romantic love.

And I can guarantee you that almost every couple up and down our suburban street is doing much the same thing. My neighbors are ferrying kids to soccer practice, searching for lessons on Khan Academy, worrying about their kids' performance in school, and trying to stay afloat financially. We're living family-first marriages that are largely about the kids, the finances, and the family. Marriage is not about "me." It's about "we." What's happening now in the culture at large, at least for married couples with kids, is a shift away from the soulmate model toward a family-first model that incorporates many classic goods from the older, institutional model of marriage. Of course today's model is more egalitarian than the one that dominated the 1950s (or the 1850s, for that matter), but it's still much more family-centered than the soulmate model of the 1970s.

This dynamic is reflected in the deep decline in the divorce rate among college-educated couples, even more left-leaning ones, since 1980.[36] It also came through loud and clear in a recent essay in the *Atlantic* by liberal journalist George Packer, talking about his experience navigating family life as a parent in New York City:

> When parents on the fortunate ledge of this chasm gaze down, vertigo stuns them. Far below they see a dim world of obesity, divorce, stagnant wages, rising morbidity rates, and they pledge to do whatever they can to keep their children from falling. They'll stay married, cook organic family meals, read aloud at bedtime every night, take out a crushing mortgage on a house in a highly rated school district [and] pay for music teachers and test-prep tutors.[37]

His comments indicate the ways in which more and more married parents now see that giving their kids the gift of a stable family is protective in today's increasingly uncertain and unequal world. At some level, most of us married parents know—even if only tacitly—that our children are significantly more likely to graduate from college, steer clear of poverty, and avoid a visit to the local psych ward if we can keep things together on the home front. We also know that, financially, sticking together is the wiser course. We recognize that the 401(k), the house, and fun summer vacations depend in large part on keeping our marriage together.

Finally, many married men and women know that the whole family is stronger when marriage grounds it—that the kids, the parents, the grandparents, and other kin have much to gain or lose, depending on the state of the union. There is a recognition that from birthday parties to Christmas dinners, it's all better together—when *both* sets of grandma and grandpa are part of the picture.

Lisa Lee represents the contemporary appeal of the family-first model for a growing share of married parents. While acknowledging that "personal growth" and "growth together as a couple" is important to her and her husband, these are not their main focus. Rather they "have this kind of family enterprise [mentality], and the purpose of it in a lot of ways is to ensure that our kids do 'okay.'" Lee adds, "I love my husband, of course, and I'm deeply emotionally attached to him. But that's not the overwhelming purpose now." Their current overwhelming purpose is, instead, forging an economic and parental partnership for the good of "the kids."

Lee, a left-leaning, college-educated Asian American wife and mother, is not alone in her prioritization of family needs. Fully 73 percent of husbands and wives in the California Family Survey said they think that marriage is primarily about "kids, money, and raising a family together" (family-first), leaving only 27 percent to believe that marriage is primarily about an "intense emotional/romantic connection" (soulmate). Today, as figure 5.1 indicates, for those Americans who actually end up tying the knot, the dominant model of married life isn't the soulmate idea; it's family-first.

The California Family Survey further reveals that the family-first model is especially appealing for Asian Americans (82 percent), religious people (79 percent), Conservatives (80 percent), and the college-educated

FIGURE 5.1: MORE HUSBANDS AND WIVES EMBRACE FAMILY-FIRST MODEL OF MARRIAGE THAN SOULMATE MODEL

Share of husbands and wives who embrace family-first vs. soulmate model

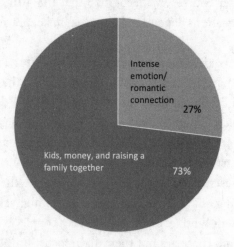

Based on married adults aged 18 to 50. Source: IFS California Survey (2019).

(78 percent), among spouses ages eighteen to fifty-five. By contrast, the soulmate model is disproportionately endorsed by liberal and secular married Americans.

On March 13, 2020, my wife informed me that our Saturday date night was off: our governor had declared a state of emergency. A few days later, we found ourselves barely managing to homeschool six children, work two jobs, and run our household on lockdown. I knew that the loss of a regular date night—the linchpin of the more romantic side of our marriage—was going to be the least of our marital challenges that spring.

Scenarios like ours—some much, much harder, with millions of parents losing jobs, heading to the front lines to battle the virus, or grieving the loss of loved ones—played out in homes across America in 2020. As for me and my bride, we didn't enjoy a date night out for nearly three months that spring, but we *were* able to deliver food, some socially distanced conversation, and air hugs from the grandchildren to my homebound seventysomething in-laws on a regular basis. And to be honest, those visits were much more memorable than the date nights we forwent, and yet another reminder that my marriage's best moments are ones when it's not all about me.[38]

The bigger lesson here is that the soulmate myth—the idea that love is primarily about feeling a passionate connection to our beloved that makes us feel happy—is a dead end for today's husbands and wives, in at least three ways. First, embracing the idea that marriage is all about "me"—your own happiness, your own pleasure—appears to increase the odds that you land in divorce court. Second, seeing marriage primarily as an intense vehicle for emotional or romantic fulfillment, rather than as an institution that advances many goods, from the welfare of your children to the size of your 401(k), is an extremely imprudent approach to handling family life in the twenty-first century. Finally, the paradox of marital happiness is that husbands and wives who don't seek to be "in love" but instead recognize that "love is a decision" to care for their spouse, their kids, and their family are more likely to find themselves happily married.

So how, specifically, are husbands and wives who eschew the soulmate model for the family-first model forging strong and stable marriages? To that question, we now turn.

CHAPTER 6

WE BEFORE ME

Looking Out for Number One Is a Recipe for Marital Failure

In the run-up to the 2018–19 college basketball season, the Duke Blue Devils were heralded as a "superteam" by SB Nation's Ricky O'Donnell.[1] Headed by the legendary Coach K (Mike Krzyzewski), Duke had landed the top three freshmen recruits—more than any other college program in the country—and seemed poised to dominate college basketball that year as the number-one team in the AP college rankings. A few months later, with March Madness about to begin, the Blue Devils were expected to win a sixth national NCAA title. But then they were knocked out in the fourth round.[2]

In Duke's final minute against Michigan State, the Blue Devil's number-one recruit, R. J. Barrett, kept the ball to himself. Rather than pass to his open teammate, Zion Williamson, Barrett tried to run right through two defenders and land a layup. But he missed the basket, and Duke fell to their lesser rated but more experienced opponent.[3] Barrett's play was consistent with this observation by the sports journalist Luke Mullin: "As is the territory that comes with being the best player in college basketball, Barrett gained a reputation as being selfish with the basketball by not passing to Williamson. He has a tendency to lock in on his defenders and will try to beat them individually, rather than passing the ball."[4]

Duke's ignominious end was partly blamed on Coach K's habit of pursuing a "one-and-done" strategy, where Krzyzewski skimmed off the best high-school superstars and then gave them a year of playing college hoops to show off their individual talent before they headed off to the NBA.[5] While Duke did not lack individual skill and ambition, it did lack players with maturity and a commitment to teamwork.

The team that did go all the way that season was the University of Virginia Cavaliers. UVA did not have nearly the talent nor the reputation of Duke heading into the season.[6] The Cavaliers had been embarrassed the previous year as the first number-one seed to lose to a number-sixteen seed in the opening round, a loss that led to diminished expectations on the part of many fans, journalists, and sports aficionados. But under the leadership of coach Tony Bennett, the Cavaliers were determined to launch a second shot at the tournament in the spring of 2019.

The Cavaliers' teamwork was built around Bennett's distinctive philosophy of play, his "Five Pillars," derived from his Christian faith. Those pillars are: humility (don't think too highly of yourself), thankfulness (be thankful in all circumstances—including the hard times, because there is great wisdom in those experiences), passion (have a plan and a purpose, throw yourself into the game, and don't be lukewarm), unity (stick and work together, don't divide our house), and servanthood (take care of your brother).[7] With these principles, Bennett aimed to make his Cavaliers "team-first players."[8]

In the spring of 2019, this strategy was put to the ultimate test. Powered by a relentless defense, unwavering work ethic, and selfless team-first play, the Cavaliers beat team after team in the NCAA tournament, often coming from behind to win in the final seconds of the game. Finally, on April 8, 2019, UVA made its way to Minneapolis to contend for the championship game against Texas Tech. And again, the Cavaliers found themselves behind by three points, with twenty-two seconds left to play.

At that moment, Ty Jerome and De'Andre Hunter—two of the team's starters—found themselves running down the court. When they first met on the court years earlier, the two players had not liked one another. But after fighting in the basketball trenches for years under Bennett's leadership, their feelings had changed. Hunter put it like this: "He's my brother now. I'd go to war with him. I love the dude."

Jerome felt the same way. "We're best friends, literally brothers," he said. "We still have days where we'll piss each other off all the time. That's what family does, but at the end of the day, I'll do anything for him, and I know when it comes down to it, he'll do anything for me."[9]

This brotherhood paid big dividends in the championship game. As Jerome drove down the court, he came within striking distance of making a basket. But instead of taking it for himself, he passed the ball to Hunter ("Jerome gives it up," in the words of the CBS commentator), who was standing just outside the three-point line. Hunter put the three-pointer in, tying up the game sixty-eight to sixty-eight, with just twelve seconds to go. Jerome's pass and Hunter's basket sent the game into overtime, which UVA went on to win. This was team-first playing of the highest order.

The divergent approaches to basketball exemplified by Duke and UVA in 2019—and between R. J. Barrett's and Ty Jerome's game-changing plays—are relevant for thinking about the quality and stability of marriage. Seeing marriage as an opportunity to shine, seek your own individual advantage, advance your own agenda, and protect what you have can put you on a trajectory that fosters resentment, conflict, self-centeredness, and unhappiness in your marriage—and even its loss. Taking a me-first approach to marriage is usually a recipe for disaster when it comes to marital enjoyment and stability. By contrast, a we-before-me approach—seeking unity in name and deed, regularly looking for opportunities to serve your spouse, and keeping the passion in your relationship alive—is crucial for marital success. In other words, marriages are more likely to survive and thrive when husbands and wives aim for team-first communion over me-first competition in word and deed.

SHARING IS CARING

All too often, when our ruling class weighs in to offer advice on marriage and family life today, they intervene to promote a Duke-style philosophy of marriage. Their basic idea is: Look out for number one. Make sure you have "me" time, a personal hobby, and the opportunity to put your own professional ambitions first. Make sure you do not lose your individuality. Make sure, in a word, that the "me" comes before the "we" of your marriage and family life. This is the loud and clear message proclaimed all too often by the journalists, academics, and professionals who control the commanding heights of our culture.

Take something as simple as checking accounts.

Writing in the *Huffington Post*, psychologist Stephanie Sarkis urges couples to keep separate accounts to avoid the conflict that can arise from differences in how partners handle money. "One person is usually a saver, and one is a spender" in marriage, she contends. Better to let partners handle their own money and avoid the "money arguments" that "can get heated and even lead to a breakup." In fact, she tells couples that separate accounts can not only "keep the peace at home" but "lead to more intimacy in your relationship."[10] So, separate accounts are supposed to make things sizzle.

There are plenty of other voices in the media, the academy, and the marketplace adding to the chorus of the me-first approach to money and marriage. "Getting married doesn't mean you have to merge all your bank accounts," says Ryan Frailich, a financial adviser in New Orleans. Because couples are getting married later these days, after they have gotten financially established, he thinks it is fine for them to keep separate accounts. "I see many couples have great success with a 'yours, mine, ours' system" where they keep some accounts separate and also maintain a joint account for family expenses.[11]

Still other millennials see their money as a reflection of their work, their own individual success—and they want to keep hold of this symbol of their individual accomplishment. "It's my work—it's my money," Karina Pasillas told the *Atlantic*, also noting: "When buying him gifts, when picking up the tab at dinner, I like knowing that I am also contributing to this relationship." Her approach is consistent with patterns that Fenaba Addo, a professor of consumer science at the University of Wisconsin–Madison, sees in the financial decisions of many couples: "It's about wanting to maintain one's sense of identity, individuality, and autonomy."[12]

Journalist Caroline Kitchener is a fan of this me-first approach to marriage and money. In an article for the *Atlantic*, she argues that keeping separate accounts "doesn't signal a lack of trust—to some, it's a way for spouses to show they trust each other more."[13] She thinks that couples who keep their own accounts have more opportunities to engage in complex negotiations, cover one another's expenses when one spouse's account runs dry, and "split the bill down the middle." In the progressive imagination, all this intricate, involved, and individualized accounting is supposed to make for better marriages. Sure.

As a young married man, I had a friend I will call Claire. One day she and I were talking about our young families, and she mentioned that she wanted to buy a couch to spruce up the apartment she shared with her husband and two young children. I nodded along in response to her sensible idea.

But then Claire confessed that she could not afford the couch she wished to buy. I was mystified. Although she and I both had modest salaries at the time, Claire was married to an engineer at a reputable firm. And certainly, I thought to myself, he earned plenty.

So I asked her, "Claire, can't you afford to buy a couch with the money you both make?" She responded, "Well, we have separate accounts, and I don't have enough money in my account to cover the cost of the couch." She looked slightly crestfallen.

Her response left me confused and speechless, partly because Claire was an outspoken feminist, and partly because Danielle and I handled money very differently in our marriage. We had a joint checking account, because *Mi dinero es su dinero*: my money is your money is our money. If we had enough money, and Danielle wanted a couch, she would get the couch. No questions asked. It was that simple.

But in Claire's marriage, *Mi dinero es mi dinero*. My money is my money, and your money is yours. Claire and her husband divided things up on a me-first basis. He covered the rent, she covered the utilities. I'm not sure how or who covered their children's expenses, but I could tell that their approach to marriage and money was not making her happy.

Maria Erickson's experience with love, money, and marriage could not be more different from Claire's. Maria was about to deploy for Iraq when she first had to deal with money matters with Jon, her fiancé. They were both stateside, in the Eighty-Second Airborne, and they had split up preparations on the day they were getting ready for their deployment. He was chemically treating their uniforms for potential gas attacks, and she went shopping to get items they needed for Iraq. Her list included inexpensive items, like toiletries, as well as some high-end items, like ballistic glasses for the two of them.

"They were really expensive—something like $160," Maria recalls. So when she returned with the items, she gave Jon his glasses, told him the cost, and made it clear that she expected him to pay her back. But he just kissed her on the forehead and said, what's "yours is mine, and mine is yours. And now we're [going to be] married, and it's all equal."

At the time, this was a hard pill for Maria to swallow. After all, "I hadn't grown up like that," she said, recalling that her parents kept separate accounts and spent as they pleased on a me-first basis. But she later realized that Jon's team-first approach to money was for the best. The "irony," Maria notes, was that she had brought college debt into the marriage, and he hadn't—and he was happy to use their newly merged money to pay off her debt. "That was my first lesson that no matter what, we would be in it together [financially]. Everything would be mixed, everything would be combined, and [we] would operate as one unit."

"I wasn't really comfortable at first [with this model] but I'm so grateful for it now," Maria says. She reports that their approach to money fueled a virtuous cycle of communication, trust, and mutual dependency in the financial arena, which is one reason she now feels rock solid about her marriage to Jon.

Claire and Maria's divergent experiences are not atypical. One University of Colorado–Boulder study found that shared accounts "increase feelings of financial togetherness—making purchases and financial goals feel shared."[14] This same study also found that couples who pooled their money were the most satisfied in their relationships, compared both to couples who kept their accounts separate and couples who used both joint and separate accounts. Couples who only kept their money separate were more than 20 percent more likely to divorce or separate, compared to couples who pooled at least some of their money.[15]

The effects of a me-first money strategy seem to fall especially hard on women. A Cornell University study found that keeping separate accounts was particularly bad for wives and girlfriends: "Individualistic arrangements appeared to undermine women's relationship satisfaction and reduce feelings of intimacy, sexual compatibility, and satisfaction with conflict resolution."[16] No doubt this is partly because women tend to earn less in their marriages. Like Claire, then, wives in relationships where money is not shared are more likely to end up feeling short-changed, literally.

Married Americans who are religious or conservative like Jon and Maria are especially likely to pool their money, according to the 2022 State of Our Unions Survey. But the shared-accounts-make-better marriages story is not all about "selection effects," where the types of husbands and wives who keep separate accounts are just less marriage-minded to begin with, or where husbands and wives who are in marital trouble are more likely to set up separate accounts. A fascinating new study from Indiana University randomly assigned newly married couples to (1) joint checking accounts, (2) separate accounts, or (3) whatever they wanted to do, and then tracked them for two years. Guess which couples thrived in what the study called the "connubial crucible"?

"After two years, couples in the Joint [checking accounts] Condition exhibited significantly greater relationship quality than couples" in the other two conditions, reported Jenny Olson, a professor of marketing at Indiana University, and her colleagues. She went on to speculate that "our intervention may have shifted couples from a more exchange view of their marriage (mine-and-yours) to a more communal view (ours), which is linked to greater marital quality."[17]

Despite what the *Huffington Post* and financial gurus like Suze Orman want you to believe about money and marriage, it turns out that thinking in terms of *our* money—not *my* money and *your* money—is more conducive to forging a strong and stable union. And it is not just money. Couples who do and hold more things in common—from last names to Facebook profile pics[18]—are more likely to flourish.

Our YouGov survey found, for instance, that couples who share the same last name had a stronger sense of their identity as a family and were significantly more likely to be happily married and less likely to have plans for divorce.[19] Not surprisingly, more-educated, secular, and left-leaning women were more likely to have kept their own last names or hyphenated them.[20]

None of this surprises Maria, who is well educated but no feminist.

"I have a picture I took the first time I wore the Army uniform with [his] name on it. I was so happy we were a team," she recalls.

She thinks that women who don't take their husbands' names miss one point of marriage, namely, forging a unified family identity around a common last name. "When I took his name, it was for me a sign that we're a team now, and I didn't want to hold on too tightly to all of the things that had to do with just me, myself, and I." To be sure, she also knew it was her decision to make: "I also knew that I was marrying someone who would not demand of me that my identity be absorbed into his," she added, "so I give it freely."

Like the Virginia Cavaliers, Maria and Jon's experience is that taking a team-first approach to marriage and family life, from money to family names, has been a winning combination. Sharing is caring, after all.

SERVICE WITH A SMILE

"Little Self-Care Tips for a Happier Relationship." "How to Prioritize Self-Love while You're in a Relationship." "The Unselfish Art of Prioritizing Yourself." These three headlines—from the popular online magazines *Bustle*, the *Financial Diet*, and *Psychology Today*—convey a powerful message I have encountered countless times in pop culture and from journalists and relationship gurus: *Tend to your own needs. Protect your boundaries. Make sure you're not taken advantage of.* These are all consistent with the kind of expressive individualism that has taken a powerful hold of our culture since the 1970s.

When it comes to marriage and relationships, the assumption here is that it's best to take a me-first, exchange-based approach. "Self-care leads to a happier relationship," Teresa Newsome at *Bustle* assures us. "Because being in a relationship isn't about becoming a pleasing machine that works for everyone but yourself. You deserve self-care, damn it!"[21] Newsome urges her readers to get their own hobbies, cultivate friendships outside of their marriage, and set their own goals. You doing you, after all, is "really healthy for your relationship."

Also, "be sure to get your wants and needs met." Don't forget, the "speakers in the car are yours half of the time, remember that so is the TV, the credit card, the vacations, the weekends, and the home. And so is the free time." If you take this kind of tit-for-tat approach to your relationship, Newsome promises, "you'll be so full of joy and relief that it will spill over into your relationship."

Maria's husband, Jon, would not score high in Teresa Newsome's book. Between working as a lawyer at the Pentagon and focusing on Maria and their four kids most of the rest of the week, he does not have a lot of time for hobbies, guys' nights out, or his own individual goals. "I don't pursue a lot of hobbies that would take me out of the house," he says, adding, "I don't play golf. I've got a wife and kids, and I like to have my wife and kids around. If I want to see the boys [his friends], they can come over after church, and our families can hang out."

Jon's family-first orientation has also had a big effect on his approach to his military career. In the military, the "drive for promotion makes you have to compromise not just your family time but your values, who you are as a family," reports Maria. Officers often accept deployments or assignments offered to them by their superiors because they do not wish to let them down, and they want to rise through the ranks. But often these deployments and assignments impose real hardships on families, translating into extended absences or frequent moves, both of which take a toll on family life. But Jon has taken a different path.

"Everyone [else] was afraid to tell their bosses no" when it came to these opportunities, recalls Maria. But Jon turned down voluntary deployments and assignments from his superior that would have taken him away from Maria and the kids. He would say to his superiors, "I hope you understand, it's just a family decision. I'm just doing this because that wouldn't be right for my family."

Maria is grateful that Jon has taken this family-first approach. In the military, she reports, "I see all these people really, truly killing themselves and running their families and wives . . . into the ground." She, by contrast, is secure and happy in the knowledge that she and the kids are more important to Jon than his success in the military.

This is not to say that their marriage is frictionless. One thing that Jon struggles with now is Maria's desire to host large social events at their home on a regular basis. (She is a focal point for social activity at their local Catholic church in Annandale, Virginia.) This can cause heartburn for Jon, a self-described introvert and neatnik. There are times when he wants to object to the regular gatherings she hosts or with-draw from preparing for them. But he knows that "when I'm selfish, I'm unhappy." By contrast, even though "all this kind of [socializing] wears me out, and it's not what I would pick . . . when I'm unselfish about that, when I'm generous and don't bring Maria down by com-plaining or by grumbling in the lead-up to an event, I'm always happier for it," he says. By Maria's account, Jon is a good sport about helping her to host large events, and it is one more reason she and Jon are happily married.

Their experience points to an important truth about married life. Husbands and wives who couple a strong we-before-me mentality with a willingness to sacrifice for one another tend to do much better in mar-riage. This attitude removes marriage from the sort of individualistic, tit-for-tat exchange approach that is running so many marriages into the ground today. The we-before-me mentality, psychologist Scott Stanley notes, changes a "relationship from an exchange market where two in-dividuals [are] competitors to a non-competitive relationship that [can] maximize joint outcomes."[22] In such team-oriented marriages, husbands and wives are more likely to respond to the needs of their spouse as they are manifested rather than only do something for their husband or wife in response to something they have done for them.[23]

FIGURE 6.1: COUPLES WHO EMBRACE "WE BEFORE ME" HAPPIER, LESS PRONE TO DIVORCE

Marital quality and perceived stability among husbands and wives (%), by mentality with which they identify

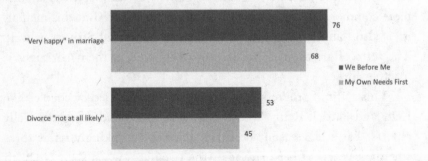

Among married adults aged 18 to 55. Source: State of Our Unions Survey (2022).

Among the "joint outcomes" maximized here are marital quality
and stability. In fact, figure 6.1 shows that husbands and wives who
have a "we-before-me" mentality and reject the view that you have to
look after your own needs first in marriage are more likely to report they
are happily married and their marriage is not likely to end in divorce.[24]
The links between a we-before-me mentality and higher-quality, more-
stable marriages persist, even after controlling for factors like education,
income, and race.[25]

Thinking about your marriage, your spouse, and your family as a
priority—and coupling this with a willingness to make sacrifices for
them—fuels a life-giving cycle in married life. In fact, my own research
indicates that being generous in your own marriage is a better predictor
of your own marital quality than how generous your spouse is.[26] This
sacrificial spirit also sends an important signal to your spouse that he
or she is your priority. Stanley and his colleagues report that "sacrificial
behaviors may be highly salient symbols of devotion between partners,
leading to greater levels of trust and reciprocated sacrifice, ultimately
creating greater relationship quality."[27] It's no wonder, then, that a spirit
of sacrifice leaves couples better off.

There is one big caveat to all this: marriages where sacrifice seems
to go largely in just one direction. Back in the day, in all too many marriages, this spirit of sacrifice often went chiefly in one direction, usually
from wife to husband. When this spirit of sacrifice is not mutual, marriages can run aground.

But in general, husbands and wives who embrace a mutual sacrificial ethic and a team spirit tend to be more happily and stably married.
And as Jon and Maria's example suggests, this team spirit is slightly
more common among conservative-minded couples.[28] But this mentality is also found among plenty of progressive-minded Strivers as well.
The term of art they use to describe teamwork in their marriages is
"partnership."

This spirit of progressive partnership is exemplified by couples like
Kelly and Patrick Reilly, who live outside Richmond, Virginia. Kelly
reports that a big reason she survived what she jokingly refers to as
"the dark years" of her marriage—the two years when she gave birth
to two baby boys in eighteen months, held down a demanding job at

an accounting firm, and struggled to keep the spark in her marriage alive—was that her husband, Patrick, did not assume that family life was primarily her job. After their boys were born, Patrick jumped in to do what needed to get done, from the dishes to the laundry.

He would go into the basement, "play music and have a drink," and do the laundry, she recalls. This gave her more time to spend with their young boys at the time, time that she treasured.

For Kelly, who always wanted to combine work and motherhood, her husband's partnership on the home front has been integral to her happiness at home and her success at work. "I am so incredibly grateful for a partner who doesn't see housework and meals as helping me—it is all part of what needs to get done for the team," she says. This is one more example of how, regardless of their ideological tribe, couples who manage to prioritize a team mentality and a willingness to flexibly serve one another are more likely to thrive.

DON'T HELICOPTER THE KIDS, FEED YOUR MARRIAGE

In too many marriages today, husbands and wives get preoccupied with their work, the kids, or even a hobby, rather than keeping the communion strong in their marriage. There are plenty of couples with kids who are so devoted to helicoptering over their children—tending to every need, cultivating every talent, and removing every obstacle from their child's path—that they neglect their own union. And their marriage grows dry, desiccated, and often dies once the kids fly the nest.

Kelly has seen this pattern play out in the lives of several couples in her social orbit. With men, in her experience, the problem is more likely to be outside friendships and hobbies like golf that keep them from investing enough time in their kids and their marriage. With women, it is more often a preoccupation with the kids. "Children are a lot of work," she observes, adding that the marriage often slips into neglect once kids come along.

"If you don't foster good communication or think it's essential to spend time with each other . . . then [the relationship] will wither," Kelly notes. The passion dies—including the sexual bond. Couples who stop focusing on spending time together and cultivating their relationship often "stop having sex"—which is a "big bonding area." Sex fosters a "physical connection [that] feeds your marriage from a biology standpoint. When I hear girlfriends" say we never have sex, that's "a big red flag." In these situations, "fast forward ten years . . . the kids are out of the house" and they are divorced.

Kelly is determined that this will not happen to her and Patrick. My "philosophy of feeding your marriage [is that you] can't just allow life to get busy and ignore your relationship with your spouse and expect it to stay strong and healthy." She has kept the "zing" in her relationship by prioritizing Patrick over the kids and making sure they have time for date nights, fun, and regular sex.

"'What's more important: Your husband or your kids?' You've got to ask yourself. We love the kids, because they're our shared purpose," she notes, but "our goal is not to, you know, raise the children to end up with a shitty marriage."

When they were in the dark phase of their marriage, struggling to raise two young boys and hold down two full-time jobs, Kelly recalls being so tired that at times they could barely muster a conversation. But they were determined to keep the spark alive in their marriage—so they started doing date nights in their basement. They would pretend to go out by going into the basement, playing music, and having a drink, she

FIGURE 6.2: MORE DATE NIGHTS, HAPPIER AND MORE STABLE MARRIAGES

Marital quality and perceived stability among husbands and wives (%), by frequency of date nights

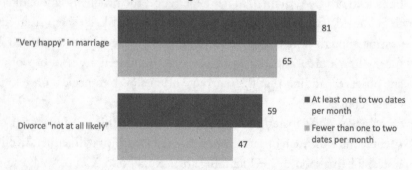

Based on married adults aged 18 to 55. Source: State of Our Unions Survey (2022).

recalls, "and try not to talk about the kids." This was the start of weekly date nights for them, because, in her words, "'we' matter."

Now that their kids are older and independent, they have graduated to weekend concerts, hikes along the James River, and regular bike rides, both with an eye to sustaining their relationship and their physical health. "We're taking care of ourselves physically through good sleep, exercise, and good food," she reports, adding that it allows them to bring their "best self into a relationship."

Kelly and Patrick's dedication to maintaining a sense of emotional communion and intimacy through regular date nights and outings has paid large dividends for their marriage. She reports that her marriage is a "10 on a scale of 1 to 10."

They are not alone. In the State of Our Unions Survey, as figure 6.2 illustrates, husbands and wives who have a date night at least once a month are happiest. Net of controls, they are almost twice as likely to be very happy in their marriage, compared to their peers without regular date nights. In fact, regular date nights are one of the strongest predictors of marital happiness in the survey.[29] Moreover, a National Marriage Project report showed that the probability of divorce for couples who set aside such "couple time" at least once a week was about 25 percent less, over a five-year period, than of those who did not have such regular couple time.[30]

While we cannot know how much of this link is causal, there is no doubt that husbands and wives who make an active effort to keep the embers in their marriage burning by doing date nights enjoy higher-quality marriages. Date nights seem to be particularly valuable if they introduce novelty into a couple's relationship, steer clear of contentious topics, and allow a couple to temporarily escape from the stress of parenting and work. They also send a signal to each spouse that their marriage is valued, "that we're together [on a date night] because our relationship is that important," as Kelly notes.

Date nights are more common among the Faithful, who have the motivation to make them a regular habit, and Strivers like Kelly and Patrick Reilly, who have the resources to afford them. But they do not just seem to translate into better marriages; they also appear to fuel a stronger sex life.

"When you feel supported as a female and loved generally, then you feel sexier. You're more comfortable in the bedroom," Kelly observes. Going out and doing things that are physically active with Patrick makes her more inclined to have sex and enjoy it. "I think you feel sexier and want to have sex more when you're not stressed, you're not depressed, you're not feeling lonely and unloved. So if you're around someone who you're laughing and having fun times with and enjoying time with, and you're not exhausted or physically unwell, then I think that naturally lends itself to a much more vibrant physical relationship for sure."

There is a definite connection between date nights and sexual frequency and satisfaction. Figure 6.3 indicates that husbands and wives who have regular date nights are markedly more likely to have sex at least once a week and are 20 percentage points more likely to say they are very happy with the quality of their sexual relationship. These are significant differences between the two groups, even controlling for factors like race, gender, and income.[31]

Sexual satisfaction, not surprisingly, is also a strong predictor of relationship quality and marital stability. Couples who have sex at least once a week are 22 percentage points more likely to be very happy in their marriage and 19 percentage points more likely to report that divorce is

FIGURE 6.3: MORE DATE NIGHTS, GREATER SEXUAL FREQUENCY AND SATISFACTION

Sexual frequency and satisfaction among husbands and wives (%), by frequency of date nights

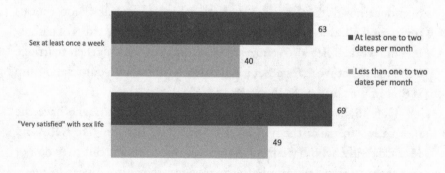

Based on married adults aged 18 to 55. Source: State of Our Unions Survey (2022).

"not at all likely" for them. A large body of research indicates that regular sex predicts better health, more happiness, and stronger marriages.[32] In our survey, regular marital sex predicted overall happiness about as strongly for women as it did for men. Good sex equals greater satisfaction with life, it would seem, for many men and women.

Furthermore, sexual satisfaction is driven not just by frequent date nights but also by many manifestations of the we-before-me orientation to marriage. Couples who identified more with a "team" mindset, who regularly sacrificed for one another, and, yes, who shared the same bank account and last name, were more likely to be satisfied with their sex.[33] It turns out that putting "we before me" doesn't just boost your odds of being happy in your marriage; it also seems to boost your odds of enjoying *eros* in a deeper and more profound way in your union.

THE BOTTOM LINE

Although the idea that you should "look out for number one" took off in the 1970s, this me-first mentality continues to have a lot of cachet in the popular and elite culture. From the big screen to the mainstream media, we're often fed the message that we should have more "me" time, our own bank accounts, and plenty of opportunities to put our own professional ambitions first. I can't tell you how many stories I've read in mainstream publications in recent years talking up—to quote one *New York Times* op-ed—the desire to "self-actualize," to stop "subjugating the self in service of the family,"[34] and to enjoy more "hours alone," all by authors who, frankly, ended up divorced. Articles like these are suggestive of why elite injunctions to take a me-first approach to money, last names, love, and life should all be greeted with skepticism.

The bottom line is that from the workplace to the bedroom, men and women who put their marriage bond over their own self-interest are usually rewarded with a union that is better and stronger. In different ways, Strivers, religious people, and more conservative-minded Americans are more likely to embrace different aspects of a team-first marriage. Clearly, those who cultivate a spirit of communion in word and deed enjoy markedly happier and more sexually satisfying marriages—most of the time.

CHAPTER 7

THE PARENT TRAP

The False Notion That Kids Make
Life and Marriage Miserable

The 1970s weren't just the decade when divorce surged; they were also the decade when childbearing slumped, so much so that America's fertility rate fell well below the replacement rate (2.1 children per woman) for the first time in the nation's history.[1] The portrait of parenthood painted in Ridley Scott's award-winning 1979 movie *Alien* was a perfect fit for the decade's anti-natalist tenor, as movie critic Sylvia Maixner has noted: "*Alien* is all about pregnancy, early childhood and how strange and horrifying it is that these things [children] end up in and out of a lot of us."[2]

Alien begins with its crew emerging from interplanetary slumber to answer a distress signal from a mysterious planet, LV-426 (LV, Maixner points out, could be short for "love"). They encounter the wreckage of a ship with a cache of alien eggs. A parasite emerges from one of the eggs, attacks a crew member, and manages to *impregnate* him, via his throat, with an alien baby.

A day later, the baby alien emerges from the man's chest in a gooey explosion of blood and guts. The crewman dies in childbirth, and the newborn alien proceeds to roam about the spaceship, dealing death and destruction as he quickly grows into a man-size killing machine.

Dissension flourishes on board the spaceship as the crew debate how best to handle the creature. Before they can figure this out, almost all the crew members are brutally killed. Finally, Ripley (played by Sigourney Weaver), the single crew member to survive the beast's continuous assaults, manages to expel the alien from her escape pod with a grappling hook and burn it alive in space. The movie's climactic conclusion could not be more anti-child.

Alien punctuated the anti-natalist character of the "Me" Decade with its harrowing depiction of parenthood as unimaginable physical trauma, confusion, chaos, a Hobbesian struggle of all-against-all, and death. Not exactly something the ordinary mortal would wish to tackle.

But in the 1980s, amid President Reagan's Morning in America, the country swung away from this view and back toward a more child-friendly ethos. The fertility rate, for instance, headed back up, hovering around the replacement level of 2.1 children per woman, and it stayed there until 2009.

In the last decade, however, fertility has taken a nosedive again, reaching a record low of 1.6 children per woman in 2020.[3] To be sure, the changing economic landscape, including the financial fallout of the Great Recession, had a hand in emptying cradles across the country. But cultural change is also afoot, with a large minority of Americans becoming increasingly ambivalent, indifferent, and even hostile to parenthood.

Part of what is happening is that, once again, the journalists, academics, and storytellers that control the heights of our culture too often tell us that parenthood makes us miserable, it will torpedo our marriages, and it's especially bad for the environment. "American Parents Are Miserable: Moms and Dads Alike Face a Massive 'Happiness Gap,'" said *Salon*, spotlighting a recent sociological study.[4] The *Washington Post* weighed in with more negative news, this time about combining wedlock and childbirth: "Why Having Children Is Bad for Your Marriage."[5] And, not to be outdone in anti-natalist messaging, NBC News piled on with this headline: "Science Proves Kids Are Bad for Earth. Morality Suggests We Stop Having Them."[6]

Lurking beneath these dark "parenthood is a trap" takes are three pervasive cultural forces: individualism, hedonism, and workism. Kids, after all, make tons of demands on parents that limit our individual options, choices, and freedom—and force us to grow up. *Time* made this abundantly clear in a cover story on "The Childfree Life," which depicted a beautiful couple vacationing in the tropics with this subheadline: "When having it all means not having children."[7] Kids limit our ability to enjoy *la dolce vita*—from that impossibly romantic Caribbean beach vacation to the hip new restaurant with rave reviews in your town center. When you have a crying baby or a truculent toddler, it is much harder to eat out, vacation, and pursue your hobbies to your heart's content. "An impromptu trip to Paris, skydiving lessons, or a cute convertible for two might be out if you have a baby at home," emphasized NBC's *Today Show*.[8]

Children also make it harder to lean in at work, especially for women. COVID, for instance, summoned up a legion of stories from media outlets like the *New York Times* describing how the pandemic "scarred" women, "dealt a blow" to them, and took them "ten years back," as the pandemic forced many parents, especially mothers, to devote more time and care to their children.[9] Even President Biden got in on the act, tweeting out: "Nearly two million women in our country have been locked out of the workforce because they have to care for a child. . . . My Build Back Better Act will make caregiving accessible and affordable and help them get back to work."[10] The takeaway from all this? Nothing could be worse than being stuck at home with your children, away from the thing that matters most: your job.

Given these kinds of messages, it is no accident that ordinary men and women seem to value parenthood less than they once did. A recent Pew poll found that more than half of adults agreed that having a job or career they enjoy is "essential" to living a fulfilling life. But only about one in five felt the same way about having children.[11] A Wall Street Journal/NBC News poll found that only 43 percent of Americans now place a high value on having children, down 16 points from 1998—and Generation Z and millennials were the least likely to say that having children was "very important" to them.[12]

Not surprisingly, not only is fertility falling but childlessness is also rising. Demographer Lyman Stone, as noted in chapter 1, predicts that childlessness is now surging in the rising generation—with about one in four young women today destined to have no children.[13] These trends are emblematic of the ways in which the American heart has been closing to children in recent years.

But are contemporary men and women right to steer clear of parenthood when it comes to marriage today? How does the "parent trap" take jive with the actual empirical data? In this chapter, we explore the links between parenthood, happiness, loneliness, and meaning. We also explore how parenthood is linked to the quality and character of today's marriages. The picture of parenthood painted here is not nearly as alienating as the one conveyed by Ridley Scott's famous 1979 horror sci-fi film *or* our increasingly anti-natalist culture.

LESS "ME" TIME, BUT MORE MEANING (AND HAPPINESS)

There are lots of reasons men and women end up childless today. They couldn't find the right partner. Started too late. Not fertile. But one of the striking features of our individualist age is that many young men and women now discount the importance of having children or decide to be child-free by choice.

From celebrities like Sarah Silverman to ordinary women like Jenna Johnson (below), a growing number of Americans are willfully steering clear of parenthood. "I have had to decide between motherhood and living my fullest life, and I chose the latter," tweeted Sarah Silverman in response to questions about her family future.[14] One reason more young adults are steering clear of parenthood, as Silverman's comment suggests, is that they are taught to see parenthood as unattractive because it necessarily infringes on their individual choices, desires, and agendas. Less time for career, for fun, and for relaxation. There's a lot less "me" time when you are a parent, especially a mother. Less money, too, to spend on things you like, like travel and eating out.

Not surprisingly, young adults influenced by this mindset are embracing the decision to delay or forego parenthood in record numbers. Take Jenna Johnson, a New York City resident, who likes the freedom found in childlessness. "I get to do all sorts of things: buy an unnecessary beautiful object, plan trips with our aging parents, sleep in, spend a day without speaking to a single person . . . go out for drinks with a friend on the spur of the moment," Johnson told *Time*. "My plans—

professionally, daily, long-term, even just for vacation—are free from all the contingencies that come with children."[15] No kids, in her book, means more freedom, more fun. In other words, individualism plus hedonism.

But childlessness is also being elevated now not just as an obstacle to professional success or an expression of selfishness but as the *moral choice* in a world where children are depicted as a threat to the environment. In a recent essay for the *Nation*, journalist Katha Pollitt asked, "Does the world need more people?" adding, "Not if you ask the glaciers, the rain forests, the air, or the more than 37,400 species on the verge of extinction thanks to the relentless expansion of human beings into every corner and cranny of our overheated planet." Representative Alexandria Ocasio-Cortez, in a 2019 Instagram Live session, said issues like these lead "young people to have a legitimate question: Is it OK to still have children?"[16]

Concerns like these are common among childless adults. A recent survey from Morning Consult found that one in four men and women without children indicated that climate change was a factor behind their childlessness.[17]

Lili Roquelin, forty-one, is a married New Yorker motivated by a combination of environmentalism and individualism to steer clear of motherhood. "I have many more things to explore on my journey," she told the *New York Times*, "that do not involve raising other suffering human beings on an out-of-supplies planet."[18] Roquelin is also a musician with a new song out called "Childless." The song's lyrics run as follows: "I don't need a baby to be happy. . . . Your fulfillment comes when you follow your bliss."[19]

But *are* parents today less happy and leading less meaningful lives than their childless peers? Plenty of media coverage and scholarship makes it seem like childlessness is the better path. Recall that *Salon* headline: "American Parents Are Miserable: Moms and Dads Alike Face a Massive 'Happiness Gap.'" In the article, Kali Holloway stressed that "raising kids can sometimes be a real drag" before summarizing studies indicating that parenthood is linked to "lower levels of happiness," "life satisfaction," and "mental well-being."[20]

Holloway's article is based on a 2016 research study delivering sobering news about parenthood from family scholars at the University of Texas–Austin, Wake Forest, and Baylor University. They reported that American parents were 13 percentage points less happy than their childless peers, a fact they attributed to the lack of work-family policies like paid parental leave and childcare subsidies in the United States. "Having kids in the US is brutal," said Robin Simon, a Wake Forest sociologist who coauthored the study.[21]

Simon also reported that US parenthood is not linked to a greater sense of purpose in life. "I thought at least purpose and meaning in life would be higher for parents, and we find it's just flat," she told the *South China Morning Post*. "There is joy to having kids. But I think that for most people, the stresses that are associated with having kids overshadow those joys."[22]

Studies like this suggest that parenthood is a trap, likely to leave fathers and mothers feeling miserable and meaningless compared to their childless peers. There is only one problem with this handwringing about parenthood: it no longer fits the data.

While it is true that surveys conducted in the twentieth century often indicate that parents are more likely to report less happiness than their childless peers, today that is most definitely not true.[23] Research by both economist Chris Herbst and the Institute for Family Studies suggests that the happiness tide has turned in recent years in the direction of parents, especially those who are married.[24] For instance, a 2021 YouGov survey shows that childless Americans are now more likely to report that their lives are lonely, and less likely to report that they are meaningful and happy. A clear majority of men and women (nearly 60 percent) ages eighteen to fifty-five who do not have kids report that they are lonely some, most, or all of the time.[25] As figure 7.1 indicates, only a minority of their peers with children, 45 percent, report this level of loneliness.

Parents are also more likely to report their lives are meaningful, as figure 7.1 shows. This dovetails with a recent Pew survey, which found that the "most popular answer" to a question about what gives Americans' lives meaning was family related: "Americans are most likely

FIGURE 7.1: LIFE FOR PARENTS IS LESS LONELY, MORE MEANINGFUL, AND HAPPIER

Percent of adults by parental status

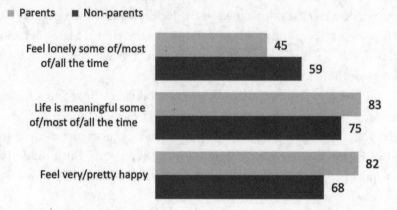

Based on adults aged 18 to 55. Source: IFS/Wheatley Institute Family Survey (2021).

to mention family when asked what makes life meaningful in [an] open-ended question, and they are most likely to report that they find 'a great deal' of meaning in spending time with family in [a] closed-ended question."[26]

The 2021 YouGov survey also indicated, unlike plenty of media coverage, that parents are generally happier than nonparents. Eighty-two percent of parents ages eighteen to fifty-five are "very happy" or "pretty happy," compared to 68 percent of their childless peers. In fact, childless men and women are also more likely than parents to say that their lives are sad most or all of the time.[27] As noted above, earlier research using older data often indicated that US parenthood predicted less happiness.[28] Fast forward to 2021, and what we see is that now this pattern appears to have reversed. In other words, today's men and women in their prime who have children report the *greatest* happiness and the *most* meaning in their lives, and these findings hold up even after controlling for factors like education, race, and age. They are also true for men *and* women ages eighteen to fifty-five.[29]

Katherine, a married mother of two young children in Virginia, gives us insight into why this is the case. On the one hand, she acknowledges that she had more free time and more opportunities to do fun things—from window shopping to eating out at "fancier restaurants" to following her favorite bloggers—when she was childless. She was able to live a more hedonistic life, the kind of life celebrated by cultural elites like Sarah Silverman, when she was single and childless in her twenties.

Today, there is no question her "life is harder now that I have kids." A crying baby, dirty kitchen, or toddler tantrum disrupts her days on a regular basis. The care and attention her two young kids require each day have forced her to "really die to myself and become selfless."

But, she insists, this death-to-self has given way to a newer, fuller, and yes, even happier life.

"I do find a lot of purpose and meaning in the mundane day-to-day [activities of family] life, as well as the more exciting times when my kids hit certain milestones or when you have a really great moment with one of them," observed Katherine, who is also a teacher. Seeing her children learn to walk and talk, not to mention celebrate Christmas, gives her unmeasurable joy. And compared to her single self, she is less lonely and has fewer "moments of sadness."

In fact, fascinating new psychological research indicates that the portion of stress and suffering Katherine endures as a parent may heighten her experience of meaning in life—and even happiness. In his aptly titled book *The Sweet Spot: The Pleasures of Suffering and the Search for Meaning*, psychologist Paul Bloom argues that there appears to be a U-shaped curve in terms of suffering and psychological well-being. Too much suffering, or unrelenting suffering, of course, can give way to despair and unhappiness. But *too little* suffering, too much living for pleasure and the self's desires and projects, can lead to a sense of meaninglessness and unhappiness as well.[30]

One experiment assessing people's resilience found that the "most positive reactions weren't from those with no stress in their life or with lots of stress in their lives; they were from those who were in between, in the sweet spot," writes Bloom.[31] Moreover, "the pain has to have meaning" to be truly valuable.[32] Bloom's book suggests that parents like Katherine often benefit from mixing a measure of suffering and stress with a measure of meaningful connection with their children. In other words, parents' lives are richer for the inevitable ups *and* downs of family life.

For Katherine, it is true that the move to motherhood has required sacrifice, suffering, and stress. Her life is less under her own control than it used to be. In that sense, the narrative in our culture tracks with her experience. But, in line with Bloom's thinking, motherhood has also made her life more meaningful—and has left her feeling more compassionate, flexible, and connected. "I think there's a deeper fulfillment there," she said. This is where today's dominant narrative falls apart. And judging by the YouGov survey, Katherine is no outlier in reporting more happiness today as a thirtysomething mother than she would have as a childless young adult.

Not only do parents like her often enjoy a greater sense of meaning and solidarity in their homes, but they also get unique opportunities to forge connections with others outside of the home, especially in a world where so many of our social ties have withered in the face of political polarization and enticing electronic alternatives to in-person activities. From soccer to school plays to visits to the local park, children force you out of your home and off your screen into the presence of other people. For instance, Katherine's happiness with life is also "fuller" because the transition to parenthood has enabled her to plug into a mother's group at her local church, which has left her feeling more connected to the women in her religious community. As Jennifer Senior observed in her book, *All Joy and No Fun: The Paradox of Modern Parenthood*, "children give us structure, purpose, and stronger bonds to the world around us."[33]

WHEN BABY MAKES THREE

We should not, however, minimize the difficulties of what scholars call the "transition to parenthood." For many men and women, marital quality often takes a nosedive after the arrival of the first baby. Late nights, little sleep, less sex, and lots more household responsibilities to argue about—all these things can take a toll on the average marriage. Not to mention recalibrating who does what when it comes to paid work and housework, as couples rearrange their work and family lives post-baby.[34]

Dynamics like this help explain that *Washington Post* headline: "Why Having Children Is Bad for Your Marriage."[35]

These dynamics certainly played out for Danielle and me, as well. But for us, the biggest dip in our marital happiness came not with our first child, whom we adopted when I was twenty-nine, but the birth of our twins when I was thirty-nine. We had already adopted five children and thought we were done. I was completely unprepared for the double dose of diapers, late-night feedings, and childcare that hit in 2009, right as the Great Recession took hold, which took a toll on our family finances.

I navigated the first year with the twins with difficulty. Overwhelmed with the responsibilities of fatherhood, I was often distracted, snappish, and unhappy. I was less affectionate and less emotionally present as a husband. Not surprisingly, there was plenty of bickering, long silences, and sober stares between Danielle and me. My happiness—and our marital quality—took a definite dip that year.

My experience in that chapter of my marriage dovetails with what psychologist Matthew Johnson wrote regarding marriage and parenthood in his *Washington Post* article:

> The relationship between spouses suffers once kids come along. Comparing couples with and without children, researchers [have] found that the rate of the decline in relationship satisfaction is nearly twice as steep for couples who have children than for childless couples . . . Worse still, this decrease in marital satisfaction probably leads to a change in general happiness, because the biggest predictor of overall life satisfaction is one's satisfaction with their spouse.[36]

"Beyond sexual intimacy, new parents tend to stop saying and doing the little things that please their spouses," noted Johnson, adding, "Flirty texts are replaced with messages that read like a grocery receipt."[37] Amid all the practical challenges of family life, "Parents often become more distant and businesslike with each other as they attend to the details of parenting."[38] And at the extreme end, about one in ten mothers *and* fathers struggle with postpartum depression.[39]

All this sounds pretty dark for married men and women thinking about having a baby. But couples often see their marital fortunes stabilize, albeit at a lower level, after they adjust to the new challenges of being mothers and fathers and get into a new groove that *combines* their identities as husband and father, wife and mother.[40]

This was certainly true for me as our twins moved into the toddler years. Once they started walking and talking, they became comparatively easy. That's because they spent a lot of time playing with one another. In fact, because they entertained and socialized with one another, they ended up requiring less work than our other children as they moved into the pre-K years. It also helped that as they got older, the twins ended up charming parents, grandparents, teachers, and even neighbors with their antics (trying to trick us about who was who), good cheer, and good behavior. Last fall, for instance, the twins delivered homemade ice cream to one set of older neighbors and homemade cookies to another set, bringing untold joy to the neighborhood and pride to their parents. And every night, one twin tracks me down wherever I am in the house and gives me a kiss goodnight before heading off to bed. Needless to say, the twins have brought a big boost to my own sense of meaning and happiness with life—and Danielle's.

My experience is emblematic of a broader pattern. One review of the parenting literature noted that "many initial challenges encountered at the time of new parenthood are transient in nature," with couples eventually adjusting and reaching an equilibrium in their relationship after kids come along.[41] In the 2022 State of Our Unions Survey, there is, surprisingly, no real difference in marital happiness between parents and nonparents ages eighteen to fifty-five. Seventy-five percent of married fathers and 72 percent of married mothers are at least "very happy" in their marriages, compared to 72 percent of husbands and 71 percent of wives who are childless. Controlling for factors like age, education, and income, these differences are insignificant.[42]

Moreover, looking beyond just marital happiness, what we now see is that married parents are *happier* with their lives than their married peers who are childless, especially after they have moved beyond the age associated with challenges posed by young children.[43] Today, as figure 7.2 shows, married adults with children are happiest. Specifically,

82 percent of married dads and 86 percent of married moms are "very" or "pretty happy," according to a recent survey. But only 68 percent of husbands and 78 percent of wives without children report an equivalent level of happiness. Both married fathers and mothers are happier than their childless married peers. These happiness premiums persist after controls for race, education, gender, age, and income.[44]

So even though children are often a strain on marriage, and they seem to lead to a dip in marital quality, the overall picture of marriage and parenthood is rosier than the popular press would suggest. To wit: the happiest group of American men and women in their prime (eighteen to fifty-five) are those who are *married with children*. To be sure, we do not know precisely why this is the case today. It may be in part that happier people today are more likely to have children—what scholars call the selection effect. But it is clearly no longer the case that parents are more miserable than their childless peers.

FOR THE SAKE OF THE CHILDREN

It's not just the presence of children that can influence married life but the way that parents think about children. Today, a large share of

FIGURE 7.2: MARRIED PARENTS HAPPIER

Happiness by marital and parental status (%)

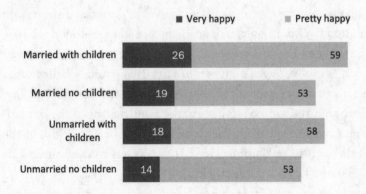

Based on adults aged 18 to 55. Source: IFS/Wheatley Institute Family Survey (2021).

Americans does not believe that one of marriage's primary aims is to provide the ideal environment for the rearing of children. When reality star Kristin Cavallari divorced her then husband, former NFL quarterback Jay Cutler, she said this about her decision:

> The scariest thing that I've ever done is get a divorce, but it's been the best thing that I've ever done, and that has really jumpstarted my journey of self-love and figuring out who I am now. . . . My kids have inspired me to become the best version of myself. . . . Being able to be energized and love myself so I can love on my kids—and support them and encourage them—that's the most important thing.[45]

Cavallari's view here is emblematic of how some people today embrace divorce as a positive good for the kids. It was not always this way. A half century ago, for instance, many endorsed the norm that parents should do all they could to avoid divorce "for the sake of the children," whereas today only a minority take this view.[46] Likewise, only a minority of Americans—41 percent—took the view that children are "very important for a successful marriage" in 2007, compared to a clear majority, 65 percent, who held that view in 1990, according to the Pew Research Center.[47] Today, secular and liberal married Americans are especially likely to disagree with the idea that "one of marriage's key purposes is to give children the best shot in life."[48]

But a large minority of husbands and wives in America dissent from the conventional wisdom on marriage, divorce, and parenthood today—and their marriages look different consequently. For instance, 37 percent of husbands and wives ages eighteen to fifty-five strongly believe that one of marriage's key purposes is to give children the best shot in life. Wives like Sarah Brown, no stranger to the family chaos of the last half century. Her mother left her father when she was two, in 1980, at the height of the divorce revolution. Her father was left to raise three kids on his own—and he did not do a good job.

As a school-age girl, for instance, Sarah was often left for days at a time in her dad's home near Diamond Head in Honolulu, Hawaii, while he traveled for business across the Pacific. One day when she thought that her father was traveling for work, thirteen-year-old Sarah went with friends to the state fair. As she and her friends were leaving the fair, she caught sight of her father arriving at the fair with his girlfriend. When he saw her, he said, "Oh, do you want to go in with us?" But Sarah could tell he was just saying it to save face. Her dad did not really want her to break in on his romantic reverie.

"No, I got to go," responded Sarah flatly, not wishing to turn the encounter into an awkward situation. But below the surface, she felt a mix of outrage, alienation, and deep sadness. "I was gutted because that [going to the fair] is something I felt like" should have been done as a family, she recalls, and yet here she was not even knowing her dad was on the island. "That was really hard and sealed the deal on my independence and determination that I will be different."

That day, Sarah concluded that "I have no family, so I'm going to have to make my own," she recalls, adding, "Nobody is going to make my family for me, so we're going to do this right and make sure [the] man that I end up marrying one day is a good man and we do it well."

The man this forty-three-year-old Dallas wife and mother went on to marry is a standup guy, Barry, whom she met at a Baptist church in Virginia. Barry now pastors a church in the Dallas suburbs. In the early years of their marriage, they struggled because Sarah did not handle conflict well. With no good model for conflict and compromise to fall back on from her own childhood, she alternated between lashing out at Barry and shutting down emotionally when conflicts arose in their marriage.

But Sarah and Barry kept working on their marriage, in part because she was committed to giving her three daughters what her own parents had not given her: a stable and secure family life. Sarah's view was that "for the sake of the children who are vulnerable and dependent on adults . . . adults have an obligation and responsibility to work out their personal struggles for the sake of maintaining a healthy family." She did not "follow the belief that marriage is meant to make me happy. . . . It has crucial elements of loyalty and commitment."

In fact, in the difficult early years of her marriage, one word that she never used with Barry was *divorce*. "Because divorce is not an option, when Barry and I are in conflict, we don't have to fear the threat" that one of them could leave, she said. It "really removes that worst fear"—that one of us "will abandon the family"—and signals that "we're together, we're not going anywhere."

The mutual dedication that Sarah and Barry Brown have to one another and to their daughters has paid substantial dividends. Their daughters get to see that "Dad and I are best friends," she reports. "When we hug, the girls are like, 'Come on!' But I'm like, 'You would much rather see this than the opposite.'" Sarah is grateful for the rock-solid marriage they have forged "on the other side of those struggles in the early years [around] emotional intimacy, physical intimacy, relational intimacy, and communication." She sums up the current state of her union this way: "My marriage is awesome . . . but not perfect."

Across America, married fathers and mothers like Sarah who completely agree that "one of marriage's key purposes is to give children the best shot at life" are 40 percent more likely to report that they do not see divorce in their future.[49] However, taking this child-centered view of marriage is not linked to greater marital happiness, perhaps in part because married parents who take this view may be more likely to persevere in their unions even when they are unhappy. Husbands and wives who are religious and right-leaning like Sarah and Barry, as well as Asian Americans, are especially likely to embrace family-first views like this one.[50]

However, Sarah and Barry also devote a lot of time to doing things together as a family with their daughters, partly because Sarah wishes to give her kids a different life from the one she experienced growing up. It turns out there is also a strong thread binding together family time and high marital quality in today's marriages. For instance, husbands and wives who report above-average "fun" time with their children—doing things like camping, boating, hiking, or playing sports together—are 10 percentage points more likely to be very happy. Surprisingly, those who indicate above-average time devoted to household chores as a family benefit even more; they are a full 17 percentage points more likely to be very happy. So family chores trump family fun time when it comes to predicting marital quality.

Devoting more time to doing things together as a family is more common among Strivers—including liberal ones like Patrick and Kelly from chapter 6—as well as the Faithful, and it is a strong predictor of marital quality, and of reduced worries about divorce, net of basic controls.[51] These findings suggest, as Sarah's life also indicates, that having the strong sense that your marriage matters for the sake of your kids, and devoting time to fun activities and household work with them, makes for stronger marriages.

LIVING THE (INDIAN) AMERICAN DREAM

Husbands and wives who prioritize the welfare of their children and take a dim view of divorce are, not surprisingly, less likely to land in divorce court. No group is as adept at avoiding divorce in America as Indian Americans. Today, an astonishing 94 percent of Indian American parents are stably married, much higher than the American average of 63 percent.[52]

Ajay Anand, a fifty-two-year-old neurosurgeon in Loudoun County, Virginia, has two theories about Indian American marital exceptionalism. The stability of Indian American marriages is rooted in familism and child-centeredness, according to this married father of three young men. In the Indian American subculture, you have "a family where you take care of your parents, no nursing homes. You have a tight bond and an arranged marriage [for spouses]. You don't get a divorce," he says, adding, "It's a scandal, a mark of shame."

Pooja Mamidanna, an Indian American family therapist, agrees that familism plays a central role in Indian family life: "With [Indian] family, it's a very strong collective unit," she observed, adding, "It's not I vs. you. [It is a] collectivistic family dynamic that exists. It's 'we come together' first. So, it's not even about putting yourself first. It's putting your family first."[53]

The cultural power of familism takes divorce off the table for the vast majority of Indian American couples and maximizes their intergenerational family solidarity. A related reason Indian Americans are committed to stable marriage is that they see the institution as key to their own children's success. "You're focused like a laser beam on those kids to get them educated and make them productive," Ajay says. "There's an understanding of the reality that to be successful you have to have a successful family."

In his view, following "the success sequence"—getting an education,

FIGURE 7.3: EDUCATION AND MARITAL STATUS, BY RACE/ETHNICITY

Percent of US adults who are college educated, married

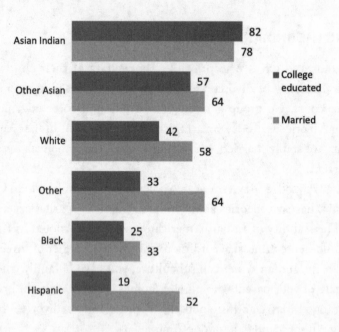

Based on American adults aged 25 to 55. "Other" includes mixed race, Pacific Islander, and Native Americans. Source: American Community Survey, 2019 (IPUMS).

working full-time, and marrying before having children—is integral to ensuring that Indian children have an outsize shot at the American Dream: "I know that Indian American marriages are more intact because they do the things you hear all the time: finish school, get a job, get married, raise kids. The Indians . . . not only finish school . . . [we] get college, go [get a] master's degree. Get a high-paying job. Have your kids. Get them educated. Have a family, take care of your grandparents. It's all those things, like quadrupled. Not only how to not [end up in] poverty [but] how to bust out of it and conquer the world."

Ajay's perspective on Indian success dovetails with the research. Indian Americans now top the charts in income. Median family income among Indian Americans ages twenty-five to fifty-five was $133,130 in 2019, well above the White median income of $86,400. Indian Americans also have higher incomes than other Asian Americans, Hispanics, and Blacks. And, as Ajay suggests, education and marriage do indeed figure prominently in Indian American success.

No other racial/ethnic group of Americans is as well educated as Indian Americans. Eighty-two percent of Indian American adults ages twenty-five to fifty-five are college educated, compared to just 42 percent of Whites, as figure 7.3 shows. Moreover, no other group of Americans is as likely to be married as Indian Americans: 78 percent of Indian Americans ages twenty-five to fifty-five, compared to 58 percent of Whites. Both education and marriage help explain the income gap between Indian and White families. After controlling for education, the White–Indian gap in average family income shrinks from $61,868 to $36,628. When marital status is also controlled in a regression model, the gap falls to $28,410.[54]

Ajay also believes that Indian success in life and family depends upon rejecting the worst features of contemporary American family culture: that Americans are too cavalier about marriage, expect too little of their children academically, and are too permissive with drinking and partying on the part of their kids and themselves. "Parents around here in [Leesburg] would say. . . . 'work hard, party hard.' No!" he says. "My wife and I were raised in Hindu families and so we weren't able to go party and carry on."

When Ajay's boys were younger, the couple decided to stop socializing with some neighbors whose weekend parties involved lots of drinking. Ajay and his wife, Binita, had enjoyed spending time with their neighbors but worried about the implicit message this kind of socializing would send to their sons: "'Oh, where's mom and dad? There's a babysitter because we're going off to a party with our friends,'" he recalled. "But we said, you know what, we got to cut off all these relationships. Because [that's] not a right model for our kids." This perspective also colored how they responded when the boys were invited to late-night parties in high school: "We knew that it would only be a bad thing for our boys; so they didn't participate in that."

Needless to say, Ajay also does not adhere to the soulmate model of marriage ambient in pop culture. "So, happiness is not my goal," he said, adding, "Having my soulmate as my wife is not my goal." Instead, "modeling for them" the importance of family, education, and hard work has been "something that we thought was extraordinarily important" about married life.

The Indian case is archetypal to what we see among Asian American and religious families more generally. As noted in chapter 2, both of these groups enjoy markedly higher levels of marital stability and lower levels of divorce.

That's partly because familistic beliefs—that children are one of life's greatest joys, for example, and that divorce should be avoided at all costs when children are involved, unless there is domestic violence—are more common among both these groups. Asian Americans, for instance, are 7 percentage points more likely to agree that divorce should be avoided when kids are involved, and religious Americans are 16 percentage points more likely to report that one of life's greatest joys is having children.[55] Attitudes like this help explain why parents like Ajay and Binita have gotten married and stayed married.

Higher levels of family stability in service of a child-centered, family-first culture are not without their costs. Ajay, for instance, acknowledges that there are downsides to the Indian focus on family stability. He's seen abuse among some of his Indian peer marriages and his share of difficult marriages.

But on balance, Ajay is glad that the familistic ethos found in his family and so many Indian families has given his children a strong start in pursuit of the American Dream. Binita and Ajay are proud that all three of their sons are recent graduates of the state's top university, UVA, and off to successful professional starts. The sacrifices they made for their sons are already bearing visible fruit.

It doesn't hurt that he and Binita are also, like most Asian American and religious husbands and wives, not just stably but happily married. Like many of the masters of marriage, they have discovered that one of the key ingredients of a strong and stable marriage is seeing that a core purpose of marriage is focusing on a project bigger than yourself: providing a strong and stable foundation for your children to flourish. For them, parenthood has not been an alienating trap but a path to deep joy.

CHAPTER 8

THE "MAYBE I DO" MENTALITY

No Way to Protect Your Marriage

In Greek mythology, Sirens were beautiful sea nymphs who lured sailors off their intended course with their fetching appearance and enchanting songs. Any sailor succumbing to their charms would run aground on their island home, never to be heard from again. The Sirens' island, Homer's *Odyssey* tells us, was a macabre sight: piles of bones, with the flesh of recent victims rotting in the open air.[1]

To protect himself from the charms of the Sirens, Odysseus had his crew bind his body to the mast of his ship before sailing by their island. As they passed by, the Sirens' song was more beguiling than anything else he had encountered in his life: "Famous Odysseus, great glory of Achaea, draw near, and bring your ship to rest, and listen to our voices. No man rows past this isle in his dark ship without hearing the honey-sweet sound from our lips. He delights in it and goes his way a wiser man."[2] Overcome by the power of the Sirens' song and beauty, Odysseus strained to break free of his bonds. Heedless of the consequences, he longed to go off course in pursuit of these beguiling creatures.

But his fellow sailors refused to release him. Eventually, Odysseus's ship moved out of range and out of danger. He had avoided a catastrophic temptation that would have destroyed his entire crew, and he was free to continue his journey toward his home, wife, and family.[3]

This is an example of one man's effort to take dramatic actions to protect his future self from a foolhardy choice in the moment—taking up with the Sirens—that would have led to a disastrous destination. One of the core functions of a healthy culture is to build institutions, norms, and customs that similarly protect us from the various Siren songs we encounter in our lives.

Marriage is one such institution—found across cultures and from time immemorial—designed to "constrain your future actions so that you can make long-term plans that heavily affect other people—your spouse, but also your future children—without them having to constantly worry about you running off to any Siren you hear," in the words of psychiatrist Scott Alexander.[4] Marriage functions as both a symbol and a vehicle for living out your commitment to your beloved, and as a publicly celebrated arrangement, it is recognized as such by you, your spouse, your family, and your friends.

One reasonable critique of Odysseus would be that he only *needed* to be bound to the mast because he was determined to hear the Sirens' song for himself. All of his men passed through safely with their ears plugged with beeswax. In real life, paying attention to Sirens as you pass their island often doesn't work out so well.

But a more common critique of this fable from *modern* love gurus would be that Homer should have been more understanding of Odysseus's desire to sample forbidden fruit. How can we truly create an inclusive society if we disapprove of Siren relationships? Isn't mentioning the rotting bone piles a little judgy?

TIES THAT BIND

The norms and customs of one of our civilization's oldest institutions are designed to keep you from falling prey to the Sirens that will confront you in life's journey, tempting you to abandon the commitment you made to your husband or wife. Today, they range from classic enticements—another lover—to more contemporary temptations—a devotion to career so strong that it leads you to ignore your marital promises entirely. The vows taken at a wedding—"Till death do us part" and "forsaking all others" and "to love and to cherish"—point us to some of the most important norms and social practices that have traditionally made marriage such a powerful force for commitment.

But all too many of the storytellers who now dominate our cultural platforms are dedicated to deconstructing and demolishing the very norms and customs that sustain marriage. They do so in the name of a kind of "expressive individualism" that wishes to deny the self none of the Sirens that might appear along the path of life. Let's look at a couple examples.

A *Times* advice columnist scolds a mother for not being "open-minded" toward her adult daughter's boyfriend—who is married to someone *else*. This woman is instructed by the *Times* that she must find out what her polyamorous daughter "likes about this arrangement and how it satisfies her" and make her peace with the arrangement.[5]

An *Atlantic* editor defends her divorce from the father of her three children but acknowledges that she still loved her husband when she left him—and that he had done nothing to justify her decision to break their bond. But she was following a higher purpose. She'd come to realize that the man "was standing between me and the world, between me and *myself*." Divorcing her husband opened new possibilities. By her account, she might have more time to devote to book writing, opportunities to try out sex with new partners, even the chance to "microdose."[6] Sirens, all.

Much of this liberationist project took off in the 1970s, championed by the young and the well educated. College-educated Americans, for instance, were the first ones to embrace the idea that divorce laws should be more permissive. Only in later years did a large share of less-educated Americans follow their lead.[7] Today, a growing minority of Americans do not believe that marriage is a permanent commitment, and a growing minority also do not believe that sexual fidelity is required of marriage.

The State of Our Unions Survey finds, for instance, that 36 percent of married Americans ages eighteen to fifty-five think that marriage is only "for as long as you feel fulfilled," rather than taking the view that "marriage is for life—unless there is abuse or adultery." The share of American adults ages eighteen to fifty-five who respond that "a married person having sexual relations with someone" else is "always wrong" dropped 6 points over twenty years, to 73 percent (from 1998 to 2018), according to the General Social Survey. Support for marital permanence and fidelity is lowest among the rising generation—young adults ages eighteen to thirty-five, as well as among left-leaning and secular adults. Today, for instance, only 51 percent of liberals say that infidelity is "always wrong," compared to 89 percent of conservatives.[8] In other words, when it comes to fidelity and divorce, many Americans today are inclined to more of a "Maybe I Do" marital ethic. But cracking open the door to the Sirens, it turns out, often has unintended consequences for the quality and stability of your marriage. The elite fantasy that good marriages and Siren romances can coexist happily is just that: fantasy.

BROKEN VOWS

It was love at first sight for James Clay, a handsome redhead from eastern Kentucky. The moment he saw Savannah volunteering at his school, James had one word for her: "supermodel." He recalls, "I just couldn't believe how beautiful she was, and I really didn't think I had a chance." But Savannah caught sight of him in the gym where he taught phys ed, and she struck up a conversation. This turned into many more conversations, a long-distance email relationship after she moved back to Ohio to finish school, and, finally, an engagement.

Their courtship led to a storybook wedding at a country church outside Lexington, Kentucky. The day is seared in James's mind: "She came down the aisle and it just, it was amazing. It brought me to tears. She was absolutely gorgeous. And, you know, [her] smile was big as the day."

The wedding did not simply reinforce a soulmate model of marriage—that marriage is all about good feelings, being perfectly suited for one another, and living life "happily ever after." James's father, a Baptist pastor, preached a sermon underlining the idea that hard days lay ahead and divorce was not an option. "You know that marriage is not a contract, it is a covenant," James's father told those assembled, adding, "and no matter what, [marriage is about staying together] in sickness or health, till death do you part. You're going to be true and faithful to each other." He emphasized that disappointments, struggles, and conflicts are part of married life in the real world.

But James did not take his father's words too seriously on that wedding day. "Being a young man, you think you're gonna live on 'love' forever," he recalls. Had he been more reflective about his own family life growing up, however, he might have realized his dad knew what he was talking about. In the mid-1980s his father had lost his job, which threw the family into poverty and emotional turmoil. James remembers getting teased at school for wearing secondhand clothes and used sneakers: "They would make fun of me and say stuff about me when the teacher would leave the room."

This experience of childhood poverty drove James to focus on financial success as an adult. He was intent on making sure that he, Savannah, and their two sons would not encounter the hardships he experienced as a child. He taught PE during the day and then launched a successful business on the side making T-shirts. It did very well. "I basically idolized money," he recalls, "and I did so because of fear of lack. . . . I just wanted more and more and more and more."

But James's success came at a cost. Working long hours meant he did not spend much time with his sons—or his wife. "I sacrificed my relationship with my family, my kids and my wife, to make more money."

Meanwhile, Savannah, who taught first grade at a different school, was striking up a friendship with another teacher, Wade. Wade taught in the class next door and would often chat with Savannah. "We just talked over time, just developed this trust and this friendship," she recalls, and over time their friendship turned more romantic. They exchanged "flirty words," "inappropriate conversation," and "we started sensing each other's attraction to each other and we weren't really shy anymore and just said what we wanted to say."

"When he opened that door to my [class] and walked in, I all of a sudden had these butterflies in my stomach," Savannah remembers. And that attraction eventually turned physical. As she looks back on the affair, Savannah attributes part of it to the fact that "James put work in front of me," and she felt like "I'm raising two children alone, eating dinner alone, going to bed alone" as her husband focused on building his business. Her affair started in part because there was a "void that I was trying to fill in my heart and in my life of that attention and that affirmation and the confirmation that I wasn't receiving at home."

Like their wedding day, the day James learned that Savannah was having an affair is also seared into his mind. He'd been doing yard work out back and came in for a cold drink to discover her on the family couch, red-faced, crying. She said, "We have to talk." She gradually admitted that she was "getting some attention" from a colleague at work—and then this devastating coda: "I like it." At first, she only acknowledged hugging and kissing Wade, but eventually, as they talked and then fought, the whole truth came out.

In the wake of Savannah's revelations, James felt myriad emotions: shame, humiliation, despair, and anger. At one point, he decided he was "done": "I didn't necessarily want to divorce my wife, but the pain was so bad that I didn't see any other option," he recalls. James headed over to his parents to tell them, "I can't stand to [stay] here, I'm divorcing her."

But his father said, "Don't throw your marriage away." He advised James to take the situation "one day at a time" and "see if we can make it thirty days, and take it from there." Because he respected his father, James reconsidered.

One factor that pushed him to reconcile was thinking about his sons. "I was thinking, I don't want my kids to be suitcase kids and [their] lives [to] be destroyed. The question about my kids played a huge role in it. I was like, I love my children. I want them to be raised the way I was raised and . . . not see their parents give up in a relationship." Motivated by his concern for his kids, as well as his faith, James managed to reconcile with Savannah.

Of course, plenty of other husbands and wives do not survive infidelity. Consider Nicole Brown's story. One day, she found herself in the shower FaceTiming an old boyfriend, barely making any noise.

"Why? Because my husband and kids were in the next room, completely oblivious," she recalled in an article about her virtual affair. Like Savannah, she connected with a man during a difficult moment in her marriage. In this case, an old flame she had been following on social media offered her the attention and affection she was not getting from her husband at the time. Her marriage did not survive this electronic entanglement, which never led to an in-person affair but nevertheless broke the bond of trust between Nicole and her husband.[9]

But how common are such infidelities—of both the new, virtual kind and the old-school IRL (in real life) varieties? Studies suggest that about one-quarter of ever-married Americans admit to having sex IRL with someone else while married.[10] Men are more likely to stray than women. One recent study found that "20 percent of men and 13 percent of women reported that they've had sex with someone other than their spouse while married."[11] When it comes to virtual infidelities, which are less common, about 5 percent of currently married Americans report they have had cybersex, and 11 percent admit they have had sexual talk online with someone besides their spouse.[12] Here again, husbands are more likely to stray than wives, with 16 percent of husbands reporting any sort of electronic sexual dalliance, compared to 8 percent of wives.[13]

Fidelity of the IRL and virtual kinds does not just vary by gender; it also varies by other factors. As figure 8.1 indicates, according to the General Social Survey, religious husbands and wives are less likely to stray, with 11 percent of those regularly attending services reporting infidelity, compared to 17 percent who rarely or never attend. Asian American husbands and wives are also markedly less likely to cheat.

Spouses who hold more familistic attitudes—who believe that infidelity is "always wrong" and think "divorce should be more difficult"—are clearly less likely to break their marital vows. For instance, 9 percent who took this view of infidelity reported cheating, compared to 43 percent who said that infidelity was just "sometimes wrong" or "not wrong at all." Conservative spouses are also less likely to report cheating, in part because they tend to be more religious and familistic.

One reason infidelity matters, of course, is that it dramatically increases the odds of divorce.[14] In her research on this subject, my colleague Wendy Wang found that Americans who reported cheating were more than twice as likely to say they had divorced. In her words, "Among ever-married adults who have cheated on their spouses before, 40 percent are currently divorced or separated. By comparison, only 17 percent of adults who were faithful to their spouse are no longer married."[15]

Of course, infidelity still exacts a serious toll on marital quality for those who choose to remain together. That's because, regardless of the state of the marriage prior to the adultery, breaking the fidelity norm ushers in thoughts and feelings of betrayal, distrust, and anger—not to mention worries about abandonment.[16] Succumbing to this kind of

FIGURE 8.1: WHO CHEATS?

Percentage of ever-married adults reporting infidelity

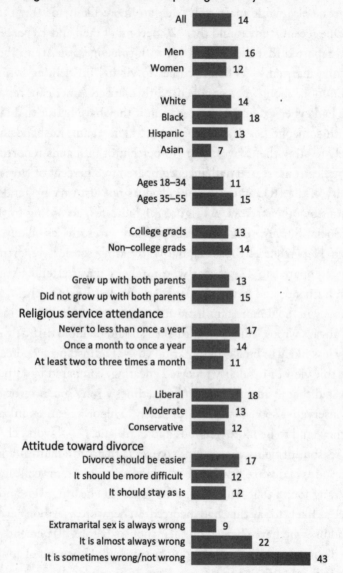

All 14

Men 16
Women 12

White 14
Black 18
Hispanic 13
Asian 7

Ages 18–34 11
Ages 35–55 15

College grads 13
Non–college grads 14

Grew up with both parents 13
Did not grow up with both parents 15

Religious service attendance
Never to less than once a year 17
Once a month to once a year 14
At least two to three times a month 11

Liberal 18
Moderate 13
Conservative 12

Attitude toward divorce
Divorce should be easier 17
It should be more difficult 12
It should stay as is 12

Extramarital sex is always wrong 9
It is almost always wrong 22
It is sometimes wrong/not wrong 43

Based on ever-married adults aged 18 to 55. Source: General Social Survey, 2014–2018.

Siren, in other words, leads all too many marriages to a shipwreck of one kind or another.

In the aftermath of her affair, for instance, Savannah recalls that the quality of their marriage—and their sexual relationship in particular—nosedived. "For me, it was hard because I felt so guilty," she said, adding that the infidelity "overtook our [sexual] lives. His frustration, anger, and hurt, and my guilt was just killing it. We still [had sex] once in a while, but it was nothing like it was before."

The data tell a similar story. In the 2022 State of Our Unions Survey, husbands and wives who reported an affair were 20 percentage points less likely to be "very happy" in their marriage and 21 percentage points less likely to be confident that their marriage would not "end in divorce." In fact, even after controlling for factors like education, race, and income, infidelity is one of the strongest predictors of lower marital quality and greater worries about future divorce in the State of Our Unions Survey.[17]

GOOD FENCES MAKE FOR GOOD MARRIAGES

Today it is not just these clear breaches of marital vows that can bring trouble to marriages; it is also what might be called "lesser infidelities," situations where husbands and wives are paying too much attention to what scholars call "attractive alternatives,"[18] either in real life or online. Letting your mind wander regularly to a pretty colleague at work, chatting up the charismatic coach of your son's soccer team Saturday after Saturday, or following an old flame on Facebook can all corrode the quality and stability of your own marriage. Paying attention to these alternatives tends to make you less engaged in and more unhappy with your own marriage, in ways that can exceed your baseline level of dissatisfaction even if you do not engage in infidelity.

Why is this? Psychologist Scott Stanley has observed that husbands and wives who do not erect "good fences" between themselves and the "alternatives" they encounter in their social and professional worlds enjoy weaker and less satisfying relationships. Without such fences, there is always a temptation to focus too much on the "green grass" in someone else's yard—to appreciate someone else's looks, charisma, humor, professional success, or personality—and discount the good things about your own partner.[19]

This temptation is especially great when our own relationship has grown full of "weeds": those frustrations, difficulties, or serious problems that spring up in any relationship. The problem with looking over the fence, according to Stanley, is that not only are we more likely to fall into infidelity, but we're also less likely to invest in the partner we're already with. Hence, proper fences between ourselves and attractive alternatives keep us from dwelling upon them or devoting too much time or attention to them. Instead, focus on making your own lawn greener, especially if it is looking a little brown. "Most lawns," Stanley observes, even those overrun with weeds, "respond well to tender love and care."[20]

Stanley once counseled a married man who was attracted to a woman he had met at the gym. "They talked as they worked out, and quite a friendship grew," Stanley noted. This man's wife did not work out with him, which was a source of "resentment for him." But to protect himself from deepening a tie that he feared would threaten his marriage, the man "decided to plan his workouts so that he and the woman would not work out together. He could still say 'hi' as he came and went, but he *planned* for them not to be together in the way that caused him the most trouble." In other words, this man erected a relational fence to protect the commitment he had to his wife.

This kind of strategy is also relevant to online relationships. The iFidelity Survey found, for instance, that men and women who erect "iFences" online that prevent them from engaging emotionally or sexually with "attractive alternatives" are markedly more likely to enjoy more stable and satisfying relationships. Fence crossing, from sexting to following old flames on social media, is associated with lower-quality marital relationships. For instance, 67 percent of husbands and wives who are following an old flame on Facebook or Instagram are "very happy" in their relationship, compared with 75 percent of those who do not do this.[21]

From this survey, I cannot tell if relationship troubles push people to ignore fences, or failing to erect such fences leads men and women into trouble. I suspect it's a bit of both. What is clear, though, is that husbands and wives who don't engage in secret emotional or sexual relationships with others online, or follow old flames on social media, enjoy markedly higher-quality marriages.

Consider Kelly's husband, Patrick Reilly, a tall, handsome, and well-spoken redhead in sales from Richmond, Virginia, who has been happily married for more than twenty years. He meets a lot of people, plays guitar in a band on the side, and travels a lot for work, all factors that boost his risk for infidelity. But he's intentional about protecting his marriage in real life: "When I'm meeting new people in my line of work, I talk a lot about my wife and kids. I want them to know I'm a family man." This is one way Patrick throws up a symbolic fence around his marriage. And it doesn't prevent him from having business meals with colleagues of the opposite sex—though he does not meet for drinks with female colleagues while away on business.

Patrick, who is neither religious nor politically conservative, also has rules governing his online interactions: "My wife is tagged in a majority of my posts, my status is listed as married, and interactions online are treated the same way as if in-person. I do not follow old girlfriends, as there is a reason that they are in that category!" The fence he maintains in the real and virtual worlds between himself and attractive alternatives is one reason Patrick's marriage is so strong, both because it keeps him focused on his wife and because it affords her an extra measure of emotional confidence in their relationship.

Husbands and wives like Patrick and Kelly who adhere to classic fidelity norms report stronger and more stable marriages. Kelly says, "I appreciate the way he is careful; it gives me a sense of security." Kelly's perspective is also borne out by the data. For instance, according to the 2022 State of Our Unions Survey, 55 percent of those who avoid following old flames online report that it is "not at all likely" their marriage will end in divorce, compared to 45 percent of those who do follow their exes. And married Americans who say that infidelity is "always wrong" are happier in their marriages, with 63 percent of those who take the classic view on infidelity reporting they are very happy in their marriages, compared to just 56 percent of those who take a more permissive position on infidelity, according to the General Social Survey.[22]

Husbands and wives like the Reillys who prioritize fidelity in word and deed enjoy more security knowing they "mutually support each other, work as a team, and have a clear future together," according to Stanley. Conversely, those who take a more casual approach to this kind of commitment are less likely to feel secure in their relationship and to invest practically and emotionally in one another.[23]

In recent years, Americans' commitment to sexual fidelity and monogamy has slipped. This drop has been especially noteworthy among young adults and progressives—egged on by countless social-media influencers and journalists eager to evangelize on behalf of some new, fashionable relationship option. These groups are especially likely, for instance, to report being open to polyamory.[24] But these departures from the classical norm of "forswearing all others" put husbands and wives at needless risk of wandering toward Sirens in the real and virtual worlds who will destroy their unions. And they make it less likely that the kind of trust, intimacy, and mutual commitment needed for a marriage to flourish are on hand.

FOR AS LONG AS OUR LOVE SHALL LAST

Our culture today teaches that embracing a "till death do us part" ethic can be an obstacle to living your best life and love. After all, if your husband or wife is not facilitating your "voyages of self-discovery and personal growth,"[25] you should feel free to move on. You need only remain married for as long as you're able to maximize your own feelings of fulfillment or your own agenda.

The critically acclaimed movie *Marriage Story* gives us one Hollywood view of how this ethic fuels marital instability in the twenty-first century. Consider how Scarlett Johansson's character, an actress named Nicole Barber, talks to her divorce attorney, Nora Fanshaw, played by Laura Dern, about why she thinks her marriage to Charlie Barber— a theater director whose professional plans do not perfectly dovetail with her own—needs to end:

> **Divorce attorney:** To me, like, you did your time in New York [where her husband works as a director]. He can do some time here [in Los Angeles, where she is acting], no?

Nicole Barber: He always said we would, but he never did.

Divorce attorney: How old's your son?

Nicole: Henry's eight. He likes L.A. I don't know if it's fair to him [to get divorced].

Divorce attorney: I want you to listen to me. What you're doing is an act of hope. Do you understand that?

Nicole: Yeah.

Divorce attorney: You're saying, "I want something better for myself."

Nicole: I do.

Divorce attorney: And this right now is the worst time. It will only get better.[26]

The message conveyed by the divorce attorney in this scene is that marriage should not be an obstacle to personal and professional fulfillment. Likewise, when it doesn't seem like your marriage is allowing you to grow, you should feel free to seek "something better for [yourself]"—even when it may not be "fair" to your child. The movie does show the emotional wreckage left by such an approach. The divorce attorney's words, however, outline a philosophy that has become all too common in our culture.

For many observers on the left, this less-committed approach to marriage is a feature, not a bug, of contemporary married life. Stephanie Coontz, the doyenne of feminist family history first introduced in chapter 5, believes that less commitment and easier divorce make for higher marital quality in today's unions. Making "marriage itself more optional and more contingent," as Coontz puts it, has *increased* the odds of marital bliss—in her words, establishing marriage as "more intimate, fair, and protective"—for those lucky enough to find and keep a spouse today.[27]

However, her view here—that a more permissive approach to divorce has helped us climb new heights of both marital satisfaction and self-actualization in recent years—is not borne out by historical or contemporary evidence. What happened during the divorce revolution of the 1970s and in its immediate wake, as Americans took a "more contingent" approach to marriage, is that average marital quality in the United States

fell. About 65 percent of husbands and wives ages eighteen to fifty-five
were "very happy" with their marriage in the early 1970s, but only about
59 percent of them were very happy by the late 1980s, according to the
General Social Survey.[28]

What is especially striking about this decline in marital quality is
that, according to progressive logic, marital quality should have improved
in the 1970s as fewer and fewer Americans married and many suppos-
edly subpar marriages were dissolved. Based on this line of thought, the
remaining marriages, the cream of the marital crop, should have trended
in a markedly happier direction. But instead, reports of marital happiness fell during and immediately following the "Me" Decade.

What proponents of the progressive view did not anticipate is this:
if your parents, best friend, and sister all get divorced, your confidence
in your own marriage is likely to take a hit. That's because how we
think about and approach our own union is deeply affected by what we
see happening in the marriages of our friends and family members.[29]
Worries about the future of your own marriage, in turn, reduce your
sense of emotional security, willingness to invest in your relationship,
and happiness in your own marriage. Consequently, marital happiness
fell for many ordinary couples, even though on the whole, fewer men and
women were marrying, and more were divorcing.

This very same dynamic plays out among today's husbands and
wives, as figure 8.2 shows. In the State of Our Unions Survey, husbands
and wives who reported that "marriage is for life—unless there is abuse
or adultery" were more likely to say that they were significantly satisfied
("very happy") in their marriages, compared to those husbands and wives
who said that "Marriage is for as long as you feel fulfilled," even net of
controls for factors like race and education.[30] Not surprisingly, conservative and religious husbands and wives are especially likely to embrace
the idea that "marriage is for life."[31]

Obviously, even with controls in place, we cannot make strong causal
claims with this data, given that men and women in happier marriages
may be more likely to embrace an ethic of marital permanence due to
the higher quality of their marriages. But research tracking more than a
thousand husbands and wives *over time* by sociologists Paul Amato and
Stacy Rogers is more conclusive: "People who adopted more favorable

FIGURE 8.2: HUSBANDS AND WIVES WHO THINK MARRIAGE IS FOR LIFE ARE HAPPIER

Percentage of husbands and wives very happy in
marriage, by opinion about marriage

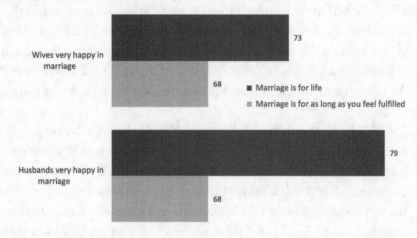

Among married adults aged 18 to 55. Source: State of Our Unions Survey (2022).

attitudes toward divorce tended to experience declines in relationship
quality, whereas those who adopted less favorable attitudes toward divorce tended to experience improvements in relationship quality or at
least a slowdown in the gradual decline in marital happiness and interaction that characterizes many marriages."[32]

So we have no evidence to support the idea that adopting a "more
contingent"[33] ethic of marital commitment is linked to happier marriages. Quite the contrary. Instead, we see that husbands and wives who
embrace a classic ethic of marital commitment are more likely to be more
satisfied.

The marriage of Jon and Maria Erickson, our Eighty-Second
Airborne couple, is emblematic of this dynamic. I asked Maria how she
thought about divorce. "We've never even said the word," she responded,
noting later that they don't see divorce as an option: "I liken it to someone who is just sure that they're never going to commit a felony. We
are one thousand percent sure [we're not going to divorce]. I love that
gift that we can give to our children that we are never ever going to get

divorced. So, we set out with that resolve and . . . it only strengthens our marriage through trials. As trials come up, or disagreements, there is heartbreak and compromise, but it's never fatal."

Couples who share the kind of deep commitment that Jon and Maria have for one another typically enjoy a greater amount of other marital goods: more trust, more emotional security, more mutually beneficial investments in one another and the marriage (both financially and emotionally), more fidelity, and a clearer vision for a joint future.[34] All of this translates, for the average couple, into higher levels of marital quality.

This has certainly been the case for the Ericksons, who are happily married, even through a life that has included its fair share of stressors—from multiple deployments to Afghanistan, Iraq, and Germany to the challenges that come from raising four children together. Through it all, they've taken solace in the knowledge that divorce has never been on the table. And when I asked them separately to rate the quality of their marriage from one to ten, they both picked ten.

"WE WANT PRENUP": IS PLANNING FOR DIVORCE A SMART MOVE?

The prenup (prenuptial agreement) is a prime example of where men and women's thinking about divorce has practical relevance to the conduct of married life. Plenty of voices in pop culture, the media, and family law are emphatic prenup boosters.

Kanye West urged men to protect themselves financially by getting a prenuptial agreement before tying the knot in his hit single "Gold Digger." In his words:

> Holla, "We want prenup! We want prenup!" (Yeah!)
> It's somethin' that you need to have
> 'Cause when she leave yo' @$%, she gon' leave with half

And it's not just megastars with messy marital histories that flag prenups. The financial guru Suze Orman is also a fan, though her endorsement of this legal strategy is more measured than Kanye's. "I get too many emails from older women and men telling me that they've just lost everything because of a divorce," she told CNBC, adding that people can protect themselves from financial ruin by specifying how assets and debts will be distributed if their marriage breaks down. In her view, couples should not fear broaching the sensitive subject of a prenup, because if "you cannot talk money to the person that you are about to marry, you are doomed for failure, because money is going to run through your relationship more than anything else."[35]

Plenty of family lawyers are also enamored of prenups, noting how it makes the divorce process much smoother. "The process may seem annoying, expensive, and even unnecessary, but if there's a divorce, a well-drafted agreement can be worth its weight in gold," says Elizabeth Green Lindsey, an Atlanta family lawyer and president of the American Academy of Matrimonial Lawyers.[36]

Prenups are especially attractive to men and women who are professionally successful and marrying older, those from affluent families, those marrying a second time, and those marrying with children. Once the exclusive domain of the rich, the use of prenups is on the rise—according to one study, prenups are up 62 percent in recent years.[37] Today, 7 percent of married individuals have a prenup, according to the State of Our Unions Survey.

The sentiments driving this uptick in prenups were well articulated on the social media platform Reddit. One Redditor said: "Nobody plans on crashing their car, getting cancer, or having their house burn down, but they still get car, health, and home insurance." Another Redditor described it as "an insurance policy that ensures we would both land on our feet" if they divorced, adding, "Saying a pre-nup is a go-bag is like saying a will is a death wish."

But other Redditors were more skeptical. They worried that signing a prenup sends a bad signal about the future of your marriage. "LOL nothing says, 'I'm not committed to this relationship' like having a pre-nup," wrote one member. Another said he would never sign a prenup, underlining the way in which the document signals less commitment: "If an average person asks to sign a prenup, to me that's a sign they already have one foot out the door."[38]

This debate was echoed among the respondents we spoke with.

Anita Agarwal, a successful accountant from Richmond, Virginia, viewed her prenup as a good way to protect her wealth if her marriage were to end in divorce. As an accountant marrying at forty-two, she had a bigger nest egg than her husband, and she wanted to make sure "whatever is my asset before marriage is mine if things don't go right." She added, "the way it was written here in Virginia is that if I have $10,000 in Apple stock right now [and it] grows to a million in ten years' time and we decide to divorce, that million dollar stock from Apple is still mine, which I completely appreciate." The prenup, from Anita's perspective, is "such an amazing protection tool."

Anita does not think the prenup poses a threat to her marital success. In fact, she is proud of her husband, who helped her negotiate the details of the prenup with her family lawyer. It was an amicable experience that made her "think much more highly of him."

By contrast, Jon Erickson is not a fan of prenups. He views this legal strategy as a bad sign heading into marriage. It is likely to be an expression of a "fear of being hurt" that signals an underlying distrust that could prove corrosive to the future of the marriage. A prenup is "basically just saying, 'I'll marry you, but I'm already planning that it's not going to work out. So, let's get our divorce paperwork done ahead of time just so the divorce will be easier.'" This is why Jon and Maria did not even consider a prenup.

Jon's views were echoed by Laurie Israel, a family lawyer outside Boston, who thinks prenups are "bad for marital health" and mentions two reasons. First, "it promotes distrust and feelings that the beloved is callous and unloving." Second, the process of getting a prenup "can change the chemistry and dynamic of a committed relationship as well. The memory of the negotiations, which often happen after the engagement, and sometimes days before the wedding, is corrosive. I think that in these cases divorce becomes more probable." According to Israel, "A prenup changes the entire connection and contract of a marriage by taking away one of its major pillars: building a secure financial future together."[39]

Her views are consistent with findings in the State of Our Unions Survey. Husbands and wives with prenups expressed lower levels of commitment, happiness, and confidence in the future of their marriage.

For instance, 84 percent of husbands and wives without a prenup are "very committed," compared to just 70 percent of their peers with a prenup. Likewise, those without a prenup are 10 percentage points more likely to be "very happy" in their marriages, compared to those with a prenup. And only 40 percent of husbands and wives with a prenup report that it is "not at all likely" their marriage will end in divorce, compared to 53 percent of those who did not get a prenup. These differences are all statistically significant after controlling for confounding factors like race, education, income, and age. And women with prenups are especially likely to be less happy, compared to their peers without prenups.[40]

Since this survey did not track couples over time, we cannot determine if prenups cause less commitment, more unhappiness, and greater marital instability, or if they are just indicative of greater problems heading into marriage. Regardless, if your goal is to forge a strong and stable marriage, the evidence collected here suggests you should feel free to ignore Kanye West's prenup advice.

TOGETHER BOUND

What is the strongest predictor of a high-quality marriage? This question was taken up by more than eighty scholars from around the world, analyzing more than eleven thousand couples and using forty-three different datasets. Using artificial intelligence to explore relationship quality across these datasets, these family scholars, led by psychologist Samantha Joel, found that the best predictor of a relationship's success is "perceived partner commitment (e.g., 'My partner wants our relationship to last forever')."[41]

This finding parallels the results of our YouGov survey of two thousand husbands and wives across America in the 2022 State of Our Unions Survey. Husbands and wives who "completely agree" that they are "committed" to their spouse are markedly happier in their marriages than those who do not express complete agreement with this question. Net of socioeconomic controls, these married men and women are about five times more likely to be very happy in their marriages, and four times more likely to report that it is "not at all likely" their unions will end in divorce, compared to other husbands and wives who are not as committed.[42] In fact, this indicator of commitment, which is most common among Conservatives, is one of the strongest predictors of marital quality and perceived stability.

Husbands and wives who embrace classic fidelity norms—like the idea that "marriage is for life"—are also significantly more likely to report they are "completely" committed, according to the survey. Apparently, when you embrace fidelity (like Patrick does for Kelly), and marital permanence (like Maria does for Jon), you send a signal to your beloved: "I love you. I will be there for you. You can count on me. My love will not be hijacked. I'm in this marriage till death." When you intentionally keep the Sirens at bay, in other words, your bond becomes not just stronger but sweeter in return.

The apostles of easy divorce and flexible fidelity understand none of this. They are under the illusion that marriage in recent decades has become, in the words of Coontz, both "more fulfilling" and "more effective in fostering the well-being of both adults and children than ever before in history." She believes "fulfilling and fragile seem to 'go together like a horse and carriage'" in today's marriages.[43]

But Coontz is wrong on both counts: there is no evidence that ordinary marriages were made more fulfilling by the growing fragility of our unions in the 1970s, or that husbands and wives who take her contingent view of commitment are happier today. That's because, in the real world, it's actually commitment and contentment that "go together like a horse and carriage" in marriage.[44]

CHAPTER 9

TO PROVIDE, PROTECT, *AND* PAY ATTENTION

What *Really* Makes Her Happy

Macarena Gomez-Barris "seemed to have it all—a brilliant career, two children, striking looks," in the words of *Oprah* magazine, which profiled her in 2008. The thirty-six-year-old Latina had fled Augusto Pinochet's military dictatorship as a child and built a new life in the Golden State. While pursuing a graduate degree in sociology at UC Berkeley, she met a handsome fellow exile from Chile, Roberto Leni, out dancing one night at a club in San Francisco. "We had instant chemistry, and he was my soul mate," Gomez-Barris recalled. They married, had a son, and headed south when Gomez-Barris was offered a position teaching sociology at the University of Southern California.

But her rising professional fortunes did not translate into happiness on the home front. "The trouble began after they moved to Los Angeles, where their daughter was born and Gomez-Barris's academic career took off," reported *Oprah*, noting that Roberto was the one who took on the primary domestic role as the caretaker and homemaker. This arrangement made Gomez-Barris, a feminist, uncomfortable in ways that must have surprised her.

"I was in the more powerful role," said Gomez-Barris. "I made more money and was struggling to balance my work and home life."

Macarena became "immersed" in her professional world, Roberto observed, and he felt marginalized in their new Southern California world. "She lived and breathed USC," he told *Oprah*. "All her friends were professors, and eventually I was obsolete. I'm nothing the system considers I should be as a traditional man. I'm not ambitious. I don't care that much about money. I was brought up among torture survivors, and the most important values were in the emotional realm of human experience, to soothe and support."

Roberto's sensitive spirit was not enough for Gomez-Barris. "Someone had to care about making money to support our family," she said. Her frustrations with Roberto led her to leave him for someone more ambitious and decisive, someone she said "took the initiative and was the most take-charge person I'd ever met."[1]

In the annals of "revealed versus stated preferences," the professor who publicly embraced feminism but privately left her husband for failing to be masculine in spirit and substance has got to rank up there.[2] But is Macarena Gomez-Barris's marital history indicative of any broader social trends when it comes to the stability and quality of married life today?

The conventional wisdom, as conveyed by the media and ivory tower, would be no; stories like Gomez-Barris's tell us very little about the ways in which men and women generally experience marriage and family life in the twenty-first century.

BLANK-SLATE FEMINISM

Since the second-wave feminism of the 1960s and 1970s, we've been told by many progressives that what really makes today's woman happy is a kind of fifty-fifty equality where husbands and wives split paid work, childcare, and housework on a roughly equal basis. Now, in the wake of third-wave feminism, we're getting the message that embracing a more "fluid" approach to gender identities and roles—including models where she works and he stays home, as Macarena and Roberto did—can also be the way to go.

These varied expressions of what I call "blank-slate feminism"—the idea that there is no fundamental difference between men and women[3]—point us toward somewhat different ideals. But what unites these various expressions is the objection to an old idea: that there is any biological reality undergirding the average gender differences between men and women that we see and experience in the real world, including in marriage and the family. Assumed instead is the notion that classic masculine and feminine virtues—not to mention the gender roles of yesteryear—have no appeal for today's woman, including in marriage.

Instead, what is supposed to make the contemporary heterosexual wife happy is an egalitarian or nontraditional marriage, and family life with a sensitive man. "We have every reason to believe that new values about marriage and sex roles will make it easier for parents to sustain and enrich their relationships," wrote Stephanie Coontz in *The Way We Really Are: Coming to Terms with America's Changing Families*.[4] A fifty-fifty approach to dividing up both breadwinning and homemaking is best for today's marriages, many journalists, academics, and relationship gurus assure us. Writing in *Men's Health*, for instance, Paul Kita talked up a new book, *Fair Play*, that encourages couples to aim for rough parity in their relationships unless they wish to "risk frustration, resentment, and divorce."[5]

By contrast, women stuck in more traditional family arrangements are, according to feminist writer Jill Filipovic, likely to be struggling with practically every emotional malady known to woman, from "depression to anxiety to anger," and, according to her, don't even "smile or laugh a lot."[6] The message is clear: traditional virtues and roles make today's women miserable.

The same goes for the twenty-first-century family man as well. In a day and age when Harry Styles gets plaudits for wearing a dress in a *Vogue* cover shoot, we are told that men who break free of outmoded gender roles and virtues are more likely to flourish—including within their families. This message comes through loud and clear from the ivory tower. "Husbands Who Have Wives Who Outearn Them Are Happier than Those Who Don't," *Slate* says, spotlighting a recent study from the University of Connecticut.[7] The study's authors assure us that the "performance of masculinity is harmful to men," adding that "decoupling breadwinning from masculinity is associated with concrete benefits for both men and women."[8]

In fact, men in egalitarian relationships enjoy "more sex, and better sex," reports the *Guardian*, because "choreplay" is the best kind of twenty-first-century foreplay: "a woman who isn't so totally knackered from working all day, picking up the kids, cooking dinner, feeding, bathing and putting the kids to bed all on her own, is much more up for sex in the evenings."[9]

Sheryl Sandberg, then the COO of Facebook, and Adam Grant, a University of Pennsylvania professor, struck a similar note in a *New York Times* article entitled "How Men Can Succeed in the Boardroom and the Bedroom." "Equality is not a zero-sum game" for men, they wrote, adding that "when men do their share of chores," they enjoy happier marriages and lower divorce rates, and even "live longer."[10]

Today's ruling class makes a public show, then, of celebrating gender equality, gender nonconformity, and the abolition of traditional roles and styles of masculinity and femininity. But as we shall see, the expressed preferences of our elites often look different from their revealed preferences. When it comes to gender expectations, as with so much else, members of our ruling class often talk left but walk right.

STRONG *AND* SENSITIVE

Kaitlyn is no conservative. She is a successful thirty-two-year-old patent lawyer at a top firm in Atlanta with a law degree from Duke, a resolute supporter of LGBT rights, and a Biden voter. In many ways she looks and talks like the archetypical young professional woman blazing a successful path in major metros across America today.

But when she opened up to me about what made her husband, David, attractive, her perspective did not sound progressive at all. In a college class more than a decade ago, Kaitlyn recalls listing her top ten traits for a husband. Number one? "Number one for me was ambition," she told me, adding that her husband, who is now putting in long hours at a start-up company, definitely fits the bill. She also admires that he is "masculine, in that he is confident in what he does" and "strong—it's nice that he can pick up the heavy box that I can't pick up."

She described a similar admiration for some of her previous male coworkers in Brooklyn, New York. Although these New Yorkers dressed more "metrosexual," these men also manifested "confidence" and physical strength in ways she appreciated: "I think there is something to be said about someone who is bigger and stronger [that makes men] appeal more."

When asked if David's appeal was also tied to his ability to provide, Kaitlyn laughed and said, "I would like to say 'no,' but I know deep down [the answer is] 'yes.' And it's not just the current company [he's working at], it's the idea of if he lost his [current] job, he would be able to get another one." She likes knowing that the burden of providing would not "all be on me."

Grace could not be more different than Kaitlyn. She's a newly married evangelical conservative working in marketing and living in the Nashville suburbs. Yet the way she talks about her husband reminded me immediately of Kaitlyn. She likes that her husband, John, told her that "my goal is to provide for you and for our family, so that you can work if you'd like to, but you don't have to." Grace, who is twenty-six, also appreciates the way he is "very confident," with an "air of masculinity [that] really appealed to me." But John's appeal to her is related to his ability not just to provide for but also to protect her.

One Friday night in Washington, DC, Grace and John were heading to Metro Center to switch lines to catch a subway home after dinner and drinks. It was late, and there was only one other couple and what appeared to be a homeless man in their subway car. Grace and John were enjoying the ride, snuggling, and "jamming to music together" on their phones. But when they came into the Gallery Place station, the couple in their subway car left in a hurry. And as the car left the station, the single man got up and moved in their direction in a menacing way. As he got closer, they took out their earbuds to hear him say, "Hey, I need you to give me your wallets, give me your bags."

At this point, John put one arm around Grace and, standing up, raised his other arm in the direction of the man. John started yelling at their assailant, putting his body between the man and Grace.

"Luckily, at this point we had arrived at the [Metro Center station], and the doors opened," Grace explained. "John was trying to raise a ruckus now . . . to get people aware of the situation, yelling 'Why are you trying to rob us?!'" Keeping himself between Grace and their assailant, John led her to safety on the subway platform, which held a number of other late-night riders.

"That was definitely a bookmark moment in moving forward in our relationship," Grace said. She remembers thinking, "'Gosh, this guy, he cares for me so much he would put himself in such danger when we didn't know where this situation could escalate to.' I was so grateful." The fact that John wanted to "protect me was huge" in solidifying her interest and attraction to him. Like many of the happily married women I spoke with, Grace stressed how much her husband made her feel "safe." This, then, is another key ingredient for her and many other women when it comes to forging a successful marriage.

Ambitious. Good provider. Strong. Protective. Safe. These are the kinds of words that came up when I asked not just Kaitlyn and Grace but other contemporary wives to explain what they admired about their husbands and what attracted them to the men in their lives in the first place.

Even though Kelly, the accountant from Richmond, leans left on social issues, she also underlined the importance of her husband Patrick's masculinity—which she described in terms of his "strength, protective-ness, confidence"—in describing her attraction to him: "One of the things that immediately attracted [me to him was] I felt so safe when he would put his arms around me," she said, also noting, "you know, the world's a dangerous place. It's nice to have strength added to the equation." In other words, when it comes to finding a mate and sticking with him, many women appreciate qualities that have been classically understood as masculine.

Acknowledging the enduring appeal of a masculine spirit—not to mention men's traditional roles as providers and protectors—for modern women runs against the grain of much of our culture today. TikTok stars inveigh against "toxic masculinity" in relationships, garnering more than two billion views.[11] Academics tell us that "conformity to traditional masculine norms is negatively associated with intimate relationship sat-isfaction, especially the satisfaction of women."[12] The women on *The View* tell us they would be "thrilled to make more than" their husbands.[13]

The takeaway in much of our discourse on gender and relationships is that traditional expressions of masculinity, at best, have nothing to do with forging strong marriages and are, at worst, an obstacle to good relationships. Masculinity is unimportant, unnecessary, or even toxic for today's wife.

Cultural critic Aaron Renn has a different view. He thinks what anthropologists refer to as "hypergamy" (marrying up in status) is still a factor when it comes to female attraction, marital quality, and marital stability. This is the idea that women prefer to marry up—to be with men who have more money, status, or strength than they do. So Renn thinks women are typically happiest with men who embody masculine traits like protectiveness and strength and/or bring substantial economic or social resources (money, status) to the table. For women married to men who lack these traits and/or resources, "unhappiness and marital dysfunction often result."[14]

The enduring appeal of hypergamy, by Renn's account, is both biological and social, rooted in nature and nurture. Evolutionary psychologists like David Buss think the hypergamy dynamic emerged out of millennia of human evolution. "Women worldwide prefer to marry up," Buss observes, adding that this orientation emerged over time because women solved "the adaptive problem of acquiring resources in part by preferring men who are high in status." By contrast, those "women in our evolutionary past who failed to marry up tended to be less able to provide for themselves and their children."[15]

On the other hand, sociologists like Yue Qian think women's preoccupation with men's financial prospects is a consequence of the fact that men continue to make more money than women in the marketplace, rather than an evolved psychological sex difference. Hence, today's women continue to "maximize their gains from marriage" by gravitating toward men who make more money than they do.[16] Renn and Qian are undoubtedly both right: the roots of women's interest in men who are more masculine or can marshal resources—which continues today—are both biological and social, a combination of nature and nurture.

Male breadwinning, for instance, remains a powerful draw for women when it comes to choosing a life partner. In a recent study of marriage trends in the United States, Qian found "the tendency for women

to marry men with higher incomes than themselves [has] persisted."
What's more, this tendency was true even for the growing number of
women who are marrying men with less education than themselves.[17]
Male strength is also enticing, with one study reporting that estimates
of "physical strength determined over 70 percent of men's bodily attractiveness" and another finding that "strength/muscularity" is a "consistent
predictor of both mating and reproduction."[18] Other research confirms
that industriousness, ambition, and good financial prospects increase
men's appeal as a mate.[19] In other words, even in the twenty-first century,
men's ability to provide and protect predicts women's interest in making
it permanent.

A masculine spirit is also linked to marital quality. Today, wives
who rate their husbands 9 or 10 on a 0-to-10 scale regarding how
"masculine" they consider them are slightly more likely to say that they
are happily married, compared to wives who give their husbands lower
ratings on this trait, according to the 2022 State of Our Unions survey
of more than a thousand wives. They are also, as figure 9.1 indicates,
markedly more likely to report that divorce is "not at all likely" for them.
Wives are also happier when, like Grace and Kelly, they describe their

FIGURE 9.1: WIVES MARRIED TO MEN RATED HIGH IN MASCULINITY ARE HAPPIER AND LESS DIVORCE PRONE

Percentage of wives "very happy" in marriage and "not at
all likely" to divorce, by whether they give a top rating for
masculinity to their husband (9 or 10 out of 10)

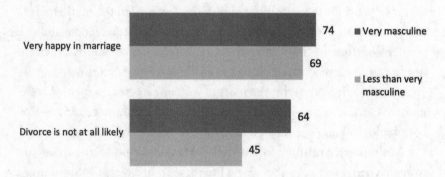

Based on wives aged 18 to 55. Source: State of Our Unions Survey (2022).

husbands as "physically strong" and "protective." (Reports of husbands' strength and protectiveness are higher among more conservative and religious wives.[20]) These findings suggest that virtues that have been classically understood as masculine, like strength and protectiveness, are still linked to happier and more stable marriages in the twenty-first century.

But what about role performance, given that so much has changed in recent decades when it comes to gender roles? Wives are happier when they give their husbands top ratings for being "good breadwinners," but the precise division of who earns what is not a significant predictor of marital quality, which suggests that the division of earnings may be less important now than it used to be.[21]

But we see a different story when it comes to men's work status if we look at marital quality for married mothers with children at home. Married mothers are significantly happier when their husband is employed full-time, compared to working less than full-time or not at all outside the home, as figure 9.2 makes clear. This suggests that a husband's job status is more important than his relative income for today's married mothers. And here, religious and college-educated wives are especially likely to have a husband employed full-time.[22] The bottom line is there is a link, even in today's marriages, between a woman's perception of her mate as classically masculine, both in style and some substance, and her happiness.

But in other respects, the predictors of her happiness are more contemporary. Married women want their man to be not just classically masculine but a "mate who is willing to invest" in them practically and emotionally, as psychologists Pelin Gul and Tom Kupfer have noted.[23] Kaitlyn, the liberal lawyer, doesn't just appreciate the "financial security" that David brings to their marriage but also his willingness to have "good days of phones down, [focusing] on us having real conversations that aren't focused on work." Days where she has his full attention, days where they are connecting emotionally.

Likewise, evangelical conservative Grace appreciates the ways in which John leaves her feeling "truly cherished." He makes sure that her car always has gas in it, devoted hours online to helping her find the right job when they moved to Nashville, and plans a new date night for

FIGURE 9.2: MARRIED MOTHERS HAPPIER WHEN HUSBANDS EMPLOYED FULL-TIME

Percentage of mothers "very happy" in marriage, by husband's employment status

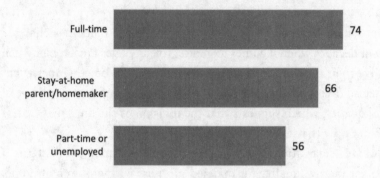

Based on married women aged 18 to 55 with children under age 18 at home. Source: State of Our Unions Survey (2022).

her every week. It could be a visit to the Nashville Farmers' Market, or line dancing at the Wildhorse Saloon, or trying out a new restaurant with glowing reviews online. She also likes the way he listens in a proactive way: "I feel so grateful that he asks [about] my needs and really listens and then [acts on] them." All of these moves signal John's willingness to invest in her.

His attentiveness translates into greater marital *and* sexual satisfaction for her. "For me and—for what I can assume—most women, it's the whole experience of what led up to [sex]. Like, did we have a nice romantic dinner? Were we chatting and sharing what's going on in our hearts?" observed Grace. "I think it involves being vulnerable and open with one another emotionally beforehand. Then after, it's important to remain physically close—snuggling and feeling that physical proximity of intimacy."

Grace is not alone in her preferences. My own research indicates that one of the strongest predictors of a wife's overall happiness is her husband's affection and understanding.[24] Likewise, according to the State of Our Unions Survey, her reports of his love and respect are very

FIGURE 9.3: WOMEN'S MARITAL HAPPINESS, BY MEN'S PROVIDERSHIP AND EMOTIONAL ENGAGEMENT

Percentage of wives very happy in marriage and sexual relationship by reports of their husband's providership and attentiveness

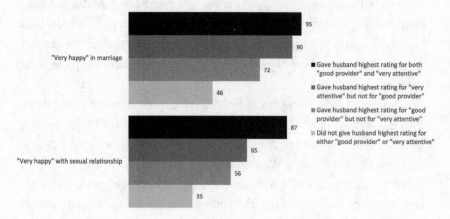

Based on heterosexual wives aged 18 to 55. Source: State of Our Unions Survey (2022).

predictive of her happiness in marriage, as well as her sexual satisfaction. This is not particularly surprising. But what is surprising is the way in which his provision and his attentiveness interact here. Wives are happiest when they report that their husbands are both good providers *and* emotionally engaged.

Specifically, the happiest wives are the ones who "strongly agree" that their husbands are good providers and very attentive.[25] As figure 9.3 indicates, wives are happiest in marriages where they give their husband high marks for both these traits, but those who give their husbands high ratings for attentiveness but less than the top rating for breadwinning are also quite happy.[26] Women are less likely to be happy in marriage to a man they do not rate as "very attentive"—especially if he is also not seen as a good provider. This tells us that the kind of hypermasculinity but low emotional investment trumpeted by some on the far right, like Andrew Tate, does not foster happy marriages among American wives.

Similar patterns apply to sexual satisfaction, as figure 9.3 also shows. Wives are most sexually satisfied in marriages like Grace's, where the husband is viewed as a good breadwinner *and* emotionally engaged.[27] John's attentiveness to designing diverting date nights, for instance, sets the stage for her sexual satisfaction. Such efforts matter, as one study found, because "sexual satisfaction is more likely to emerge" in marriages "marked by high levels of generosity, commitment [and] couple-centered quality time."[28] Indeed, wives who say it is "definitely true" that their husband is "generally romantic before initiating sex" in the State of Our Unions Survey are 31 percent more likely to be very happy in their marriages.[29]

Note also that even among women with more feminist sensibilities like Kaitlyn, sexual satisfaction and marital quality are all higher when they are married to men they rate as good providers, as long as those men are also attentive.[30] Women are drawn to men who are "willing to invest"—both financially and emotionally.[31] Today, religious and conservative wives are especially likely to give their husbands top marks for providing *and* attentiveness.

MEN (NOT) AT WORK

His breadwinning does not just loom large in her marital quality; it also plays a signal role in their marital stability. Because of my work, I know plenty of men who have seen their marriages end in divorce. Lots of factors figure into the breakdown of these marriages, but one that I have observed over and over is a problem with his financial support of the family. This includes entrepreneurs who land in divorce court soon after their companies go belly-up, husbands with their head in the clouds and their feet not firmly planted in full-time work, and men who get off to a slow start professionally and never really hit that strong and steady stream of money.

A large body of research indicates that men's work matters a great deal for their marital prospects and stability (as well as their sense of self-worth). Men who are employed full-time and well paid are more likely to be viewed as attractive prospects for marriage, to get married, and to stay married. The opposite is true for men who are not gainfully employed. A Pew study found that "finding someone who has a steady job" is important for 78 percent of single women, compared to just 46 percent of single men.[32] A Harvard study by sociologist Alexandra Killewald found that when a wife loses her job, there is no consequence for the marriage. But when the husband is not employed, his risk of divorce shoots up 33 percent. Killewald noted that her findings are consistent with the idea that "breadwinning remains a central component of the marital contract for husbands."[33]

Men's earnings also seem to matter for marital stability, and in ways that, again, seem to differ from the earnings of women. Take the work of University of North Carolina sociologist Rosemary Hopcroft. She discovered that higher-earning men were more likely to get and stay married. Hopcroft found, for example, that "for men the probability of divorce declines as income rises, such that men in the highest income category are about 37 percentage points less likely to divorce than men in the lowest income category [but for] women the probability of divorce increases as income rises."[34] To be sure, the different story for money and women's divorce pattern is related, in part, to the fact that women who are looking to leave a marriage tend to increase their work effort. But if her research is any indication, it looks as if for husbands, but not necessarily wives, excelling at breadwinning reduces your odds of divorce.

All this is consistent with Hopcroft's observation regarding the etymology of the word *husband*: "It derives from two words, 'hús' (from the Old Norse for house) and 'bóndi' (from the Old Norse for occupier and tiller of the soil), and its original meaning was a man who had a home and therefore could marry and support a family. The word thus embodies a principle common in preindustrial England and Europe 'that a man might not marry until his living was assured.'"[35]

It's also consistent with findings that owning your own home reduces your risk of divorce by more than 30 percent.[36] Clearly, having a husband who is a good breadwinner and owning a shared home are stabilizing forces not just in preindustrial England but also in today's marriages.

SEX APPEAL

So, on average, women enjoy happier (and more stable) unions when married to men who are good providers *and* emotionally engaged. What about men? What makes them happy?

Our thinking on these questions is often derailed by culturally fashionable ideas with considerable currency in the academy and media but little basis in the real world. Plenty of academics, professionals, and journalists discount the idea that husbands have, at least in some respects, somewhat different needs in marriage compared to their wives. The most obvious example here involves sex.

Economist Marina Adshade, who writes regularly for academic and popular audiences on relationships, did a popular TED Talk on men, women, and sexual desire. She noted that many people think women are less interested, biologically, in sex than men are. "But that's not right, and it's time we evolved in our thinking," she said. To Adshade, it is an "entirely false societal belief" that "women are biologically less sexual than men."[37]

Like many feminists, Adshade is keen here to minimize the biological differences between the sexes—in this case, regarding sexual desire. Her view seems to be that once you dispense with all the antiquated cultural baggage in our society regarding gender, men and women are about equally interested in sex.

This idea would come as news to my fiftysomething friend, who came to me with a confession one afternoon as we met for coffee. My friend, whom I will call Ben, told me he was struggling with something in his marriage. He explained with a rueful look that the gap between his and his wife's libido was large. Ben seemed both frustrated and sheepish. "I am trying to find outlets, give her the space she needs," Ben told me. "But I don't know what to do." This gap in sexual desire was clearly affecting the character and quality of his married life.

In fact, many of the men and women I spoke to for this book touched on a gender gap in sexual interest. When asked what makes men (and her husband, in particular) happy in marriage, the first thing Kaitlyn said was this: "I mean, obviously, men and sex, I think [it] is important." "Physical intimacy is big," said Grace, striking a similar note, adding, "I've only been with one man, but I'm assuming it's probably [the case for men] across the board. I also notice a difference when we haven't been intimate for a few days versus when it's more regular. He's a lot more responsive to me."

Kelly, the accountant from Richmond who leans left politically, had a similar view. She pointed out a humorous meme that Patrick had sent to her: "One side of the page is filled with all the things you have to do to satisfy a woman—you know, candy, flowers, flattery, spending time, holding hands, listening, trying to share your feelings, taking her out to eat, you know, blah, blah, blah, blah, blah—on the other side, it just says, you know, 'How to Please a Man: show up naked.'"

Note, however, that Kelly does not think that men's interest in sex is simply physical. It's mental and emotional, too: "That sharing of yourself at an intimate level, physically, does so many things. For the man, it's an acceptance and, you know, it's a reinforcement of his masculinity and prowess. . . . And it also is a form of trust. . . . So I think it does many things beyond the chemistry of, you know, reinforcing the bond."

For a range of reasons, then, sex plays a core role in the quality of a man's marriage. A good sexual relationship is not just physically pleasurable, it also makes a man feel connected, respected, worthy, even . . . manly.

This is not to say that sexual satisfaction is not important for women; in the State of Our Unions Survey, her sexual satisfaction is also highly predictive of her marital happiness. But husbands and wives, on average, approach sex differently. A meta-analysis of more than two hundred studies found, for instance, "a stronger sex drive in men compared to women," with men being more likely to "think and fantasize about sex" and "experience sexual affect."[38] Likewise, Harvard evolutionary biologist Carole Hooven notes that, because men average about ten to twenty times the amount of testosterone, which fuels libido, as women, their interest in sex is typically markedly higher than a woman's.[39] Studies across dozens of countries indicate that "men everywhere reported a higher sex drive," even if the size of this "sex gap" varies from one country to the next, as Hooven pointed out in her book, *T: The Story of Testosterone, the Hormone that Dominates and Divides Us*.[40]

Husbands are much more likely to report initiating sex in marriage today, compared to wives, according to the State of Our Unions Survey. More than 50 percent of husbands said it is "mostly" or "definitely true" that "I usually initiate sex first in our relationship"; only 15 percent of wives said the same. This is a clear and dramatic difference between husbands and wives.

Conversely, the survey also indicates that the marital happiness of wives is more closely tied to reports that a spouse is "considerate when I am not in the mood for sex" than is the case for husbands.[41] All this suggests some important gender differences in spousal orientations to sex. It also indicates that an ethic of sexual generosity—where both husbands and wives recognize they approach sex somewhat differently and aim to be sensitive to the different needs and expectations of their spouse—is likely to foster higher-quality marriages.

Husbands and wives who navigate all this reasonably well and manage to cultivate a sexually satisfying marriage enjoy markedly higher levels of marital satisfaction. Specifically, husbands who are very happy with their marital sexual relationship are 92 percent more likely to be very happy with their marriages in general, whereas wives who are very happy in their sexual relationship with their husband are 90 percent more likely to be very happy in their marriages. This indicates that even though the desired frequency varies between husbands and wives, success at building a satisfying sexual life is about equally important for them both.

Sex is by no means everything, of course, for today's husbands. Other factors play a crucial role in his marital quality. Although Martin Jones, a forty-one-year-old African American husband and father of three, mentioned his wife Kimberly's beauty as his first point of attraction to her, he then went on to mention two other factors that keep him happy in his marriage today: "To feel respected. To feel a sense of closeness. So, to use the word intimacy, which is not just physical or sexual, but just closeness. When I feel like we're distant, when we both acknowledge, you know, we've been like two ships passing in the night, neither of us tends to feel particularly happy about that."

Kelly's husband, Patrick, has a similar view to Martin's, even though they have dramatically different family-work arrangements and worldviews (Patrick leans left politically, Martin right). Patrick gives his marriage a 10 for its quality, attributing it in part to Kelly's "caring" and "positive" spirit. "She always finds the silver lining," he said, also noting that "she's more of the sweet, loving person [whereas] I'm the tough-love person."

Although men like Martin and Patrick occupy opposite ends of the ideological spectrum, when it comes to describing what they appreciate about their wives, they (and other happy husbands) used words like *beautiful*, *pretty*, *sweet*, *kind*, *caring*, and *respectful*. In general, husbands who describe their wives as more "feminine" in the 2022 State of Our Unions Survey are happier in their marriages. Beyond that, describing their wife as "respectful," "sexually responsive," and "loving" are, respectively, the top three predictors of men's marital happiness in a series of questions where we asked both husbands and wives to assess how much their spouse embodied a series of gendered traits.

For men and women alike, reports of love and respect are among the top three predictors in this list of nine traits—which indicates how much emotional engagement matters for both husbands and wives in today's marriages. But for men, sexual responsiveness makes it into the top three (for women the third trait is rating their husband a "good breadwinner").[42] In other words, while the character and quality of a couple's sexual relationship matter today for both husbands and wives, we have evidence that sex is more salient for men in marriages than for their wives.

CHOREPLAY ANYONE?

Speaking of sex, there are plenty of voices in the culture telling us that the division of housework and childcare is highly predictive of a good sex life (and a happy marriage) for today's married Americans.

"Couples Who Share Housework Have the Most Sex and Best Sex Lives," read a recent *Washington Post* headline.[43] Studies find, the *New York Times* assured us, "that the happiest and most sexually satisfied couples are now those who divide housework and childcare the most equally." And *Quartz* reported that "couples who strike a division of household labor that feels fair to both parties report happier relationships and better sex."[44]

Does a fifty-fifty approach to housework and childcare translate into happier marriages and better sex? Is "choreplay" a thing? Kelly does not think so. "It is not, you know, do 'x' during the day, and therefore 'y' will happen at night in the bed." From her perspective, a good sexual relationship flows more from a sense of "emotional safety," his "affection," and being "comfortable and confident in the person you're with."

Martin smiled at the notion that "choreplay" would lead to sex in his marriage. Not so for him. By his account, taking initiative—like planning a fun date night—and being extra emotionally attentive were much more important in setting the stage for sexual intimacy than who did what in the home. In the State of Our Unions Survey, we found no relationship between the division of housework and the frequency of sex, sexual satisfaction, or marital quality.

But caring for the kids is a different story for the married parents in our survey. In general, married fathers and mothers who share between 40 percent and 60 percent of the care of their children are better off. For couples like Kelly and Patrick, where both spouses work full-time or embrace an egalitarian division of labor, wives told me they are especially happy when their husbands take an active role across the family front. "You know, I've heard of people that have husbands who, you know, the wife's working her ass off and the husband just sort of sits by—that's just not the kind of relationship we have." Patrick is "all-in," according to Kelly, when it comes to sharing the work of the home *and* caring for their two sons.

But for couples where the wife stays at home or works part-time, or who lean right culturally, like Martin and Kimberly, things look a little different. What is important is not that they share household chores on a roughly fifty-fifty basis but rather the sense that he is "on duty" when he's home: especially that he is practically and emotionally engaged with the kids on weeknights and weekends.

When I spoke to Kimberly one Tuesday night, Martin was bathing the kids and putting them to bed, which he does most nights so she can relax and recharge. She describes Martin as "so hands-on," mentioning his commitment to caring for the kids, along with his willingness to clean up after the kids and kitchen when needed, handle the garbage, and make sure their cars are filled up. Moreover, the last time she was pregnant, he did all the cooking and cleaning. Kimberly is grateful her husband is "super hands-on" when he is at home.

But theirs is not a fifty-fifty relationship. Since she started staying home, she does most of the housework, and he catches up on office paperwork in the evenings. Kimberly's fine with this, given that he is now the sole breadwinner. She also appreciates that he encourages her to see friends and attend local lectures: "Martin's very much like 'Okay, alright, you want to go out, go do something, hang out with your friends.'" In her book, their relationship is fair, in large part because her husband is a good provider, concerned about her well-being, and emotionally and practically engaged with her and the kids when he is home.

More generally, the research indicates that across ideological lines, what matters for husbands and wives is a subjective sense of "fairness" and "sharing" responsibilities as a couple or family. How couples define fairness depends on their paid work arrangements and ideology. Splitting housework fifty-fifty is not important per se for marital or sexual satisfaction; it really depends on a couple's expectations going in. But in our survey, sharing the care of the kids is predictive of greater marital happiness and sexual satisfaction *across* the ideological spectrum. And married moms report more frequent sex when the care of the kids is roughly shared.[45] Here, we have more evidence that wives of all ideological stripes are more likely to thrive in their marriages, sexually and otherwise, with a man who is present, emotionally and practically, to them and their kids.

BREADWINNER MOMS

Over the course of her two marriages, Brittany has been the primary breadwinner most of the time. Sometimes this has worked out fine, but other times, it has been a source of struggle for this White, thirty-eight-year-old married mother. Her first husband, Chuck, was a stay-at-home dad for most of their marriage. He was often jealous of all the opportunities she had to socialize at work, even as she was "jealous of the time he got to spend with our son."

Her second husband, Dan, has only worked intermittently, while she has worked as a manager at Panera Bread for most of their time together. This has been a source of friction for them, because when he is not working, Dan struggles personally—to meet other people, live a regular schedule, and not feel "guilty about spending money" that Brittany has earned. By contrast, when Dan is working, he's happy to socialize with coworkers, and there are no fights about money. In fact, for the brief period when Dan worked and Brittany did not, she did not witness "the resentment in our relationship," adding, "He was very proud to be bringing home the paycheck, and I didn't feel that same fear of asking for help with paying the bills."

Brittany's experience with men and work is all too typical of the relationship realities, both within and outside of marriage, in many poor and working-class communities. In today's postindustrial economy, men without college degrees are more likely to struggle to find a job, keep a job, and even simply show up on time for a job. This is partly the fault of our economy and educational system. Today's schools and marketplace are often unfriendly toward the kinds of skills and interests that young men who are not on the college track bring to the table. For instance, men who wish to work with their hands or rely on their physical strength make a lot less money now than men who sit in front of a screen all day.[46] What's more, the women in their lives are often doing better in today's service economy than they are.[47] It's no accident that marriage is in much worse shape in working-class and poor communities, ravaged in recent decades by globalization, automation, and schools that neglect boys not on the Striver track.[48]

But the problems that women like Brittany have with the men in their lives also have roots in the culture—and bad public policies. Parents and teachers, not to mention pop culture and government, do not demand much of our young men, nor do they give them a clear roadmap for how and what it means to be a man. We are in the midst of a masculinity crisis, where too few teenage boys and young men have any clear sense of identity that would orient them toward productive adulthood and equip them with the skills they need to reach that destination. Too many of our young men end up coddled by parents or mates and/or addicted to what the historian David Courtwright calls "limbic capitalism" in the form of gaming, porn, vaping, or weed, all of which sap their drive to get a job, keep a job, and succeed at work.[49] Courtwright describes "limbic capitalism" this way in his book, *The Age of Addiction: How Bad Habits Became Big Business*: "a technologically advanced but socially regressive business system in which global industries, often with the help of complicit governments . . . encourage excessive consumption and addiction. . . . They do so by targeting the limbic system, the part of the brain responsible for feeling and for quick reaction, as distinct from dispassionate thinking."

Moreover, family instability and absent fathers have left too many men bereft of a role model and life coach, floundering in both their work and their love lives as they move into adulthood.[50] Brittany, for instance, has witnessed a "gap in a desire or motivation to work" between young men and women in her workplace and extended family; she attributes it in part to the many homes without fathers where boys did "not necessarily [see] a role model working all the time."

This dynamic puts the women in these men's lives in a real bind. Because while they are getting established at work and thinking about love, marriage, and forming a family—that is, "busy becoming women"— too many of the men in their lives "seem content to idle in Guyland indefinitely," as sociologist Michael Kimmel observed.[51]

Concretely, this means too many situations like Brittany's—where *she* works and *he* free-rides or just works intermittently. In many such homes, moms not only bring home most of the bacon but also do most of the housework and childcare, *even* as the men have the lion's share of screentime.[52] Needless to say, this unfair pattern fuels resentment and acrimony. And because men without college degrees are less likely to

FIGURE 9.4: BREADWINNER MOMS MORE COMMON AMONG LOW-INCOME FAMILIES

Percentage of mothers who are breadwinners or co-breadwinners, by income quintile, 2022

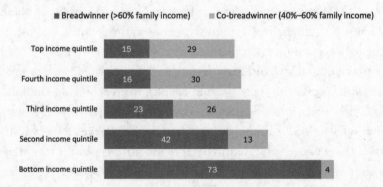

Based on women with children under age 18 at home, including single, cohabitating, and married women, among families with positive income in the past twelve months. Source: Current Population Survey, 2022 (ASEC, IPUMS).

be working full-time, families headed by such "female breadwinners," where she works and earns more than he does, are concentrated among the poor and working class.

Take a look—in figure 9.4—at the link between class and all bread-winner moms—married, cohabitating, or single (who make 60 percent or more of their family's income). Female breadwinners are much more common among the poor and working class, with 42 percent of working-class and 73 percent of poor families led by female breadwinners.

These breadwinner moms have been heralded by media outlets like the *Washington Post* and liberal think tanks like the Center for American Progress as a mark of our gender progress.[53] But in the real world, many female breadwinners are more often to be pitied than praised, especially when they head up a household marked by the absence of a second parent, or by a man who is more devoted to his Xbox than the needs of his family. There are exceptions, of course—I know men in good marriages who have taken turns in their marriages as stay-at-home dads. But the large rise in female breadwinners should give us pause. More than 70 percent of breadwinner moms are unmarried moms.[54] In all too many cases, these families are a sign not of female triumph but of male disengagement from American family life today.

VIVE LA DIFFÉRENCE

What's striking about these findings is how often they contradict so many of the dominant narratives, influenced by some variant of blank-slate feminism, emanating from the ivory tower, think tanks, and media. We hear from prominent academics, like Stephanie Coontz, the feminist historian, that a traditional division of domestic labor fosters "marital discord, preventing heterosexual couples from achieving the kinds of egalitarian relationships that are now associated [with] the greatest marital satisfaction."[55] Brookings scholar Richard Reeves tells us in the *Atlantic* that college-educated marriages are stronger and more stable today in part because they are "the most egalitarian about gender roles." He writes elsewhere that the idea that contemporary marriages still rely upon a "breadwinner-or-bust model" is "bordering on nostalgia."[56] And from Kate Mangino in the *Atlantic*, we learn that men *like* rejecting traditional scripts, because it allows them to be "their own authentic self—they don't have to perform masculinity and feel like a failure if they don't make a certain amount of money; they have a fantastic relationship with their partner."[57]

Despite being the group most likely to profess progressive gender ideas like these *and* to be publicly dismissive of the idea that men should be breadwinners, guess which group is the least likely to dispense with a male breadwinner in the privacy of their own homes? Yes, the upper-middle class—those in the top 20 percent of families for income. What's ironic, then, about claims like the ones made above is that no class is more *reliant* on male breadwinners in their own families than the very class most likely to publicly dismiss their importance.

All this was unintentionally telegraphed in a recent study from the left-leaning Center for American Progress, which reported that as "family income increases, the rate of breadwinning mothers steadily declines."[58] What we have here is another example of elite hypocrisy around marriage. Our ruling class talks left about gender roles in the public square even while they are more likely to walk right inside their own McLean McMansions, Central Park penthouses, or Silicon Valley manses—not to mention the comfortable cul-de-sacs of Loudoun County, Virginia, Montgomery County, Maryland, or Morris County, New Jersey. This is partly because women in these communities have access to the kind of men—ambitious, hardworking, successful breadwinners—who remain privately appealing to them, even if they are not supposed to say so in public. These are men like Kaitlyn's husband, David, introduced at the beginning of this chapter. In fact, a big reason that Striver wives like Kaitlyn are happier and less prone to divorce than their working-class and poor peers is that they are more likely to have husbands who are gainfully employed.

More generally, what we see is that even in twenty-first-century America, elite and ordinary women typically prefer more masculine men to get and stay married to. These are men who are strong, ambitious, or high status, whom they view as "good providers" and "protective." Such men give their wives *choices*—especially about whether to work full-time or part-time, or to stay at home, especially when they become mothers—and make them feel physically and emotionally safe. They also make it easier for them and their kids to flourish. That's why today's wives are more satisfied in marriages where the men measure up. That's provided, of course, that such men also meet more contemporary standards when it comes to manifesting love and respect for them and their children. In other words, today's women are happiest with good family men, men who can be counted upon to excel as breadwinners *and* engaged husbands and fathers.

For their part, husbands also value the expressive dimensions of married life today—they are more likely to flourish when their wives are "respectful" and "loving." Being an engaged father is also associated with being a happier husband today. But the classic expectation that sex matters more for husbands than for wives also remains true today, even in the twenty-first century. Likewise, modern husbands who report their wives as more "feminine" are also happier.

This is not to say that many husbands and wives want to turn the clock back to 1955, or that more people would flourish if we did. The truth is that when it comes to men, women, and marriage, what has emerged in the twenty-first century as most conducive to strong and stable families, gender-wise, is a different model than prevailed in the 1950s—it is a "neotraditional" model. It is traditional in the sense that women prefer to marry and stay married to men who are reliable providers and strong protectors. Manly men, if you will. But it is "neo" in the sense that today's women have high expectations that their man will be emotionally and practically attentive to them and any children they have—and will partner *with* them at home if they work full- or part-time outside of the home. New men, if you will, in this sense.

This is partly why her report of his practical engagement in the care of the kids is now so important to the quality of contemporary marriages. Of course, another way to describe this neotraditional trend is a "family-first model of marriage," where not only women but also men are expected to attend to the home fires. The tragedy of our moment is that this model is most accessible to those who enjoy the luxury of talking left about gender roles in public even as they often walk right in the privacy of their high-end homes.

CHAPTER 10

IN GOD WE TRUST

How Religion Helps, Not Harms, Your Marriage

A Sociologist of Religion on Protestants, Porn, and the 'Purity Industrial Complex'"—so read the title of a recent interview by Isaac Chotiner with sociologist Samuel Perry in the *New Yorker*, in which the two discuss the nexus between religion, pornography, and marriage among evangelical Protestants. You can probably guess how the Christian faith—in terms of the role it plays in men's approach to pornography and married life—comes off in this mainstream media outlet. Not well.

"Pornography is leading to depression and unhappiness, and it's disrupting marriages and communities" in the evangelical Protestant subculture, Chotiner claims in his introduction. As Perry—the author of *Addicted to Lust: Pornography in the Lives of Conservative Protestants*,[1] published by Oxford University Press—puts it, Christian men using porn are afflicted by "guilt and shame that makes you feel crappy about yourself," and evangelical Protestant women "draw a hard line" against their husbands' porn use because they view it as "literally adultery, or a betrayal, or a perversion," all of which make Christian wives "twice as likely to divorce their husband because of his pornography use." And this benighted religious group has tried to establish a "purity industrial complex" made up of books, small groups, and software companies designed to help evangelical men avoid becoming addicted to porn. Of course such efforts are painted as, at best, quaintly quixotic and, at worst, corrosively counterproductive for evangelical men, women, and their marriages in this *New Yorker* interview.[2]

Perry's big insight here is that using pornography is especially problematic for Christian men because they suffer from "cognitive dissonance" between their belief that sex is sacred—and meant to be shared only with your wife—and any behavior that contradicts this belief, such as turning their attention to sexual images of women to whom they are not married. By his telling, Christian men bear a particularly heavy burden from this heightened sense of shame.[3] By contrast, secular men are much less likely to suffer any guilt from using porn, so they avoid the relationship problems founded on religiously motivated sexual hang-ups. The *New Yorker* interview leaves the reader with the distinct impression that Christian men and communities are rife with "depression," "unhappiness," and disrupted marriages, all attributable to an archaic and outmoded sexual ethic.

This is but one example of the ways in which today's media often paints a dark portrait of the role that religious faith plays in ordinary family life, much of the time working hand in hand with an academic with an axe to grind against some religious subculture or religion in general. There are plenty of other examples. Consider the way the media handled a study conducted not long ago by University of Chicago psychologist Jean Decety contending that religious children are less altruistic than children from more secular families. Decety and his colleagues claimed his research revealed that "religion negatively influences children's altruism" and challenged "the view that religiosity facilitates prosocial behavior, and [called] into question whether religion is vital for moral development—suggesting the secularization of moral discourse does not reduce human kindness. In fact, it does just the opposite" for kids.[4]

Decety offered a sweeping indictment of the role of religion in children's lives based on a study of sticker-sharing and cartoon-watching among children ages five to twelve around the globe. This academic reported, among other things, that children from religious homes were less likely to share stickers with an unseen child than children from secular homes and that religious children were more likely to take a harsher view of kids who were pushing other kids in a cartoon video. In response to Decety's study, a *Daily Beast* headline proclaimed, "Religious Kids Are Jerks," and the *Guardian* said, "Religious Children Are Meaner than Their Secular Counterparts." All because some religious kids were some- what less likely to share stickers with an imaginary playmate and because the Muslim students in the study (though the study said "religious," without clarifying) were more likely than the secular ones to advocate for firmer punishment of kids engaging in bullying behavior on-screen.

These are but two examples of increasingly common antireligious messages being broadcast by journalistic outlets and academic research. They are often motivated by concerns that religion is an obstacle to social progress on issues related to abortion, feminism, and trans rights, or that it operates as an adjunct to conservative politics in general.[5] Meanwhile, a growing number of young adults in America identify as religious "nones," often with little knowledge of religion and consider- able skepticism of the impact that religion has on relationships. So is it really the case that religion is as negative a force in American family life as its detractors and skeptics suggest?[6]

THE TRUTH ABOUT RELIGION AND FAMILY

No, the truth is that religion is generally a force for good when it comes to the quality and stability of married life, men's and women's satisfaction with their lives, and the welfare of children. The research tells us that American men and women who regularly attend a church, synagogue, temple, or mosque are significantly happier in their marriages, less likely to end up divorced, and more satisfied with their lives—and their chil- dren are more likely to be flourishing. Of course, there are exceptions to these trends, exceptions that often get prominent coverage in the media (see, e.g., the Duggars). But in general, here's what the research tells us:

GREATER MARITAL HAPPINESS. Social scientists consistently find that couples who attend church together are happier in their marriages.[7] In the State of Our Unions Survey (2022), we find a similar story. For wives, only 66 percent of those who never or infrequently attend/or do not attend as a couple are very happy in their marriages, as figure 10.1

indicates. (The middle category, occasionally attending together, refers to couples who attend services together as little as a few times a year or as much as once a month.) By contrast, 80 percent of wives who attend regularly—defined as several times a month or more—with their husbands are very happy. There's a similar story for husbands. Only 68 percent of those who never or infrequently attend, or do not attend as a couple, are very happy. By contrast, 84 percent of husbands who attend regularly with their wives are very happy. And, by the way, this happiness premium is also true for churchgoing evangelical Protestant men, who are, on average, markedly happier in their marriages than husbands who rarely or never attend.[8]

MORE MARITAL STABILITY. There is no question that faith is also a force for greater marital stability. One Harvard study found, for instance, that women who regularly attend church are about 50 percent less likely to divorce.[9] Data from the National Longitudinal Survey of Youth (NLSY97), which tracked young adults from their teens in the 1990s to their late thirties in 2019, indicate that regular religious attendance reduced divorce by about 30 percent among those men and women who had married.[10] And the State of Our Unions Survey shows us that evangelical Protestant husbands and wives who attend church together report greater marital stability than those Americans who rarely or never

FIGURE 10.1: SHARED FAITH, GREATER MARITAL HAPPINESS

Percentage reporting being "very happy" in their marriage

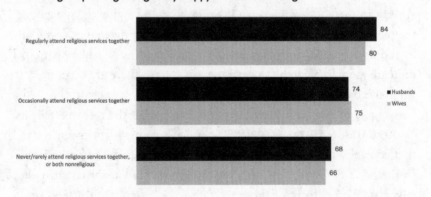

Based on married adults aged 18 to 55. Source: State of Our Unions Survey (2022).

attend.[11] So much, then, for the *New Yorker*'s insinuation that Christian marriages are rife with unhappiness and instability!

MORE HAPPINESS. The science could not be clearer. Religious Americans report more overall happiness, greater life satisfaction, more meaning, and less loneliness in their lives than their unchurched fellow citizens.[12] This pattern also is visible in the State of Our Unions Survey. Satisfaction with life is lowest among wives and husbands who rarely or never attend church or do not attend as a couple, and highest among those who regularly attend together. Figure 10.2 indicates, for instance, that less than one-third of wives and husbands who are not religious or do not attend together are very satisfied with their lives compared to 49 percent of wives and 55 percent of husbands who attend regularly as a couple.[13] We also witnessed this pattern during COVID time, when the only group that did not see a dip in its emotional well-being were those Americans who kept attending church, temple, synagogue, or mosque in person.[14]

THE CHILDREN. When it comes to kids, the research also paints a generally positive portrait. Religious parents are more likely to do chores together and attend outings with their children.[15] They are also more likely to report praising and hugging their school-age children.[16] Contra the claims made by the University of Chicago's Decety, sociologist James Davison Hunter, my colleague at UVA, finds that religious teens

FIGURE 10.2: SHARED FAITH, GREATER LIFE SATISFACTION

Percentage reported being "very satisfied" with life

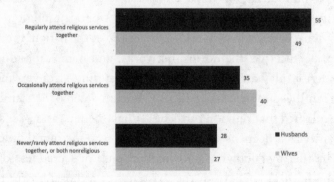

Based on married adults aged 18 to 55. Source: State of Our Unions Survey (2022).

are more likely than secular teens to eschew lying, cheating, and stealing and to identify with the Golden Rule. Children from religious families are "rated by both parents and teachers as having better self-control, social skills and approaches to learning than kids with non-religious parents," according to a nationally representative study of more than sixteen thousand children across the United States. Findings like these clearly contradict Decety's flawed study, which *was* finally retracted under pressure from other scholars.[17] But by then, the headlines had moved on; the damage was done. The bogus "findings" were now part of the social consciousness. In general, the reliable science tells us that faith is a force for *good* in children's lives.

NORMS, NETWORKS, AND NOMOS

There is no question that religious Americans generally enjoy stronger and more stable families and happier lives, provided that husbands and wives attend together. But why? Part of the story is about what we earlier called "selection effects." In this case, the kinds of men and women who select into attending religious services today tend to be more educated and affluent, for instance, than was the case in a bygone era, when the rich and poor, the working class and middle class, attended at roughly similar rates. Churchgoers also have the kinds of personality traits—such as conscientiousness—that lead to higher levels of engagement in faith *and* family.[18]

But selection is not the whole story. Embracing your faith also seems to boost your odds of forging a strong and stable family. There is no community that is more family-friendly than American religion—the churches, synagogues, temples, and mosques across the nation. From a sociological perspective, the norms, networks, and nomos found in American religion play an important role in fostering stronger and more stable families among the faithful.[19] French sociologist Emile Durkheim explained that religion furnishes rituals, beliefs, and a sense of group identity that deepens people's connections to the moral order and to one another by endowing both with a sense of sacredness. In his words, the faithful "believe in the existence of a moral power to which they are subject and from which they receive what is best in themselves."[20] This power, by his account, is realized in and through their participation in a "Church," which "must be an eminently collective thing."[21]

In most of the world's religions, the moral order of which Durkheim speaks is focused to a very great extent on how men and women, boys and girls, conduct themselves toward one another within the family. This is partly because the religious traditions that best succeed in forging strong families are precisely the ones that are much more likely to flourish across time and space.[22] Strong families make for strong faith communities, in other words, which is why the most dominant religious traditions around the world reinforce family life through norms, networks, and a nomos that sustains such families.

NORMS. It's no accident that the normative character of American religion has been deeply tied to values and virtues that prioritize family life. "The ideology of familism," observed sociologist Peter Berger, has been nurtured and sustained by America's religious traditions in ways that stress that the "family [is] the crucial social institution, both for the individual and the society as a whole."[23] Sunday after Sunday, familistic values and virtues related to marriage, fidelity, marital permanence, childrearing, and domestic life are reinforced in congregations across the United States.

As I noted in *First Things*, "Churches and synagogues give symbolic and practical support to family life. In such rites as a baptism and a bris, congregations erect a sacred canopy of meaning over the great chapters of family life: birth, childrearing, and marriage. Rabbis, pastors, and priests—particularly orthodox ones—offer concrete advice about marriage and parenthood. Congregations also have disproportionately high numbers of families who put family-centered living high on their list of priorities. These families offer moral and practical support to adults adjusting to the joys and challenges of married life and starting families."[24] In fact, religious institutions are one of the few places today where you regularly hear messages underlining the importance of marriage and parenthood, along with sermons and homilies on the virtues—from forgiveness to fidelity—that keep marriages and families strong. This is one reason why rates of marriage and fertility are markedly higher among those who regularly attend religious services today.[25] The nation's houses of worship supercharge the values required for strong and stable marriages and parent-child relationships.

NETWORKS. When Danielle and I left the hospital on a cold November day in 2009 with twin newborns, we were overwhelmed. We had a bunch of children waiting for us at home, but we were already exhausted, adjusting to the physical demands of caring for not one but two newborns. Sleep, energy, and good cheer were in short supply at that moment in our lives (especially for me, as I noted earlier).

But this season was made easier by the care and concern of our Catholic and evangelical Protestant friends. They organized a meal sign-up and delivered dinners, Monday through Friday, for a full month. And they crowded around the twins at church, saying, "What beautiful babies." Their meals, visits, and words of encouragement made this big transition less strenuous. Their presence in our lives further made it clear that we were not alone in facing this big new challenge. This gave us a measure of comfort as we transitioned from the massive demands of raising five children to the full-on seven-kid adventure we had in store.

Our experience is emblematic of the power of social networks for families in religious communities. The men and women who are regulars at churches and synagogues on any given weekend in America are more likely to be married, to have children, and to be living a family-centered way of life.[26] They are more likely to lend support and counsel to couples navigating the challenges of marriage and family life. And they are also more likely to exercise what social scientists call "social control," discouraging behavior that can derail a relationship—from infidelity to excessive drinking or drug use.[27] Having family and friends who are there for you and your marriage, especially ones who embrace a family-first mindset, can make a big difference in strengthening marriages. It certainly helped us navigate a tough transition.

NOMOS. The death of a loved one. The loss of a job. The trauma arising from caring for a daughter afflicted by bipolar disorder. What Hamlet called the "slings and arrows of outrageous fortune" come for almost all of us one day.

But men and women who identify with what Berger called a "nomos"—a meaningful sense of the cosmos, a belief that God or some supernatural force superintends the world—are better able to handle the arrows when they hit home. Those who can fall back upon a "fundamental order in terms of which the individual can 'make sense' of his life and recognize his own identity" are better able to handle stress and suffering.[28] That's in part because most faiths have prayers, rituals, and teachings that make sense of the difficult and dark moments of our lives. In Berger's formulation, they cast "sacred canopies" over our lives that make sense of death, of suffering, and of evil that we confront in our daily lives.

This is important for family men and women. That's because stress often acts like a cancer in our family relationships. The man who has lost his job and then loses his sense of dignity, self-worth, and hope tends to also disengage from family life in ways that make his wife doubly resentful. The woman who has lost her mother to a sudden and unexpected death is often in danger of withdrawing from her marriage and children's lives in ways that can lead to a vicious spiral of family dysfunction. The couple facing financial problems is more likely to succumb to a cycle of escalating marital conflict.[29]

The research tells us that faith often helps couples navigate tough times like these. Sociologist Christopher Ellison and his colleagues found, for instance, that faith "buffers the deleterious effects of overall perceived stress and role strain" in a study of more than one thousand married men and women in Texas, adding that "couples with high levels of sanctification may be more inclined to reframe economic [and other] challenges in less threatening terms (e.g., as opportunities for growth or part of a larger divine plan) and may also be better able to identify strategies for managing negative emotions or solving economic problems."[30] In fact, shared prayer is a big predictor of higher-quality marriages in the State of Our Unions Survey, especially for women.[31] In other words, more nomos means less stress, fewer marital problems, and better marriages.

A religious nomos also endows family roles with a sacred significance that fosters bigger investments in family life. Ergo, if you're a believer, you're not just parenting your child with an eye toward getting them into Harvard but also with an eye toward getting them into heaven. This helps explain why we see religious men and women typically investing more time, more affection, and more mental energy on their spouse and children than reported by their secular peers.[32]

Finally, the norms, networks, and nomos associated with faith also foster an orientation toward the future among religious adherents that encourages them to steer clear of short-term thinking and impulsive actions that harm relationships. As the psychologist Evan Carter and his colleagues observed, "Many religions teach concepts that direct people's attention to the distant future. Preoccupation with future-oriented concepts such as immortality, reincarnation, resurrection, the slow but inexorable creep of divine justice, karma, or places one might inhabit after death such as Elysium, Gehenna, Hades, Heaven, Hell, Purgatory, Valhalla, or Sheol might cause the intermediate future (e.g., 6 months from now) to feel closer . . . people who are intrinsically religious and who indicate an interest in the afterlife tend to report that the future feels as though it is approaching quickly, and that they spend a lot of time thinking about the future."[33]

This live-for-the-future mentality translates into a greater ability to resist short-term temptations—from cheating to smoking meth to sleeping in and missing work—that can bring lasting harm to your life and family. Insofar as religions enjoin vices like idleness, infidelity, and drug abuse,[34] stigmatize them socially, and attach those injunctions to ultimate consequences of the greatest significance, they boost the odds that their adherents avoid living for the moment in ways that deny them a good long-term family future.

Religious Americans, for example, are less likely to abuse alcohol and drugs.[35] This is important, because substance abuse often paves the way to marital conflict, marital dissatisfaction, and divorce.[36]

MORE FAITH, BETTER SEX?

So religion seems to help people navigate alcohol, drugs, illness, and death more successfully. But what about one of the most important *and* contested domains of our culture: Is greater faith linked to better sex?

Plenty of voices in our culture would suggest that answer is no. For instance, in his book *Addicted to Lust*, Samuel Perry—the academic featured in that *New Yorker* article on evangelicals and pornography—introduced us to two thirtysomething Georgia men, one of whom is a Christian and one of whom is not, who both turn to porn on a weekly basis.

David is depicted as tortured, deflated, and deeply unhappy because of his regular use. This White, married family man feels "like a failure" and a "horrible hypocrite." His inability to be honest with his wife about his viewing habit has "stolen intimacy" away from his marriage, and he "feels beaten down because of his inability to fully eradicate pornography from his life."[37]

By contrast, Nick doesn't "think there's anything wrong morally" with viewing pornography. He consumes material that he "considers pretty vanilla, standard fare" and comes across as comfortable with his regular use, as well as with his romantic relationship of six years. While he acknowledges that there can be "side effects" from consuming porn, including his propensity to fantasize "about other women besides my partner," he does not appear to be particularly affected by his use.[38] Even though he acknowledges some downsides, Nick by no means comes across as crippled by his porn use, unlike his fellow Peach Stater David.

In this ivory tower tale, you know which man is the "Christian" before you're even told: David.

Academic and media treatments of religion and relationships, like this one, often leave readers with the impression that conservative Christian norms about sex have a toxic effect on ordinary people's lives and relationships. Religious hang-ups about sex, we're led to believe, leave all too many men and their marriages crippled. Nick, we are informed, "feels that religion has a counteractive effect; it bottles up sexual desires and then causes frustrated people to act out sexually" by, among other things, viewing porn.[39] And, according to Perry, the "recurrent moral incongruence" of regular porn use, "along with the attendant cover-up and deceit," leads to negative "consequences for conservative Protestants' mental health and even their faith."[40] This line of analysis is in keeping with the way that our cultural gatekeepers think about faith as one of the biggest obstacles that keeps men and women from enjoying the fruits of a half century of sexual liberation.

But for all the Davids out there, there are many more men like Martin. Martin, the DC police lieutenant who is a Black conservative Christian husband and father, does not use pornography, in large part because his faith helps him steer clear of it. Even when he's on the internet, checking out his favorite news and music sites, he's careful. "I mean it's one of those things where, you know the Bible's very clear about fleeing temptation," he said, adding, "So, yeah . . . certain sites I won't go on." Moreover, Martin treads gingerly on his favored hip-hop sites and Instagram, being careful to "keep scrolling" past videos of "scantily clad women" that pop up on these sites on a regular basis.

The care with which Martin navigates the internet is emblematic of how religious husbands typically approach virtual temptations. Religious married men are markedly less likely to use pornography than their secular peers, according to the State of Our Unions Survey. Only 35 percent of religious husbands have viewed pornography in the last month, compared to 62 percent of married men who rarely or never attend religious services. Another analysis of the General Social Survey found that a clear majority of churchgoing Protestant men did not use pornography in the last year; by contrast, a majority of men who were not regular churchgoers did use porn.[41]

Religious men's comparative care regarding sex extends beyond the virtual world to the real world. Martin reports that his "faith walk" has led him to avoid situations that "could land me in a compromising situation." After he got married, for instance, Martin and Kimberly "talked about guardrails" in their relationship when it came to navigating relationships with members of the opposite sex. This included steering clear of maintaining relationships with old flames or going "out at night drinking with somebody" besides your spouse, noted Kimberly.

Their pastor has reinforced their commitment to fidelity as well, according to Martin: "He says, 'How are you doing with your marriage? How are you doing reading the Word? How are you doing with sexual purity?'" Here, then, we can see how the norms and networks associated with their Christian worldview and their church community reinforce Martin's commitment to honoring his vow of fidelity to Kimberly. This is especially noteworthy because husbands remain more likely to stray than wives,[42] and regular churchgoing is linked to lower reports of infidelity for both men and women.[43]

Beyond setting up guardrails against virtual and real alternatives to their relationship, Martin and Kimberly's faith has also been a positive force in guiding their sexual relationship. They have prayed together about their sexual relationship, and their faith fuels discussions about their mutual "needs, whether it comes to sex or emotions or whatever," according to her. When it comes to sex, she adds, "We have ongoing conversations about, 'Okay, so how often?' or 'How not often?' or . . . 'Are you fulfilled, like where [are you]?'" in terms of how the physical side of the relationship is going.

Sex is an especially sensitive issue for Kimberly, who was sexually abused earlier in her life. Her background initially made sexual intimacy with Martin difficult for her. "But that's how prayer entered, because I had some stuff happen prior to us that made [having sex] challenging for me," she noted. "I'm like 'Okay, God, you're only going to heal [me]' . . . [only] God can really, truly heal this." Prayer, then, served a nomic function for her when it came to navigating the challenge of enjoying physical intimacy with her husband. Her faith helped her work through the emotional wounds she bore from her abuse and gave her the strength to solve the sexual issue "we were having, especially in the very beginning of our marriage."

Tamara, an orthodox Jewish mother of six living in the Baltimore suburbs, was never sexually abused growing up. But like Kimberly, when I spoke with her, she conveyed the strong sense that sex plays an integral role in her marriage, and a sacred one. She was particularly eloquent in articulating how her tradition engenders a sense of sexual generosity between spouses. In Tamara's view, sex is "like the most Godly gift because it's creating—it has the potential to create another human" as well as to forge a uniquely "spiritual" connection between herself and her husband. She attaches particular significance to sex because it symbolizes the "connection between God and the world" and her relationship with her "husband in a way mirrors [my] relationship with God. And so, there's all these levels, you know, explored and discovered" in the sexual relationship that she has with her husband, Isaac.

Tamara also thinks her tradition's customs and rituals related to sex have distinctive value for women. In Orthodox Judaism, for two weeks after menstruation starts, husbands and wives do not have sex. After this period, Orthodox wives have "a mikvah, a ritual bath" that marks the transition where the couple is "allowed to be together again." From Tamara's perspective, both the time away from sex and the ritual bath, which have "been going on for thousands of years," "keep things exciting and fresh

[and] . . . sacred" in her sexual relationship with Isaac, and for many women in her tradition.

Of course, not every religious couple has a good experience with sex. Take Jason and Whitney Wilson, an evangelical Protestant couple in Florida. One morning, Whitney saw an Instagram post from a woman responding to a comment Jason had made on the platform, hinting that she had had an affair with Jason a few years before. When Whitney confronted Jason, he admitted that he had been unfaithful a while back, and later, he confessed that he was still regularly using pornography.

Whitney was shattered by Jason's admissions. "I didn't know how we were going to move forward. I didn't know if I wanted to move forward," she recalled, adding, "I was very clear at that time that he had an addiction. And he had not come to that conclusion yet, he was still very much minimizing what was going on." But as he realized the stakes might include the end of his marriage and the breakup of their family (the Wilsons have two children), Jason knew he had to make big changes.

The first major change he made was to stop keeping secrets from Whitney. "I needed to be honest and truthful and transparent with my life and what I had from my past," Jason said. "A lot of disclosure, versus discovery, versus her asking, 'Hey, tell me more, tell me this.' I was disclosing, versus [having her] discovering." Jason also purchased software to monitor his smartphone and computer, software that reported any problematic viewing habits back to Whitney. And he joined a men's accountability group that met once a week at his church to help its members be better Christians, husbands, and fathers. The men's group focused on pornography and a range of other personal and family challenges its members were facing.

Jason also sought counseling from a Christian therapist, read books recommended by his therapist, and prayed for deliverance. The counseling and prayer led him to the conclusion that his "full identity" is "in God." "Like I'm a whole and complete individual and not missing any part of me that I need to fill in some sort of way. Because I think pornography—I think drug addiction, alcohol addiction, gambling. . . . I think all of those things [are about] something missing in me that I need to be filled up in, or pain that I need to cover."

This nomic move on his part—seeing his life tied more closely to a supernatural identity—coupled with a new network, the accountability group, and new norms (including radical honesty with Whitney), enabled Jason to break his pornographic habit, save his marriage, and realize a new level of intimacy with his wife.

The Wilsons' story suggests that religion can help couples recover from "moral incongruence" between their sexual behavior and beliefs. Of course, as Perry's research tells us, this does not always happen. And religious couples struggling with a disconnect between their faith and sexual behavior are especially likely to suffer. But on average, the story about religion and sex is generally a positive one.

In fact, because sexual problems—from infidelity to pornography to misaligned sexual interest—are a major cause of divorce and marital strife, the ways in which faith directly reinforces fidelity, open communication, generosity, and above all, a high spiritual value regarding sex can be important in setting the emotional and social stage for a strong and secure physical relationship.[44] For instance, religious couples seem to recognize that he often wants sex more frequently than she does, and manifest a willingness on the part of both parties to compromise regarding this difference in desire. In fact, wives in religious marriages are more likely to report that it is "mostly" or "definitely" true that their husbands are considerate when they do not wish to have sex, compared to couples who do not share a common faith; likewise, husbands in religious marriages are more likely to report that their wives are responsive to them when they initiate sex, compared to men in marriages marked by no faith.[45]

The sacred canopy that faith casts over men's and women's lives— including their intimate life—undoubtedly helps explain why husbands and wives who share a common faith report more sex and greater sexual satisfaction than their peers, according to the State of Our Unions Survey.[46]

Figure 10.3 illustrates the relationship between religious attendance and the frequency of sex. About two-thirds of husbands and wives who attend together have sex at least once a week, compared to less than half who do not regularly attend together or at all. These differences in sexual frequency are significant.[47]

FIGURE 10.3: SHARED FAITH, MORE SEX

Percent reporting having sex with their spouse once a week or more often

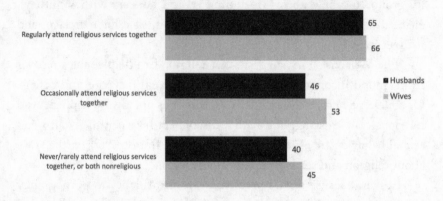

Based on married adults aged 18 to 55. Source: State of Our Unions Survey (2022).

FIGURE 10.4: SHARED FAITH, BETTER SEX

Percent reporting being "very happy" with their sexual relationship

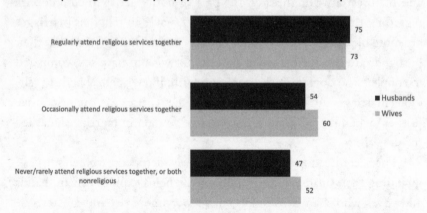

Based on married adults aged 18 to 55. Source: State of Our Unions Survey (2022).

Couples who attend together also report the greatest sexual satisfaction. About three-quarters of these husbands and wives are very happy with their sexual relationship; by contrast, those who do not regularly

IN GOD WE TRUST

attend together or at all are markedly less likely to be happy, as figure 10.4 indicates. This difference is statistically significant.[48] So, contrary to the *New Yorker*'s insinuation that faith functions as a stultifying and soul-destroying force, in the real world, couples like Martin and Kimberly are more likely to navigate the challenges associated with sexual intimacy in the twenty-first century—from avoiding infidelity to overcoming a history of sexual abuse—successfully.

To be sure, David's story shows us that not everyone's marriage benefits from faith. There is no religious magic pill that makes for good sex. But too many academic, media, and pop cultural depictions—think, for instance, of *Saturday Night Live*'s hilarious sendups of "The Church Lady" back in the 1980s and 1990s—of the relationship between religion and sex obscure this important sociological truth: for most husbands and wives, more faith equals better sex.

NO BACKUP PLAN

Critics of marriage from the manosphere—and they are legion, running from groups like MGTOW (Men Going Their Own Way) to Andrew Tate—caution or actively discourage men from marrying. Male critics of marriage note that women are significantly more likely than men to initiate a divorce, with about 66 percent of divorces being initiated by women today.[49] And they contend that many of these divorces are unnecessary and unfair.

In the words of one MGTOW adherent: "Talk to the men in MGTOW who have had their wallets ripped out their a** in family court. Go to the graves of men who killed themselves after they were unemployed and couldn't afford child support and faced jail. Talk to those men about how wonderful marriage was. . . . Ask them about the hundreds of hours they work extra each year to avoid going to prison because they owe so much child support or alimony that they gotta move in with their parents."[50]

Comments like this represent an obviously extreme perspective on the downsides of marriage. But they underline the ways in which divorce remains a risk today for women and especially for men willing to trust the marital vows. A large minority of wives and even more husbands will find themselves with an unwanted divorce, often losing their home, day-in, day-out access to their children, and a substantial share of their monthly income.

Martin is one man keenly aware of the ways in which easy divorce (so promoted in pop culture and media) poses a risk for men. "As the culture grows darker," he observed, there is a whole new genre of articles and stories in mainstream media outlets that run something like this: "I divorced my husband and left my kids to find myself." This ethos "will be as recognizable when our, you know, grandchildren look back on this period as *Mad Men* is to us when we look back on that period, right? So [then it was a] corporate executive, middle-manager [running] off with his secretary, unfaithful to his wife [whereas] our generation has, 'I blew up my marriage to drink chardonnay on Tuesday night.'"

Martin and Kimberly reject the often-trumpeted easy-divorce ethic, in part because they think "marriage is an institution created by God," as Martin noted. The door to their proverbial "house" only swings one way: "We walked through it ten years ago, and we sealed it shut." This means that when they get upset with one another, "at no point does this talk of divorce come into the picture," he said.

Kimberly has a similar view. "I don't have a backup plan, I don't have a secret account [like] I was encouraged to get when I first got married," she told me. "This is it. I'm all in." She thinks that her method is best, because she has seen "a lot of friends struggle when they have one foot in and one foot out from the beginning of their marriage." By contrast, Kimberly trusts that "God will protect and provide for me, so I don't fear what will happen in our marriage, because ultimately I know who holds me, who has me, and that's God." Her faith gives her the confidence to "trust" in Martin and in her marriage, and, unlike her struggling friends, to "be two feet in."

Her commitment to Martin and their marriage also conditions how she handles conflict in their marriage. Some of her friends have fallen into toxic cycles of ad hominem attacks, where disagreements and criticisms quickly become personal, disrespectful, and contemptuous. Kimberly aims instead to keep their disagreements calm and respectful. Because of their commitment to marriage and the Golden Rule, this is how they handle conflict: "We don't call each other out or, like, names. I don't say he's dumb. I don't call him a punk or anything like that when I'm upset. So, those things, having those guardrails, for me is helpful. . . . In our relationship . . . we try to maintain that basic line, respect, and just trust."

The general pattern where faith reduces the risk of divorce was also visible among other respondents I spoke with. Maria and Jon, our military couple from earlier chapters, are as inclined to reject divorce for religious reasons as Martin and Kimberly are, and they enjoy a similarly happy marriage.

"I was just doing pushups the other day. And I was so happy. And I tried to think, why am I so happy?" Maria recalled Jon saying. With a laugh, she noted that Jon went on to say: "Oh, I know why—it's because she's so Catholic that . . . she'll never leave me." Jon clearly derived a great deal of security from the knowledge that the Catholic faith he shared with Maria meant he did not have to worry about divorce, unlike many of his buddies from the military, who had seen their marriages collapse under the strain of multiple deployments, post-traumatic stress disorder, or falling into infidelity while stationed thousands of miles from their wives. The faith that Jon and Maria share supplies the nomos, the norms, and the network to buffer them from the stresses and temptations that can end a military marriage.

It is no accident, then, that regular religious attendance is linked to a reduction in your risk of divorce by between 30 and 50 percent. With the State of Our Unions Survey, reports that a marriage is "not at all likely" to end in divorce are especially common among husbands and wives who share a common faith. For example, 70 percent of wives who share attendance with their husbands report their marriage is stable, compared to 57 percent of those who attend without their husbands and 48 percent of those who are secular or unchurched. Wives and husbands who attend jointly are significantly more likely to report that divorce is not at all likely, compared to those who do not attend together or at all, net of standard controls.[51] At the same time, husbands who attend by themselves (a relatively rare group) are at greatest risk of ending up divorced.

The data tells us, then, that shared faith functions as a big hedge against divorce. And in a world where a large share of marriages end in divorce, this tends to brighten the horizons of wives and especially husbands who might otherwise fear finding themselves divorced, alone, and depressed.

BIRDS OF A FEATHER

What predicts obesity? Education, race, income?[52] Yes, to all these factors. But when the Yale sociologist Nicholas Christakis and his colleagues set out to answer this question, the most interesting answer they came up with was *your friends*. If your friend is obese, the odds of you being obese are 45 percent higher; and if your friend's friend is obese, that increases your odds 25 percent. "Our experience of the world depends on the actual structure of the networks in which we're residing and on all the kinds of things that ripple and flow through the network," Christakis observed.

He and his colleagues found similar results for smoking, voting, and an outcome of central concern to this book, divorce.[53] You are 75 percent more likely to become divorced if your friend is divorced and still 33 percent more likely to see your marriage end if a friend of a friend is divorced.[54] His research reinforces a central lesson of this chapter: not just the stability but also the quality of your marriage and family life depend a great deal upon whom you choose as friends. The quality and character of your community matter a great deal for the quality and character of your marriage.

In particular, the family-friendly norms and networks found in America's churches, mosques, and synagogues make religion one of the key pillars of strong and stable marriages in America today. Shared faith is linked to more sexual fidelity, greater commitment, happier wives, higher relationship quality (including greater sexual satisfaction), and more stable marriages.[55] In other words, in a day and age when the values and virtues that sustain strong marriages and families are regularly denied, devalued, and demeaned in the broader culture, and where millions see their dreams for a happy home life dashed on the shoals of me-first living or some other contemporary malady, religious faith tends to strengthen and stabilize marriage and family life by reinforcing the values and virtues that make for good families.

This does not mean that religion in America guarantees a happy home life. On any given Sunday, for instance, about one in ten husbands and wives sitting out there in the pews are unhappy in their marriage—and another 10 percent are only "somewhat happy."[56] They may be struggling with unresolved anger toward an emotionally distant husband, disappointment with a wife's lack of sexual interest, frustration with a husband's practical disengagement from family life, or even a porn habit that is corroding the quality of their marriage—not to mention their faith in God. Pastors, priests, rabbis, and imams—and lay leaders—who are serving their communities need to remember that pain and pathos are part and parcel of contemporary family life, even among their flocks.

Finally, it's not the case that the only route to building a strong family runs through your local religious congregation. Secular Strivers and Asian Americans, who are also more likely to excel at contemporary family life, as we have seen, have their own ways of forging strong and stable families. They tend to embrace family-first values and social networks in their private worlds—family-friendly communities often centered around schools, kin, or sports teams. But joining a faith where weddings and babies are celebrated, children are catechized, and fidelity is endowed with sacred significance also has its place when it comes to increasing your odds of living happily ever after. In fact, one reason that Conservatives and Strivers have stronger and more stable marriages than the population as a whole is that they are also disproportionately more likely to be regular churchgoers.

The bottom line is that family-friendly birds of a feather flock together. Pick your friends, and your community, accordingly.

CHAPTER 11

ORPHANED

How Our Political Class Fails the American Family

On a warm spring day in 2000, a who's-who audience of law-makers, lobbyists, Hill staffers, and academics gathered on Think Tank Row in Washington, DC, to hear President Bill Clinton deliver a ringing endorsement of the China trade bill. The bill was designed to bring China into the World Trade Organization and promote free trade between the United States and China.

The president's endorsement of the bill was effusive, full of extravagant promises. Free trade with China, he claimed, would advance "economic freedom," "have a profound impact on human rights and political liberty" in China, undercut China's efforts to "crack down on the Internet," and, most importantly for his domestic audience, foster a "future of greater prosperity for the American people."[1]

In retrospect, Clinton's promises ring hollow. There was no flowering of freedom in China—political, religious, or technological. And the idea that a dramatic expansion in free trade with China would be a prosperous boon for the American people would come as a rude surprise to the millions of ordinary Americans who lost their jobs because of it. To be clear, there is no question that expanding trade with China enriched many elites like the ones assembled before Clinton in Washington on that spring day. It also brought countless cheap

stuff—from sneakers (think Nike) to smartphones (think Apple)—to
our shores.

In what came to be called the "China shock," the industries and jobs
shipped to China because of this deal ended up throwing more than two
million Americans, primarily working-class men, out of work.[2] The toll
on these workers and their families was devastating. MIT economist
David Autor and his colleagues found that the China shock had "particularly negative impacts on the labor market prospects of men" across the
country, eliminating their jobs and "diminishing their relative earnings"
compared to the women in their lives. In simple terms, millions of men
lost ground as providers for their families.

The consequences for these men and their families were devastating. Areas of the country most affected by the job losses—primarily the
Midwest and Southeast—saw a decline in new marriages, falling rates
of fertility, and an increase in unwed motherhood.[3] Men and women
in these communities were also more likely to succumb to "deaths of
despair," with "a sizeable share" of the increase in fatal drug overdoses
across Middle America attributable to the China shock.[4] For millions
of middle- and working-class Americans, then, more trade with China
meant less marriage, more family instability, and a dwindling shot at
the American Dream—not to mention an increased likelihood of tragic
death.

It's fair to say the collapse of countless working-class families across
America was partly the fault of Washington elites, who naively pursued
normalized trade with China without regard for its consequences for
millions of ordinary families in Middle America. Our nation might have
gained cheap sneakers and TVs, but we lost many of the sturdy jobs that
allowed men without college degrees to provide for their families.

This failure on the question of trade with China stems in part from
a blind faith in a kind of "free-market fundamentalism."[5] According to
American Compass executive director Oren Cass, this approach to economics tends to see free trade—not to mention the free market, minimal
regulations, limited government, and low taxes—as unalloyed goods.
This idea has deep roots on the right, but in recent years, it has gained a
measure of support from center-left figures like Clinton and Joe Biden
(who also supported the China trade bill). As the Niskanen Center's

Samuel Hammond and I noted in an article for the *Atlantic*, "Our elites had too much faith in a laissez-faire ideology that sees labor markets as automatically self-correcting but, in fact, exacted a terrible toll on scores of working-class families across the United States."[6]

This is but one example of how our ruling class, both Republicans and Democrats, in both the public and private sectors, have made decisions that have eviscerated the economic and social foundations of family life for working- and middle-class Americans. We have already seen how their decisions in media, the ivory tower, and pop culture have devalued and distorted the truth about marriage and family life in our culture. But the challenges facing American families are not simply cultural; they are also political and economic. Instead of creating family-first policies, government and corporate leaders have increasingly made decisions about trade, technology, education, and welfare based on increasing their own wealth and/or social status. It is no accident that elite families have emerged relatively unscathed from the economic and cultural transformations of the last four decades, while families lower down the economic ladder, especially in working- and middle-class communities, have lost tremendous ground.

MEN OUT OF WORK

Politicians, journalists, and executives in C-suites across the country told us that free trade would fuel a virtuous cycle of economic growth and cheap consumption that would redound to the benefit of ordinary Americans. What they did not appreciate, however, is that good jobs, not just cheap goods, are fundamental to strong and stable families.[7] When large numbers of Americans, especially men, are employed in decent-paying, stable jobs, families are more likely to flourish. But that's not happening today.

The reality right now is that too many men in our country are not stably employed. The percentage of men in their prime working years, ages twenty-five to fifty-four, who are not working full-time has risen from 16 percent in 1975 to 20 percent in 2019.[8] And the share of men who have completely left the labor force in this age group, as Nicholas Eberstadt noted in his book *Men Without Work: America's Invisible Crisis*, "was three-and-a-half times greater in 2015 than fifty years earlier."[9] The numbers are even more stark for men who do not have college degrees, as figure 11.1 indicates. Among this group, the percentage of men without full-time work rose from 16 percent in 1976 to 25 percent in 2021.[10] Think about that: one in four less-educated men in their prime today, about sixteen million men, are distant from the discipline, direction, and dividends of full-time work. This is why Eberstadt thinks we are now seeing an almost Great "Depression-scale crisis in relation to men and work."[11]

Part of the story here is that many men cannot find work in our new economy.[12] Trade and automation are two major reasons for this. But we are also seeing an "eerie and radical transformation" where many men are choosing not to work full-time. You know them, you've seen them: twentysomething boys in mom's basement and fortysomething men begging for money in the median. They are part of a growing class of men living what Eberstadt calls an "alternative lifestyle to the age-old quest for a paying job."[13] This is partly a failure of personal responsibility, as scores of men have abandoned the norm of work.

But they are not solely to blame. Too many of our leading institutions,

FIGURE 11.1: GROWING SHARE OF LESS-EDUCATED MEN NOT WORKING

Percentage of prime-aged men (25 to 54) without college degree not employed full-time, 1975–2021

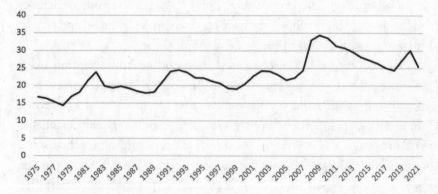

Source: Current Population Survey.

and the elites who guide them, have failed millions of men and boys in ways that have left them unprepared and unmotivated when it comes to earning a living. In particular, big education, big government, and big tech have all had a hand in the growing disconnect between men and work.

BIG EDUCATION—by which I mean the schools, colleges, and universities teaching kids and young adults—has done a notoriously bad job in recent decades of educating boys and young men. The teaching methods, substance, and ethos found in too many of our schools end up favoring girls and disfavoring boys, fueling a widening gender gap that leaves many girls flourishing and all too many boys floundering.[14] Not enough male teachers, too little recess, books that don't speak to the male imagination, and intolerance for the boisterous spirit of boys in our nation's schools are among the many factors driving "the growing epidemic of unmotivated boys and underachieving young men" in the education sector, as observers like Drs. Leonard Sax and Richard Reeves have noted.[15]

For instance, only 41 percent of college students today are men. "Men are falling behind remarkably fast" at our colleges and universities, noted Thomas Mortenson, a senior scholar at the Pell Institute for the Study of Opportunity in Higher Education.[16] But the failure of the education establishment to form young men shows up much earlier in life. Two-thirds of high-school students in the top 10 percent are girls, while boys dominate the ranks of the bottom rung, as Reeves has noted.[17] Boys have been consistently about twice as likely as girls to be suspended or expelled from school since the early 1990s.[18] And the writing proficiency of the average high-school boy now lags two grade levels behind that of his sister (i.e., a girl in the same demographic).[19]

Big education has also focused its spending and attention overwhelmingly on serving students on the "college track," a track now dominated by girls and young women. The Department of Education, for instance, spends about *seventy-nine times* as much money on colleges and universities as it does on vocational education in high schools and community colleges—now called technical education.[20] This despite the fact that only 39 percent of young men completing high school enrolled at a four-year university in 2019 (compared to 49 percent of their female peers), and that those millions of young men who aren't on the college track could benefit immensely from high-quality vocational education.[21] Big education is failing to equip many young men, especially poor and working-class young men, with the kind of vocational education they need to build useful job skills, develop a sense of self-worth based on learning a marketable trade, and get on the path to a decent-paying, stable job.[22]

This failure has had real consequences for the take-home pay of ordinary American families. Men without college degrees have seen their incomes stagnate since the 1970s. In most of these families, men are contributing *less* real income than they did in the 1970s, requiring wives to work more hours.[23] Meanwhile, the guys at the top—men who successfully jump through the hoops of our "college-for-all" education system—are contributing significantly *more* money today to their family's income than they did in the 1970s. This state of affairs means that instead of learning being the great equalizer, big education is actually contributing to increased inequality.

BIG GOVERNMENT also has a hand in the floundering fortunes of men, with policies that reward idleness and penalize work for too many young and middle-aged men. One reason the share of men unemployed during their prime working years (twenty-five to fifty-four) has more than doubled since 1970 is that growing numbers of men are living off government assistance, especially Social Security Disability Insurance (SSDI). One study found that about two-thirds of prime-aged men out of the labor force lived in a household drawing cash payments from a government disability program.[24]

Of course, many of these men have legitimate mental or medical problems that prevent them from working. But the share of prime-aged men on disability has surged even as the physical conditions of work have gotten easier in America; this suggests some men on assistance could get by without it. What is also frustrating is that the system is set up so that going back to full-time work is often a worse deal, financially, than just remaining on disability and collecting a government check.[25]

BIG TECH also is contributing to this male malaise. Big tech offers increasingly alluring electronic opiates—from Xbox to OnlyFans—that distract adolescent and young adult males from engaging with school

and work to the fullest. Their products instead appeal to their instinc-
tive interest in adventure, conquest, and sex. In his book *Boys Adrift:
The Five Factors Driving the Growing Epidemic of Unmotivated Boys and
Underachieving Young Men*, Sax notes the ways today's technology un-
dercuts male motivation in real life by offering rewards "associated
with achieving a great objective, but without any connection to the
real world, without any sense of a need to contextualize the story."[26]
Dopamine hits coming from big tech's screens tend to minimize teenage
boys' and young men's desire to hit the books, learn real-world skills, or
invest in a job, especially when it is usually easier to succeed online than
in real life.

Consider, for instance, how the rise of ever-more enticing electronic
experiences has been linked to young men's disengagement from work
in America. Princeton economist Mark Aguiar and his team found
that recreational computer time surged 60 percent for young men ages
twenty-one to thirty from 2004 to 2017. They estimate that nearly half
the decline in hours worked by men in this age group over the same time
frame can be explained by their deepening devotion to their screens.[27]

Too many of our boys and men have been captured by the "limbic capitalism" mentioned in chapter 9, a form of parasitical commerce
where companies like Microsoft (Xbox), OnlyFans, and ByteDance
(TikTok) capture and waste their time. Young men affected by "stress,
social defeat, neglect or abuse," hailing disproportionately from poor and
working-class communities, are especially vulnerable to the seductive
power of big tech's products.[28]

What's especially striking about this is so many big tech overlords
do not let their kids fall prey to the tech products they are selling to
others. Take Chris Anderson, the former editor of *Wired* and now the
chief executive of a robotics and drone company in Silicon Valley, who
was profiled for a *New York Times* story on Silicon Valley executives and
professionals who limit technology in their kids' lives.

"On the scale between candy and crack cocaine, it's closer to crack
cocaine," Anderson said, regarding tech. "We thought we could control
it," he added. "And this is beyond our power to control. This is going
straight to the pleasure centers of the developing brain. This is beyond
our capacity as regular parents to understand."

Anderson's concern about tech has led him to enforce rules for his kids that include: no phones until high school, no iPads, no social media until age thirteen, and no phones in bedrooms.[29] Anderson is not alone. Apple founder Steve Jobs famously told a reporter that his kids "haven't used it," referring to the iPad he helped invent, adding, "We limit how much technology our kids use at home."[30]

These are just three of the ways in which big education, big government, and big tech elites have made decisions (often decisions that put money in their pocket or a patina of virtue in their public profile) that have resulted in fewer men at work. As we saw in chapter 9, this disconnect between men and full-time work, in turn, has reduced the appeal and accessibility of marriage for all too many men in America—especially men who are not Strivers on the college track.

STAGNANT LIVING STANDARDS

Unemployment and underemployment for men are not the only problems facing ordinary American families. The cost of living is spiraling upward for too many working- and middle-class families, outpacing their ability to afford key aspects of family life. Sure, we have cheaper stuff—our smart TVs and telephones have never been more affordable or entertaining. But when it comes to some of the biggest and most important expenses in our budgets, many ordinary mothers and fathers are reporting that their income is not keeping pace with the rising cost of living.

One working-class Black mother in her forties from Atlanta put it this way: politicians need to "lower the cost of living, so housing and groceries and gas, everything can be affordable."[31] This theme came up over and over again in a series of focus groups convened in 2021 by the Institute for Family Studies (IFS), as working-class men and women in Georgia, Ohio, and Texas expressed concerns about the costs of childcare, housing, food, fuel, and health care.

In fact, the rising cost of providing for a family has left many of the working-class couples IFS interviewed feeling like they had no choice but to have both parents work to cover their expenses. Many of these couples would prefer to have one parent home full- or part-time. "It's been so much harder to maintain a home and home life . . . without having two incomes to complete everything," noted one Ohio focus-group participant in her early fifties. "Financially, it's become more difficult for families." She resents the time squeeze—juggling the responsibilities of full-time work and motherhood—she now faces.

Part of the problem here is that working- and middle-class Americans have seen much more stagnant income than both the rich and the poor. They've "experienced much slower income growth than both the affluent (who have seen rising wages) and the poor (who have been helped by an expanded safety net)," as Richard Reeves and Isabel Sawhill at the Brookings Institution have noted.[32] Over the last forty years, the middle class has seen their household income rise only about half as fast as the poor and the rich.[33]

For the rich, this is because our new winner-take-all economy is providing bigger financial returns to men and women with the most education and the best skills. For the poor, this is because big government is now devoting much more money to programs—from Medicaid to food stamps to disability checks—to Americans with the least income.

This is frustrating to those in the working and middle class, who often feel that poor people, working less and receiving government benefits, have a standard of living almost as good as their own. "It's like we are damned if we do, damned if we don't," said one Black working mother from Atlanta. "If we work, we don't have any type of [government] resources." This view was shared by a White middle-class mother in southern Ohio, who said, "I think the middle class is struggling more than the lower class, because the lower class has so many more opportunities for programs than the working [or] middle class."[34]

The irony here is that big government has driven up the prices of many of the goods working- and middle-class families are struggling most to afford—like childcare, higher education, and housing.[35]

Today, for instance, housing costs are outpacing inflation, especially in big metro areas such as Washington, DC, New York, and Los Angeles. This is partly because onerous environmental regulations and local zoning laws make it too expensive to build new homes people can afford. The Council of Economic Advisers found that regulations drove up the cost of housing at staggering rates in our nation's most elite metropolitan areas. Excessive regulations have led to a 150 percent premium on homes in the San Francisco Bay area. Even in Washington, DC, where the greatest concentration of political elites live, regulations are responsible for an 80 percent premium in housing costs, according to the report.[36] For dual-career, college-educated, high-powered couples, housing that is artificially scarce and overly expensive might be a headache, but many lower-income families literally cannot afford to start a family in the places with some of the best jobs and economic growth in the nation. This is one reason why fertility has fallen in communities with surging housing costs.[37]

What we have then is an economy that showers disproportionate returns to the Strivers, who have seen their real income surge by about 100 percent since 1980. Meanwhile, big government steers billions to the poor, who have seen their real income rise by about 85 percent since 1980. Families in the middle, by contrast, have only seen their income go up by 45 percent.[38] And that rise is only because they usually have both parents working, often struggling to juggle the time demands of having two full-time jobs while raising the next generation. These financial pressures not only impinge on their desire to marry and have kids but also put strains on the quality and stability of their marriages.[39]

MARRIAGE, PENALIZED

Mark and Lisa Payne could have stepped out of a Norman Rockwell portrait. This attractive working-class couple live in a modest country home in central Virginia with their two daughters, four and six years old. He works as a technician for an HVAC company based in Harrisonburg, Virginia, and she is a stay-at-home mother. Their lives are traditional in most respects. But in 2019, when I first interviewed them, they were decidedly nontraditional in one respect: they were not married.

Years ago, when the girls were very young, Mark and Lisa sat down at the kitchen table, ran the numbers, and discovered they would lose about $600 a month if they were to marry. "You're talking about $600 out of my paycheck per month for just becoming married, and at that time I was making $40,000 a year," Mark recalls thinking. "It just wasn't doable. It's either, yeah, we can get married, and I can afford that [loss of] six to eight hundred a month, but then we can't afford gas to get to work. We can't afford food to put on the table. We can't afford to buy our kids things that they need. Not just things that they want, the things that they need."

What is Mark talking about? How would marriage drive a big hole in their monthly budget, amounting to about one-fifth of their real income? At the time, Lisa and the children got their health care through Virginia's Medicaid program, as Mark's employer did not provide health coverage. If the Paynes had gotten legally married and reported Mark's income, they would have lost this crucial coverage. Purchasing health insurance for the family would have cost them at least $600 per month. "It's like if we were to get married at that point in time, we would have financially ruined our [family]," said Mark.

A Black mother in Atlanta is living a similar experience: "Yes, I chose not to marry," she said, adding, "I get a lot of assistance for my children, for myself, so if I did marry or put any other type of income in, I would not qualify for anything" from the government.[40]

A University of Virginia graduate student from Arkansas observed a similar pattern among some of his White working-class friends back home. "I continue to be amazed by the trajectory difference between my married versus unmarried friends," he told me. "I keep thinking of my high-school classmates who are basically trapped by Medicaid and other income-based programs, never to get married."[41]

In fact, more than one in ten unmarried Americans with incomes less than $50,000 report that one reason they are steering clear of marriage is that they would lose their government benefits, according to a 2021 family survey.[42] These stories and survey data show how our nation's public policies—especially our tax and welfare policies—often penalize marriage, making it financially costly for ordinary couples like the Paynes to marry.

Today, marriage penalties fall hardest on working- and middle-class families, with incomes falling between about $35,000 and $65,000.[43] They often rob such families of between 10 and 30 percent of their household income. One study lent confirmation to the UVA graduate student's observation, finding that a working-class couple with two children in Arkansas stood to lose 32 percent of their real income if they married.[44] Another study found that a $1,000 increase in the marriage penalty facing couples was linked to a 1.7 percentage point decrease in the probability a couple would marry—even a 2.7 percentage point decline for those without a college degree.[45] A different study found that mothers facing a marriage penalty related to the earned income tax credit (EITC) were 2.5 percentage points more likely to cohabit and 2.7 percentage points less likely to marry, compared to mothers who did not face a marriage penalty.[46] These are just some of the ways that big government today works against the cause of strong and stable families.

In 1997 Congress took up some of the marriage penalties facing American families—but *only* the ones facing affluent Americans. They addressed many marriage penalties embedded in income taxes for the upper half of the income distribution. But they did not tackle the penalties from programs used by working-class families.[47] And so, in a major dereliction of duty, lawmakers failed to give relief to precisely the group that needed it most, those who have faced the most economic turmoil and family instability over the past four and a half decades.[48]

BEYOND NIKKI HALEYISM

Amid all these changes, we have seen the fortunes of the American family fall dramatically, across both Democratic and Republican administrations. For instance, from 1975 to 2020, the share of children living in married families dropped almost 20 percentage points for middle-class kids and even more for working-class kids, to the point where only about two-thirds of kids in these two communities were in married homes in 2020. But for the upper class, this number barely budged, going from 95 percent in 1975 to 91 percent in 2020.[49] Democratic and Republican presidents, governors, and legislators alike have generally failed to move the dial as marriage has nosedived among the working class, even as it has remained robust among the rich. What we have on our hands is a bipartisan failure to serve families.

Many Republicans, though, have talked a good game. Back in 1992, Vice President Dan Quayle made national headlines inveighing against Murphy Brown, a TV character who had embraced single motherhood, and plenty of Republican politicians have mouthed pieties about "family values" since then.

The problem with too many Republicans is that their laissez-faire economic instincts lead many of them to do nothing or just offer empty cultural sloganeering when it comes to helping ordinary families in practical ways. They often wrongly assume that tax cuts, deregulation, and higher GDP growth will fix all the problems ailing American families. "The best way we can support the family is to reduce the size and scope of government in every direction," wrote conservative economist Anne Rathbone Bradley in 2021, adding, "Allowing markets to direct innovation will create the most productive jobs and provide families with choices that best suit them."[50]

The 2017 debate over the Tax Cuts and Jobs Act is illustrative. Senators Mike Lee (R, Utah) and Marco Rubio (R, Florida) introduced an amendment that would have made the child tax credit apply to both income and payroll taxes, thereby putting real money in the pockets of millions of working- and middle-class families.[51] Unfortunately, many of their Republican colleagues were so focused on delivering a big tax cut for corporate America that they could not bring themselves to shave off 0.98 percent of the corporate tax cut to deliver a more generous child benefit to working-class families across America.[52] For too many Republicans, practically speaking, big business takes precedence over serving ordinary families.

Today, one of the more prominent Republican voices, and a 2024 presidential candidate, is former South Carolina governor Nikki Haley. She is a talented politician and gifted speaker. Unfortunately, her approach to family policy is stuck in the past, with almost no consideration for the new challenges facing families in the twenty-first century.

In a 2020 article for the *Wall Street Journal*, for instance, Haley crowed about her Reagan-style bona fides by boasting about the "pro-market policies" she pushed as governor of the Palmetto State that "helped bring our state more than $20 billion in capital investment." She derided any efforts to advance a "hyphenated capitalism," which would mean reining in or redirecting the market with tax credits, subsidies, or mandates.[53] Haley was clearly targeting recent efforts by leaders like Senator Rubio to think creatively about using policy to strengthen the family, an approach that is clearly heresy to Haley and 1980s-style conservatives like her. Later, in the *National Review*, she lashed out at the idea of expanding the child tax credit for American families, without offering any concrete policy ideas of her own for families struggling to cover the costs of raising kids today.[54]

Haley's out-of-touch rhetoric here conveyed no recognition that the financial challenges families face today are different from the ones of the last century. No recognition that too many men are idle or presumed unnecessary in America. No recognition that marriage and fertility have fallen to record lows as families struggle to keep up with the cost of living. And no recognition that her party has largely failed to shore up the American family in any way beyond mere lip service.

It's well past time for Republican politicians to give some teeth to their family values talking points and take bold action to revive the fortunes of ordinary families in America.

BEYOND BIDENISM

Unfortunately, things do not look better on the left. There is no question that President Joe Biden's family agenda in 2021 was bold. After spending $110 billion on a one-year expansion of the child tax credit in the coronavirus relief package, he proposed spending an additional $1.8 trillion over ten years on a raft of policies in his American Families Plan, which, he claimed, would help lift the fortunes of families across the nation.[55]

One feature of his plan is to be applauded: he sought to expand the child tax credit and pay it out monthly, thereby helping millions of American families with the financial challenges of raising kids today. But otherwise Biden's plan, which failed to pass Congress, would have been a disaster for American families, penalizing marriage and outsourcing one family function after another to the state and market.

First, Biden's plan would have added yet another penalty to marriage by expanding the earned income tax credit for childless adults without doing the same for married adults, thereby adding another roadblock for couples considering marriage. His plan would have meant that these couples would stand to lose hundreds or even thousands of EITC dollars.[56]

Biden also displayed his statist colors with big new proposals for universal, public pre-K and state-subsidized day care, measures that were both designed to minimize the time young children would spend with parents or other family members. By backing pre-K for three- and four-year-olds, Biden's plan would have given big government two *more* years to mold and educate our kids. In the wake of our public school system's manifold failures to navigate COVID flexibly and effectively, along with its failure to successfully educate our kids in recent years, every parent should be highly skeptical of a big new push to give government schools two more years of our children's lives.[57]

If public policy is going to support more preschool, we need grants and vouchers that give families the choice to send their kids to a preschool of their choice, be it public, private, or religious. My own research with Albert Cheng and a team of scholars indicates that private schools, especially religious ones, do a much better job of preparing kids for marriage and family life.[58]

The most egregious part of Biden's plan was his push to get more kids out of their homes and into day care centers. He aimed to spend $200 billion on direct day care subsidies and more than $80 billion on tax credits for day care, thereby creating a powerful public policy incentive for families with two working parents over families with a parent at home.

What's more, Biden's plan to spend billions on day care ignored the fact that most parents prefer family care to day care. Andrea Nunez, a twenty-five-year-old mother in St. Petersburg, Florida, relied on family to take care of her toddler. "Both grandmas lived nearby and took turns caring for our daughter," she said. "It's great having someone you trust, knowing that she is going to be in good hands."

Andrea preferred family care to day care because "when they are a baby, it is harder to trust a childcare worker, because they have other kids they are looking after, not just ours. But being with a grandparent, they will get the attention, love, and care that a baby needs."[59]

Andrea is no outlier. "A majority of parents (58 percent) say they prefer to have their kids at home, either cared for by parents (47 percent) or a family member (11 percent)," according to a 2021 study from the Institute for Family Studies. The study also found that only 18 percent wanted their young kids to be in full-time day care.

Many working- and middle-class families want to take a more "familist" or family-first approach to caring for the youngest children in their home. By familist, I mean the idea that men and women prioritize the needs of their family over their individual desires, that families cultivate strong bonds between children, parents, grandparents, and other kin, and that the family takes the lead in caring for the dependent young and old, rather than the state (public care) or market (private care).

Andrea Nunez's approach to the care of her toddler is emblematic of this kind of familism. But this more family-first way of caring for kids was not an important priority for the White House when President Biden was assembling his American Families Plan. "We want parents to be in the workforce, especially mothers," said Susan Rice, then the head of the president's Domestic Policy Council.[60] Like many highly educated professionals, Rice was set on advancing what was recently described by the *Atlantic*'s Derek Thompson as a "workist" approach to life.[61] This is an approach that assumes that work, not family, is what provides the most meaning, status, and happiness to our lives.

In fact, it's no accident that when we look at the survey data, it is highly educated parents like Rice who are the ones most likely to prefer and use day care. As one recent survey found, working-class and middle-class parents are half as likely to *want* this kind of care for their kids as are upper-class parents.[62] Highly educated and affluent parents are also almost twice as likely to *use* center-based care, compared to poor and working-class parents, and parents without a college degree. The bottom line: day care is much more popular among Strivers than among ordinary Americans.

One problem, then, with Bidenism is that so much of his agenda is elitist and workist. It caters to the comparatively small number of upscale Strivers who value full-time work more than the family-centered care of their own young children. The desires of families who want one parent to stay home, or to have a grandparent or relative watch their child during the day, are virtually absent from family policy discussions inside the Beltway. The values of the ruling class, who dominate our public conversation about family from their perches in media, the academy, and the policy world do not represent the more family-first aspirations of many middle- and working-class families in America.[63]

The other problem with Bidenism is that it is statist, not familist. Patrick T. Brown, a fellow with the Ethics and Public Policy Center, criticized the left's statist leanings when it comes to family policy, especially "the Left's tendency to task the state with the roles traditionally understood as crucial to family life: provider, caretaker, and educator. An inadvertently revealing glimpse into this framework came from former Virginia governor Terry McAuliffe, who now-famously said the quiet part out loud during a debate: 'I don't think parents should be telling schools what they should teach.' (Virginia parents, apparently, disagreed.)"[64]

WHAT THEN MUST WE DO?

Reviving the fortunes of the American family depends on strengthening the economic, policy, and cultural foundations of marriage and family life. We must get behind policies that make it easier for working families to get ahead. J. D. Vance, author of *Hillbilly Elegy* and the new Republican senator from Ohio, has called for more "good jobs that pay a good wage," because he believes it is important that "if you work hard and play by the rules, you can support a middle-class family on a single wage."[65] His words are indicative of the state's affirmative duty to do its part to strengthen the fraying financial foundations that make a flourishing family life possible. Partly this means, at the very minimum, to "do no harm" when it comes to people getting and staying married. And, at the maximum, this means the state conveying to the culture this unheralded but perennial truth: men, women, and children are much more likely to thrive when stable marriage anchors American family life.

Obviously, the government can only do so much here. But there is a role for public policy in reviving the fortunes of the American family. Here are five ideas for policies that would strengthen and stabilize marriage and family life here at home.

1. DEFUND COLLEGE, REFUND VOCATIONAL EDUCATION

I mentioned earlier that the current educational policy landscape tilts against young adults not on the college track, who make up a large share of the young adult population.[66] This is unwise and unjust, because it robs millions of less academically inclined young men and women of the opportunity to gain a strong financial footing early in life and start to build the families they desire.

We can rework the educational landscape to favor family life by dramatically increasing the number and quality of career and technical education (CTE) programs, teaching students real-world skills from coding to car repair.[67] Career Academies, high-school programs that offer struggling students rigorous, career-oriented courses, have succeeded in boosting the earnings *and* marriage prospects of the young men who succeed in them.[68] Policymakers should lean into the success of Career Academies and other CTE models in high schools and community colleges by increasing funding and prestige for these programs.

The goal should be to design a national workforce education system that prepares one-third of adults for the middle skills market, offering skill-based certificates and job training with real value in the labor market. We should start by reallocating at least one-third of current state and federal spending on higher education to skills-based workforce education in high schools and community colleges, contingent on a commitment to tracking a program's success in placing students into good jobs, to make sure the money is going to the best programs.

Let's spend less on a bloated and inefficient higher education system and more on a vocational education system that gives more young women and especially young men a pathway into a good job—and a shot at the successful family life that its income can enable.

2. BOOST FAMILIES' FINANCIAL FORTUNES

Given the relatively stagnant wages of working- and middle-class families and the rising costs of raising children, Congress should expand the child tax credit in three ways to shore up the financial foundations of American families.

First, Congress should increase the value of the child tax credit. The federal government should extend it to parents at the rate of $350 per month for children under six and then $250 per month for children six to seventeen. For parents of young children, this will help families

cover the cost of childcare or having a parent stay at home. For parents
of school-age children, this will help parents cover the cost of expenses
like tutoring, youth sports, and food.

Second, to be eligible for the full benefit, families should be required to hit an earnings threshold of $10,000. All families that made
at least that amount (with an upper limit for the wealthiest households)
in the previous year would be eligible for a monthly child benefit for the
following fiscal year. Families whose earnings fell below the threshold
would instead receive a reduced benefit as well as continued support from
existing safety-net programs like food stamps and Temporary Assistance
for Needy Families.

Relying on a threshold-type model like this would reinforce the
norm of work for families. This is important, given the signal role that
work plays in boosting families' long-term financial well-being, lending
direction and purpose to parents' lives, and modeling to children the
importance of earning a living.

Third, Congress should emphasize the importance of the married two-parent family by adopting an explicitly pro-marriage design.
Obviously, married, two-parent households provide the best environment for children. Yet for too long public policy has penalized marriage
among lower-income parents. Policymakers should right the wrongs of
existing marriage penalties and offer a tangible validation of marriage's
value to children. To wit, married parents eligible for the child tax credit
should receive a 20 percent supplement. Skeptics of this idea should note
that a marriage-focused approach to family policy has been successfully
incorporated into the largest federal agency, the Department of Defense,
for decades. For instance, the military gives housing and health care
benefits only to partners of service members who are married to service
members, not to partners who are cohabiting with service members.

A streamlined and expanded child tax credit would support parents
financially in a way that reinforces work and marriage. Importantly, it
would also demonstrate that the country isn't committed just to lending
cultural support to its families but also to backing up that support with
the economic resources that help working- and middle-class families
invest in the next generation.[69]

3. ELIMINATE MARRIAGE PENALTIES

Too many of our public policies—from the earned income tax credit to Medicaid—make marriage a bad financial decision for couples. And the burden of these marriage penalties is concentrated on working-class couples, who have seen an outsize fraying of family life in recent years.

Policymakers need to tackle penalties in means-tested programs like Medicaid and public housing. Congress should double the income thresholds for these programs for married parents, compared to single parents. To be sure, adding a whole new group of lower-middle-income married families to these programs is not inexpensive. But it is important if we are serious about removing the government's thumb on the scale against strong and stable families.

One way to limit the costs would be to restrict threshold extensions to families with children under age five. This would concentrate the additional expenditure in the immediate years surrounding a couple's decision to marry, while also funneling additional support to married families in their highest-cost years of parenthood.

Given that Congress has already eliminated many of the marriage penalties facing upper-income families in the tax code, there is no excuse for ignoring the financial penalties facing lower-income couples, especially working-class couples, who would otherwise marry. Big government should not be in the business of discouraging ordinary Americans from getting married.

4. EXPAND SCHOOL CHOICE BEYOND THE STRIVERS

Right now, our educational system reserves school choice for Strivers; better-off families are the ones who can move to the neighborhoods with the best public schools. Or these families can turn to private schools and tutors when they are not happy with their public options. We see this pattern among countless politicians, such as Senator Elizabeth Warren (D, Massachusetts) and Congresswoman Nancy Pelosi (D, California), who profess support for public schools and oppose school choice yet sent their children to private schools. Moreover, we have learned that kids are more likely to forge strong and stable families if they are educated outside of a public school.[70]

But our educational system boxes the vast majority of poor and working-class students into public schools that fail to foster their best family future, not to mention their educational attainment. Policymakers should give families from all backgrounds the choice to find the type of environment that's best for them, opening the door to better opportunities for these kids' future families.[71]

One of COVID's silver linings is that public school failures have caused many states—from Florida to West Virginia—to expand more options for school choice to parents in their communities. One model here is Arizona, which provides educational savings accounts (ESAs) to parents who choose not to enroll their child in public school. The cash value of an ESA averages about 90 percent of what the state spends on education per pupil (or about $7,000 per child per year) and has just been made available to all children in Arizona. Parents can use ESAs for a range of private educational purposes, such as paying tuition at a local private school, private tutoring, or purchasing textbooks to homeschool their child.[72]

This model could be expanded, and other states should follow in Arizona's footsteps. Federal lawmakers should also implement a similar policy nationally, adding the federal government's per-pupil spending (currently about $1,140 per student) on top of state dollars for families in any state that chooses to pursue an ESA model.[73]

Efforts like these would dramatically expand the number of families that can afford to send their children to schools that not only offer stronger academic development but also cultivate the type of moral environment that prepares kids for marriage and parenthood later in life.

5. PROMOTE THE SUCCESS SEQUENCE

Too many of our young adults are uncertain about how to best navigate the transition to adulthood, especially when it comes to family formation. Young men and women today are less likely than older adults to believe that children need to grow up with both parents in the home, and they are more likely to believe that marriage isn't necessary for parenthood.[74] The problem, then, is that too many young adults are ignorant of the benefits that marriage affords them, and especially any kids they have.

A powerful framework exists to help more young Americans build healthy, stable family lives. The "success sequence" describes a series of crucial life decisions surrounding education, work, marriage, and child-rearing that are powerfully linked to positive economic outcomes, even in today's treacherous landscape.[75] My research with Wendy Wang finds that only 3 percent of millennials who earned at least a high-school diploma, worked full-time, and waited until marriage to have children were in poverty by the time they reached young adulthood.[76]

This success sequence offers an accessible framework, a compelling narrative, and a launching pad for teachers and mentors to help young adults approach family formation with greater clarity and purpose, without requiring them to conform to the "college-for-all" mentality. What's more, surveys indicate that the success sequence is popular among parents across both class and racial lines.[77] Policymakers should launch national, state, and local campaigns teaching students the success sequence and prompting them to think critically about the decisions that will pave their pathways to success.

Rigorous evaluations of curricula teaching the success sequence show promising results. One randomized control trial found a 46 percent reduction in teen pregnancy for a relationship curriculum teaching the success sequence.[78] Interventions like this should inspire a range of public *and* private campaigns. Private campaigns, led by churches and nonprofits, may prefer to use moral or religious language. Public campaigns will undoubtedly use a more descriptive model. A successful initiative will leave room for a wide range of approaches.

Campaigns against smoking and teenage pregnancy have taught us that sustained efforts to change behavior can work. A campaign organized around the success sequence—receiving widespread support from educational, civic, media, pop cultural, and religious institutions—might meet with the same level of success as the recent national campaign to prevent teen pregnancy, which had a hand in driving down the teen pregnancy rate by more than 75 percent since the 1990s.[79]

IN SUM

From Ronald Reagan to Donald Trump, from Jimmy Carter to Joe Biden, across Democratic and Republican administrations, the American family has lost ground. Too many on the right have had a *blind faith in the market's power* to bring prosperity and so much more to all families if the state can simply get out of the way. Too many on the left have had a *blind faith in the state's ability* to seize the core functions of families—like providership and childcare—without injury to the strength, stability, and solidarity of American family life. And yet even as the Dow stands close to its record heights, and government spending on social welfare annually tops the trillion-dollar mark, family formation in America has hit historic lows.

Policymakers in recent years have rarely pursued or prioritized *family-first* policies aimed directly at strengthening and stabilizing marriage and family life. They have not sought to protect or renew the educational, economic, and cultural foundations of family life by pursuing, for instance, anything close to a family wage. They have not eliminated barriers to family formation like the working-class marriage penalty. And they have not pursued policies that make it easier for parents to maximize their investments of time and money in their children rather than the workplace. Too often, the family has been orphaned by our political class.

The policies offered here—from an expanded child tax credit to school choice—are family-first policies, designed to make it easier for parents to provide for, care for, and educate their children; for young couples to get and stay married to one another; and for family ties across generations to remain strong. The alternative to taking policy steps like the ones offered here is to accept a world where the United States devolves into a separate-and-unequal family regime, where strong and stable families are the preserve of the Strivers, the Faithful, Conservatives, and Asian Americans—and everyone else is consigned to increasingly unstable, unhappy, and unworkable families, or no family at all. I think we can agree that such a dystopian future is un-American and unacceptable.[80]

CONCLUSION:
IN PURSUIT OF HAPPINESS

From dark portraits of contemporary family life—think *Marriage Story*—to anything-goes shows and movies—think *The Ultimatum* and *365 Days*—Netflix is not exactly known for delivering the kind of pop-culture offerings that would renew your hope in our nation's most fundamental institution or put you on a path to forging a strong union of your own.

The irony, however, is that Netflix cofounder and executive chairman Reed Hastings has built a marriage in private that seems to contradict much of the spirit and substance presented to the public by his streaming service. To be sure, he and his wife, Patricia Ann Quillin, had their challenges toward the beginning of their marriage.[1] In his book *No Rules Rules: Netflix and the Culture of Reinvention*, Hastings confessed that he and Patricia hit a wall in their marriage over his excessive devotion to work—including lots of travel away from their family—early in their marriage: "I spent half of each week away, but when my wife expressed her frustration, I would defend myself, saying that everything I did was for the good of the family."[2]

However, unlike his company's *Marriage Story*, Hastings's own marriage story has a happy ending. After seeing a marriage counselor, Reed was able to course-correct, prioritize his marriage, and go on to forge a strong and stable family—not to mention a $3 billion fortune—with his wife and two children in California. His own marriage has been going strong for more than three decades.[3]

The best description of the elite pattern manifested not only in the Hastings family but across the nation is that it is a kind of inverted hypocrisy. Classically, hypocrisy is when men and women extol goodness in public but fall prey to vice in private. When it comes to marriage and family, however, today's American elites typically do the opposite. They are *familists* in the sense that they are often deeply dedicated, in their private lives, to living family-first marriages and lives. That's a good thing. But they are also driven by progressive commitments to honor family diversity, a belief in individual choice, a desire to signal their adherence to the current zeitgeist, and an unwillingness to offend their peers. Therefore, as we have seen, these educated and affluent Americans are, at best, unwilling to stand up publicly for the virtues and values that sustain strong and stable families and, at worst, dedicated to actively speaking out against them. They are inverted hypocrites, then, in the sense that they are not willing to "preach what they practice" when it comes to articulating a public vision of marriage and family life, to use Charles Murray's phrase.[4]

Why is it a big deal that so many professors, politicians, journalists, school superintendents, technology titans, producers, and other cultural influencers in America personally tend to forge strong and stable marriages for themselves and their kids but do not lend support to a marriage-friendly ethic (or even do the opposite) in public, in their professional roles? Obviously, the Reed Hastingses of the world and their kids benefit financially, socially, and emotionally from forging strong families. In fact, almost half of the happiness advantage enjoyed by college-educated Americans can be explained by the fact that they are more likely to be married—and happily married at that—than less educated men and women.[5]

No, the problem isn't that elites have forged stable marriages for themselves and their kids in the twenty-first century. The problem is that they are not producing films, developing curricula for public schools, writing articles for the *New York Times*, or advancing public policies on Capitol Hill that conform to the truth about the realities of contemporary family life. They are not doing much of anything culturally, economically, or politically to strengthen the foundations of marriage for Americans outside of their own privileged circles. They are doing nothing to boost the financial prospects of young men in the poor and working classes or the cultural cachet of marriage in their communities across urban, rural, and small-town America. The failure of our ruling class to lend cultural and economic support to marriage and family life in these communities is a big reason why children, men, and women in them are much more likely to end up immiserated, incarcerated, under-educated, and unhappy today.

This elite dereliction of duty is also tragic for the nation as a whole because marriage plays an unparalleled role in the fortunes of American civilization. As marriage goes, so goes the American way of life. We have learned all the ways that "Life, Liberty, and the pursuit of Happiness" are more secure in a nation made up of strong families. In a nation where marriage is flourishing, men and women are more likely to welcome new life, keeping fertility at a sustainable level. In such a nation, the loss of life to the twin scourges of suicide and homicide is kept to a minimum. In such a nation, there is less need for a state that spoils, superintends, and spends to excess, and more opportunities for citizens to enjoy their liberty and exercise their independence. And in such a nation, ordinary people are much more likely to have a shot at the American Dream and, more importantly, a good and happy life. But ours is not such a nation right now, and too many of our citizens are paying a high price for marriage's falling fortunes, especially the most vulnerable.

WHY SO UNHAPPY?

Much of the public conversation about marriage and family has focused on the class divide, one of the most visible signs of marriage's retreat. But, as *Get Married* shows, culture matters as well. Religious and right-leaning Americans, not just educated and affluent Americans like Hastings, are also more likely to be married—and happily married at that. This is in large part because members of the Faithful like Jon and Maria Erickson or Conservatives like Martin and Kimberly Jones are markedly more likely to embrace the values and virtues associated with family-first marriages. In fact, we have uncovered startling

differences between conservatives and liberals, and religious and secular Americans, in how much they value the institution of marriage itself
as well as virtues like the norm of sexual fidelity in marriage. Recall,
for instance, that liberals are now 38 percentage points less likely than
conservatives to say that infidelity is "always" wrong and about 50 percent more likely to report they have had an affair. On the religious
front, we have discovered that when it comes to marital quality, husbands
and wives who share a common faith top the marital happiness charts,
with more than 80 percent of them reporting that they are at least "very
happy" in their marriages. Today, on the American family scene, we have
learned that both religious and conservative men and women are much
more likely to identify with the values and virtues that sustain strong and
stable marriages than are their secular and/or liberal fellow Americans.

These cultural divides related to marriage and family life seem only
to be growing among young men and women, especially in the wake of
what journalist Matthew Yglesias has called "The Great Awokening"—
the period since 2014 when far-left takes on gender, race, environmental
concerns, and social justice have achieved new salience among today's
progressive-minded young adults.[6] New ideas about sex, gender, and
family life—arising from #MeToo, third-wave feminism, the academy,
and especially social media, among other venues—are coursing through
young adult circles, having an outsize impact on relationships among left-
leaning and/or more secular young adults. Worries about sexual assault,
the rise of fluid gender identities, the absence of clear dating norms,
negative feelings about the opposite sex, and too much time devoted to
screens rather than in-person relationships are especially concentrated
among progressive young men and women, particularly left-leaning and
more secular-minded women.[7] What's more, young men and women of
a more secular or progressive bent are also more likely to prioritize work
and individual freedom over getting married and having children; they
are the ones most likely to buy into the increasingly popular notion that
you need not be "married to have a happy and fulfilling life," in the
words of family scholars Brian Willoughby and Spencer James.[8]

Alexandra, a twenty-nine-year-old finishing her doctorate in psychology at the University of North Carolina, describes herself as a "very
politically liberal person." She has witnessed these dynamics playing

out in eight years of dating men ranging from their mid-twenties to their early forties in and around Chapel Hill. Most of the men she has met are "either not valuing marriage at all" or have no clear timeline regarding marriage. Many of them are "much more short-term focused" in their approach to relationships—they "want to date me, they want to see how long it's going to take for me to sleep with them, etcetera." But the typical response she has gotten from men when they are pressed about longer-term plans, including marriage, is "Why can't we just date for a few years? Like it's fun for that few years?" In the main, most of the men she has dated have no interest in getting married any time soon.

Alexandra attributes these men's unwillingness to put a ring on it (in part) to three things: worries about how marriage would affect their ability to pursue future job opportunities in a different city (what she calls the "two-body problem"), the fact that "concepts of obligation and responsibility are absolutely horrible taboo words now," and a "lack of clarity about life direction," which defines the lives of many young men in her circle.

Alexandra's experiences with three boyfriends who *were* more marriage-minded only underline the challenges facing more progressive-minded women today. Her relationship with an Indian American boyfriend ended when his parents threatened to cut him off should he marry a non-Indian. She ended the two other serious relationships because of ideological differences—namely, they were too conservative for her. In one case, she reports, "it actually ended up being Donald Trump that broke us up." Because of his support for Trump, they found there was "less and less for us to talk about in common."

Or take the experience of Taylor, the thirty-three-year-old graphic designer from Denver introduced in chapter 1. When she was in her twenties, she held a more progressive view of the world that left her more skeptical of men and inclined to postpone marriage in favor of focusing on getting her career launched. "I think that a lot of the cultural war stuff [led me to] viewing men as predators," or just negatively in general, "even when I didn't really have much evidence" that they deserved to be viewed that way. Taylor thinks this perspective limited her willingness to give the men she met and dated in her twenties due consideration.

Moreover, in the progressive circles she ran in as a twentysomething, as we saw earlier, Taylor was encouraged to focus on having fun and building her career. But knowing what she knows now, Taylor believes she had the wrong focus in her twenties.

This conclusion was only cemented after observing a recent boss's approach to life and love. Her boss was "just a couple years older than I am and, you know, she was really beautiful and just very talented and friendly and outgoing," Taylor noted. The woman worked long hours, "like, eight until seven. And she had told me that she was divorced, and she was like, 'Well, I want to date people but I'm just always so busy.' And I'm just sitting there thinking like, *This [job] isn't worth it. None of this is worth it.*" Now that she is in her early thirties and single, Taylor is worried she may not be able to attain what she has come to believe is truly worth it—a husband and family.

Alexandra's and Taylor's experiences dovetail with a series of emerging trends among men and women today, insofar as the closing of the American heart is increasingly concentrated among men and women who lean left or are not religious. From 1990 to 2018, demographer Lyman Stone and colleagues found growing gaps in both marriage and childlessness among prime-aged adults by partisanship and religiosity. For instance, the gap in childlessness between secular and religious women ages eighteen to fifty-five grew from about 10 percentage points in 1990 to around 15 percentage points in 2018.[9] Another recent study of Republican and Democratic high-school seniors found that the partisan gap in desired fertility has flipped in recent years. Prior to the early 2000s, Republican high-school seniors were more likely to say they did not want children, but since 2014, Democratic high-school seniors have been more likely to report they want to be childless.[10]

This ideological and religious polarization is also apparent when it comes to dating and marriage among young adults today. For instance, one 2021 survey found that 47 percent of those ages eighteen to forty who rarely or never attend religious services were single, compared to just 28 percent of these young men and women who regularly attend.[11] Likewise, data from the General Social Survey indicate, for example, that the marriage gap between liberal and conservative women ages eighteen to forty grew from 10 percentage points in 2000 to 17 percentage points in 2021, as figure 12.1 illustrates.

FIGURE 12.1: PERCENTAGE OF WOMEN (18–40) WHO ARE MARRIED, BY IDEOLOGY, 2000–2021

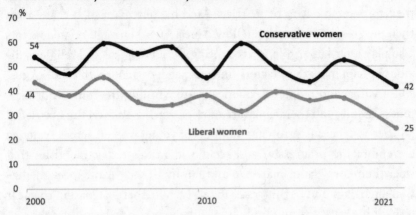

Based on women aged 18 to 40. Results for moderate women are not shown.
Source: General Social Survey, 2000–2021.

This polarization in marriage, childbearing, and singleness is note-worthy for two reasons. First, psychologists like Jonathan Haidt and journalists like Michelle Goldberg have pointed out that liberals are less likely than conservatives to be flourishing emotionally today. They are, for instance, less happy than conservatives. Haidt, Goldberg, and others believe this ideological divide in happiness has been driven largely by technological and worldview factors—e.g., liberals use social media more often and are more likely to take a more "catastrophizing" view of society—that leave left-leaning young adults vulnerable to a dark view of the world. But the growing ideological and religious divide in matters of the *heart* also looms large in explaining this polarization.[12]

When you look at reports of happiness among prime-aged adults (eighteen to fifty-five), who have been the central focus of *Get Married*, you see that conservatives are markedly happier than liberals, and churchgoing Americans also have a significantly sunnier outlook than their fellow Americans who rarely or never attend services. Unhappiness is much more common among left-leaning and secular adults. These patterns are visible in figures 12.2A and 12.2B.

What's striking about these ideological and religious divides, how-ever, is that they *shrink* when you factor in marital status and marital happiness. In fact, about one-third of the happiness advantage enjoyed by conservative and religious Americans can be attributed to the fact that they are more likely to be married—and happily married at that—than their progressive and secular fellow Americans. Marriage-related factors also play a far larger role in accounting for ideological and religious divides in happiness than factors like race, age, or gender. In other words, conservative and religious Americans are winning the "pursuit of happiness" game, and their signature move is getting and staying married.[13]

Second, because growing numbers of young women across America are embracing progressive and secular identities today, identities that steer them away from marriage and family life, we can expect the nation's marriage and fertility rates to fall even further—at least in the near term. This retreat from family life is likely to be accelerated by the fact that, according to new survey data, growing numbers of young men are tilting right,[14] influenced no doubt by manosphere figures as varied as Andrew Tate and Jordan Peterson.

This growing ideological divide means that liberal "women and conservative men who want to marry face a particular challenge: "There are not enough single partners of the correct political persuasion available to marry today," as Lyman Stone and I noted in the *Atlantic*. In fact,

FIGURE 12.2A: CONSERVATIVES MORE LIKELY THAN LIBERALS TO BE HAPPY

Percent of adults aged 18 to 55

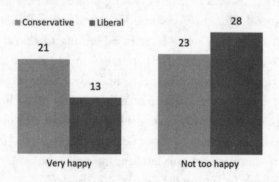

Respondents were asked if they were "very happy," "pretty happy," or "not too happy." "Pretty happy" not shown. Source: General Social Survey (2021).

FIGURE 12.2B: RELIGIOUS ADULTS MORE LIKELY THAN SECULAR ADULTS TO BE HAPPY

Percent of adults aged 18 to 55

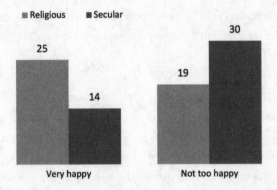

Respondents were asked if they were "very happy," "pretty happy," or "not too happy." "Pretty happy" not shown. "Religious" refers to those who attend religious services at least two to three times a month. "Secular" refers to those who attend services less than once a year or never. Source: General Social Survey (2021).

"about half of these ideologically minded young singles face the prospect of failing to find a partner who shares their politics."[15] This divide will only make it more difficult for young adults to find common relational ground, and their way to the altar, as Alexandra's experience illustrates. These social changes suggest that achieving happiness via a good marriage will likely prove even more elusive for the rising generation than it has been for millennials and Generation X.

TOWARD STRONG, STABLE, SUSTAINABLE FAMILIES

Listen not to what our elites say about marriage, family, and gender. Instead of "Do as they say, not as they do," it's "Do what they're doing, but ignore what they say." Responding in this way to the inverted hypocrisy of the happily and stably married elites among us is one of the key lessons we have learned from *Get Married* when it comes to making sense of the success of American Striver families in recent years.

So what lessons, exactly, have we learned from the marriages of Strivers—as well as Asian Americans, the Faithful, and the Conservatives covered in this book? Why are they more likely to forge happy marriages in the twenty-first century? In general, these masters of marriage are more likely to accord marriage great value, to embrace the virtues that sustain strong marriages, and to be possessed of good family men. More specifically, there are five pillars upon which they are forging strong and stable family-first marriages. They may be summarized as the following five Cs:

1. **COMMUNION.** A "we before me" approach—both in attitude and action—to marriage is key to marital success. This spirit of togetherness is marked by sharing last names and bank accounts, for instance, as well as regular date nights. Forging a sense of communion requires rejecting the individualistic ethos of our culture—which religious and conservative couples are more inclined to do—and devoting time to your better half, which—when it comes to date nights—is more common among religious and Striver couples.

2. **CHILDREN.** Prioritizing the welfare of your children is also a mark of successful family-first marriages. Husbands and wives who view raising children as a primary goal in life and spend a lot of time with their children, from frequent family chores to fun family activities, are generally happier in their marriages and less prone to divorce. This pro-child orientation is common, albeit in somewhat different ways, for all four groups who make up the masters of marriage.

3. **COMMITMENT.** Keeping divorce off the table is one key to succeeding at marriage today. And so is not crossing social, emotional, and physical lines with attractive alternatives encountered at work, the gym, or a party—not to mention online. Husbands and wives who prioritize marital permanence and fidelity are much more likely to be not only stably but happily married because shared commitment fosters trust and emotional security in your relationship. High levels of this kind of marital commitment are especially common among Asian American, Conservative, and Faithful couples.

4. **CASH.** It has fallen out of fashion to publicly discuss the (average) differences between men and women vis-à-vis marriage. But discuss them we must. For what we see is that the happiest and most stably married couples—including elite couples who often talk left on

gender issues—generally appreciate a bit of *vive la différence* in their marriages. One way this is manifested is that wives are especially likely to get and stay married to men who are good providers—a fact worth bearing in mind when couples set up their work and family arrangements. This is one example of how cash matters in today's marriages. Acquiring shared assets also strengthens marriages today. These financial realities help explain why more educated and affluent Americans enjoy stronger and more stable marriages than their poor and working-class fellow citizens, who are less likely to have resources to pool.

5. **COMMUNITY.** Husbands and wives who surround themselves with friends and family who take marriage and family life seriously are much more likely to thrive, especially in a world that discounts and disparages the virtues and values needed to create a strong family. Such communities are most likely to be found in churches, synagogues, temples, and mosques that endow marriage and family life with sacred significance and house fellow believers who take seriously the sacrifices they require. No doubt this is why no group of men and women in America are as happily married—or as happy with their lives—as husbands and wives who share a common faith. So, if you have a religious bone in your body, the data suggest that investing in your local religious congregation is likely to offer significant returns on the quality and stability of your married life.

To be sure, not every husband and wife who is successfully married has a marriage secured by all five of these pillars. But in general, marriages established on these pillars are more likely to flourish today. In turn, men and women in such marriages are more likely to thrive financially, socially, and emotionally insofar as they enjoy the benefit of a strong and stable union. In fact, *Get Married* reveals this paradox regarding the pursuit of happiness in contemporary America: individual happiness is most likely to be found not by directly pursuing it for oneself but by opening your heart to love, marriage, and living for your spouse and family.[16]

Given these truths, we must defy the progressive orthodoxies about marriage, family life, individualism, and gender that now occupy such a central place in our universities, media, pop culture, schools, and corporations, because their messages diminish our odds of forging strong families.[17] We must push back against a culture that tells our young men and women that money and work are more important than marriage and family, discouraging and diverting them from focusing on love and marriage in their twenties and early thirties, when they have the best shot at finding a spouse and maximizing their chances for marital success.[18] We must instead encourage young men and women—along with middle-aged husbands and wives navigating the challenges and occasional doldrums of marriage and family life—to reject the me-first ethos of our culture and open their hearts to a we-first approach to love and marriage built around the distinctive values and virtues embodied by the masters of marriage.

Opening the hearts and minds of young men and women to the idea of committed love and lifelong marriage will entail working with conservative cultural institutions playing a rising role on the scene, as well as engaging mainstream institutions and publications that still occupy our cultural heights. It also means supplying religious institutions—from nondenominational ministries to the Roman Catholic "Word on Fire" initiative to Jewish day schools and Latter-day Saints seminaries—with the latest information and insights about family life to improve their ability to form their flocks in a family-friendly way. This will also entail working with family-minded educators and politicians to reform America's public schools, which educate almost nine in ten American children,[19] so that they handle family-life education more truthfully.

The path toward renewing marriage also includes identifying and amplifying promising civic efforts—like Communio, a new initiative strengthening marriages in churches across America—that have been launched in the last few years to strengthen family life.[20] It means pursuing public policies that will make it easier for Americans to afford families founded upon strong and stable marriages, such as a child allowance for working families and ending marriage penalties in government programs. It means paying special attention to reviving the fortunes of boys and men, too many of whom are failing at school, work, and life, which then limits their appeal and ability to be good family men. Finally, efforts to renew and revive the fortunes of marriage in America must target especially the poor and working class—the two groups for whom marriage has grown weakest in the last half century.

In all these efforts to revive our nation's most important institution, one virtue will be particularly important: *courage*. It will take courage to publicly defy the elite "wisdom" on marriage, family life, and gender in the public square. It will take courage to fight for family policies that challenge the outdated orthodoxies of both parties. It will take courage to launch major new civic and educational efforts to put marriage within reach of poor and working-class couples across America. It will take courage to preach the full truth about marriage and family life from the pulpit. Above all, it will take courage for ordinary men and women to take a risk on lifelong love in a world where so many forces seem arrayed against strong marriages and families. But the future of the American way of life—our lives, our liberty, and the pursuit of our happiness, rightly understood—depends upon making strong and stable marriages possible for all who wish to open their hearts to lifelong love—and to the children who arise from that union.

So, for your own sake—and, indeed, the sake of our civilization— I urge you:

If you're married, honor your commitment to love and cherish your spouse and any children you may have all the days of your life.

And if you haven't tied the knot, then, with wisdom, seek out one worthy of your heart, and get married. It's one of the best decisions you'll ever make.

ACKNOWLEDGMENTS

We are "social animals," as Aristotle taught, which is why we are most likely to thrive when we have good relationships with family and friends. Not surprisingly, this book was researched and written with the help of many colleagues, friends, and family members. I'm also indebted to the institutional support provided by the University of Virginia, the Institute for Family Studies, and the American Enterprise Institute.

At UVA, I would like to thank Jenn Bair, Joyce Holleran, Simone Polillo, and Katherine Shiflett for administrative support. I'm grateful to Gerard Alexander, Mary Kate Cary, Paul Kingston, and Steve Rhoads for exchanging ideas, and to Claire Hungar, Emma Jinks, Laura LaMonica, Kyle McClelland, Dan Nakasone, Sam Richardson, and Howe Whitman for invaluable research assistance. The National Marriage Project at UVA and its many supporters (including the William E. Simon Foundation as well as Greg and Amanda Cash, Andy Krouse, Dave and Carol Myers, and Rachel and Will Ed Settle) provided vital support to this book.

At the Institute for Family Studies (IFS), Wendy Wang, the director of research, played a crucial role in investigating many of the outcomes discussed in the book. Her willingness to explore new questions about American family life—from many angles—is deeply appreciated. Michael Toscano played a central role in directing the work of IFS and provided strategic advice about how to frame the book's central arguments. Brigette Gustafson and Wendy Mason provided administrative support, and I benefited from the research assistance of Joe Bondi,

Emma Fuentes, Riley Peterson, and Elizabeth Self. I'm also grateful for the insights of Patrick Brown, Jason Carroll, Jenet Erickson, Alysse ElHage, Spencer James, Galena Rhoades, Scott Stanley, Lyman Stone, Jean Twenge, and Nicholas Wolfinger, all of whom have worked with IFS in one way or another. I appreciate Betsy Stokes for doing a masterly job editing the final draft of the manuscript. IFS board members Jeff Adams, Rachel Brough, Fred Clark, Rebecca Horner, Rick Hough, and John Stanley—as well as IFS supporters Manny and Linda Cirenza, Matt and Jennie Hantzmon, Jim and Molly Perry, Brian and Sheila Svoboda, Gellert Dornay, and Gerry Mitchell, along with the Vine & Branches Foundation and John Hood at the John William Pope Foundation—have supported the research in myriad ways. Paul Edwards at the Wheatley Institute has also provided invaluable institutional assistance. Jeff Dew furnished exhaustive analyses of the 2022 State of Our Unions Survey as well as many insights on the contemporary character of married life. I'm grateful also to Jane Lankes for reviewing General Social Survey work done for the book.

At the American Enterprise Institute, I would like to thank Arthur Brooks and Robert Doar for providing a collegial intellectual home to me in the years that the research for this book was conducted. I'm also grateful to Tim Carney, Ron Haskins, Yuval Levin, Richard Reeves, Ian Rowe, Belle Sawhill, Michael Strain, Ryan Streeter, and Scott Winship for their commitment to exchanging ideas and advancing the national conversation about American family life in the AEI-Brookings orbit. Peyton Roth and Tim Sprunt provided crucial research support at AEI.

Over the years, I have also benefited from reading and engaging with Richard Albertson, Marcy Carlson, Oren Cass, Andrew Cherlin, J. P. DeGance, Kathy Edin, Paula England, Richard and Linda Eyre, Maggie Gallagher, Alan Hawkins, Melissa Kearney, Wells King, Bob Lerman, Lisa May, Sara McLanahan, Steven Nock, Joe Price, Mark Regnerus, Aaron Renn, and Linda Waite on family matters. Needless to say, the scholars and advocates thanked here do not necessarily agree with every or any of the major claims made in the book.

Parts of this book appeared first in the *Atlantic*, the *Federalist*, *National Review*, the *Wall Street Journal*, the *Washington Post*, and especially the *Deseret News*. I'm grateful to the editors at all these publications, especially to Hal Boyd, for helping me develop my thinking on marriage and family life in the run-up to this book.

Howard Yoon, my agent at WME, pushed me hard to make this book more engaging to the general public and steered me toward Eric Nelson, my editor at HarperCollins. I am forever grateful to Howard for his patience with this project. Eric and his team, Hannah Long and James Neidhardt, helped me refine and reorganize the project; they also made many incisive suggestions to introduce new themes and angles to the book. This book is much better for their editorial interventions.

I'm grateful to my children; sister, Melissa; in-laws, Pam and Bill; and mom for their moral support and patience over the years. They have showed an unflagging interest in the project and put up with too many absences from family activities or gatherings as a consequence of my research and writing. In writing this book, I am most indebted to my wife, Danielle, for sharing her wisdom about life and love, for putting up with me when I was bogged down with writing, for her dedication to living a family-first way of life, and for always telling me the truth. *Cor ad cor loquitur.*

NOTES

Preface: Devaluing Our Most Important Institution

1. Josephine Franks, "Who Is Andrew Tate, the Self-Styled 'King of Toxic Masculinity' under House Arrest in Romania?" *Sky News*, March 31, 2023, https://tinyurl.com/WilcoxGMa.

2. Sigma Talk, "Andrew Tate on Why Modern Men Don't Want Marriage," YouTube video, December 26, 2022, https://youtu.be/W9SIxE6wWHo.

3. Richard V. Reeves, "Andrew Tate and the West's Lost Boys," *UnHerd*, October 30, 2022, https://tinyurl.com/WilcoxGMb.

4. Molly Smith, "Women Who Stay Single and Don't Have Kids Are Getting Richer," *Bloomberg*, August 31, 2022, https://tinyurl.com/WilcoxGMc.

5. Mandy Len Catron, "What You Lose When You Gain a Spouse," *Atlantic*, July 2, 2019, https://tinyurl.com/WilcoxGMd; Lauren Sandler, "Having It All without Having Children," *Time*, August 12, 2013, https://tinyurl.com/WilcoxGMe; Lara Bazelon, "Divorce Can Be an Act of Radical Self-Love," *New York Times*, September 30, 2021, https://tinyurl.com/WilcoxGMf.

6. US Census Bureau, American Community Survey, 2020. Based on women aged 18 to 55. "Mothers" refers to those with children living in the same household. Family income includes any income from family members living with the respondent.

7. US Bureau of Labor Statistics, National Longitudinal Survey of Youth, 1979 cohort (NLSY79). Family net wealth was measured in 2016 at ages 51–60, and adjusted for inflation (2020 dollars).

8. NLSY79.

9. Institute for Family Studies and Wheatley Institute, State of Our Unions Survey, 2021 (YouGov).

10. Deseret News and Center for the Study of Elections and Democracy at Brigham Young University, American Family Survey, 2022 (YouGov).

11. Bazelon, "Divorce Can Be an Act of Radical Self-Love."

12. Nicholas Zill, "Family Still Matters for Key Indicators of Student Performance," *Institute for Family Studies Blog*, April 6, 2020, https://tinyurl.com /WilcoxGMg.

13. Shannon E. Cavanagh, "Family Structure History and Adolescent Adjustment," *Journal of Family Issues* 29, no. 7 (January 2008): 944–980, https://doi .org/10.1177/0192513X07311232.

14. Camron S. Devor, Susan D. Stewart, and Cassandra Dorius, "Parental Divorce, Educational Expectations, and Educational Attainment among Young Adults," Center for Family and Demographic Research at Bowling Green State University, working paper, 2016, https://tinyurl.com/WilcoxGMh . NLSY97 analysis in chapter 4.

15. Brad Wilcox and Alysse Elhage, "Why Conservative Women Report Being the Happiest—and How You Can Be, Too," *Newsweek*, October 4, 2022, https://tinyurl.com/WilcoxGMi; Kasey J. Eickmeyer, Wendy D. Manning, Monica A. Longmore, and Peggy C. Giordano, "Exploring the Married-Cohabiting Income Pooling Gap among Young Adults," *Journal of Family and Economic Issues*, January 28, 2023, https://doi.org/10.1007/s10834-023 -09885-0.

16. Kashmira Gander, "'Deaths of Despair': U.S. Life Expectancy Has Been Falling since 2014, with Biggest Impacts in Rust Belt and Ohio Valley," *Newsweek*, November 26, 2019, https://tinyurl.com/WilcoxGMj; Meryl Kornfield, "U.S. Surpasses Record 100,000 Overdose Deaths in 2021," *Washington Post*, May 11, 2022, https://tinyurl.com/WilcoxGMk.

17. Richard Reeves, *Of Boys and Men* (Washington, DC: Brookings Institution, 2022); Vivian P. Ta, Amanda N. Gesselman, Brea L. Perry, Helen E. Fisher, and Justin R. Garcia, "Stress of Singlehood: Marital Status, Domain-Specific Stress, and Anxiety in a National U.S. Sample," *Journal of Social and Clinical Psychology* 36, no. 6 (June 2017), https://doi.org/10.1521/jscp.2017.36.6.461; "Our Epidemic of Loneliness and Isolation," US Surgeon General's Advisory on the Healing Effects of Social Connection and Community, 2023, https:// tinyurl.com/WilcoxGMm.

18. Harry Enten, "American Happiness Hits Record Lows," CNN Politics, February 2, 2022, https://tinyurl.com/WilcoxGMn; Jean Twenge, "Marriage and Money: How Much Does Marriage Explain the Growing Class Divide

in Happiness?" *Institute for Family Studies Blog*, July 20, 2020, https://tinyurl .com/WilcoxGMr.

19. Brad Wilcox and Chris Bullivant, "The American Dream Can Be Achieved If We Spend More Time Building Strong, Stable Families," *USA Today*, May 20, 2022, https://tinyurl.com/WilcoxGMp, or no paywall at https:// tinyurl.com/WilcoxGMq.

20. Wilcox and Bullivant.

21. Raj Chetty, Nathaniel Hendren, Patrick Kline, and Emmanuel Saez, "Where Is the Land of Opportunity? The Geography of Intergenerational Mobility in the United States," *Quarterly Journal of Economics* 129, no. 4 (November 2014): 1553–1623, https://doi.org/10.1093/qje/qju022.

22. Wilcox and Bullivant, "American Dream."

23. Twenge, "Marriage and Money: How Much Does Marriage Explain the Growing Class Divide in Happiness?"

Introduction: Marriage since the "Me" Decade

1. Tom Wolfe, "The 'Me' Decade and the Third Great Awakening," *New York*, August 23, 1976, https://nymag.com/news/features/45938/.

2. Dan Kois, "Free to Be You and Me 40th Anniversary: How Did a Kids Album by a Bunch of Feminists Change Everything?" *Slate*, October 23, 2012, https://tinyurl.com/WilcoxGMs.

3. Marlo Thomas, *Free to Be . . . You and Me*, vinyl record, Bell Records, 1972.

4. Susan Gettleman and Janet Markowitz, *The Courage to Divorce* (New York: Simon & Schuster, 1974), 45.

5. Nicholas Zill and Brad Wilcox, "1-in-2: A New Estimate of the Share of Children Being Raised by Married Parents," *Institute for Family Studies Blog*, February 27, 2018, https://tinyurl.com/WilcoxGMt.

6. Joseph Henrich, *The Weirdest People in the World: How the West Became Psychologically Peculiar and Particularly Prosperous* (New York: Farrar, Straus, and Giroux, 2021), 71–72.

7. Linda Waite and Maggie Gallagher, *The Case for Marriage: Why Married People Are Happier, Healthier, and Better Off Financially* (New York: Doubleday, 2000), 34.

8. David Popenoe, *Life without Father: Compelling New Evidence that Fatherhood and Marriage Are Indispensable for the Good of Children and Society* (New York: Free Press, 1996); Paula England, "*The Case for Marriage*," book review, *Contemporary Sociology* 30, no. 6 (November 2001): 564–65, https://doi.org/10

.2307/3088984; W. Bradford Wilcox, Robert I. Lerman, and Joseph Price, "Strong Families, Prosperous States: Do Healthy Families Affect the Wealth of States?" American Enterprise Institute, October 19, 2015, https://tinyurl .com/WilcoxGMu.

9. US Census Bureau, "Annual Social and Economic Supplements," https://tiny url.com/WilcoxGMv.

10. Pamela Paul, "How Divorce Lost Its Groove," *New York Times*, June 17, 2011, https://tinyurl.com/WilcoxGMw.

11. W. Bradford Wilcox and Elizabeth Marquardt, *When Marriage Disappears: The New Middle America*, State of Our Unions series, Institute for American Values and National Marriage Project, 2010, https://tinyurl.com/Wilcox GM75; US Census, Current Population Survey (2018).

12. Nicholas A. Christakis, *Blueprint: The Evolutionary Origins of a Good Society* (New York: Little, Brown, 2019), 154, 173.

13. Richard Reeves, "How to Save Marriage in America," *Atlantic*, February 13, 2014, https://tinyurl.com/WilcoxGMx.

14. The General Social Survey (GSS) is a project of the independent research organization NORC at the University of Chicago, with principal funding from the National Science Foundation.

15. I also changed identifying details of their lives to protect their anonymity.

16. Wendy Wang, "A Portrait of Contemporary Family Living Arrangements for U.S. Children," *Institute for Family Studies Blog*, April 14, 2020, https:// tinyurl.com/WilcoxGMy.

Chapter 1: The Closing of the American Heart

1. David Brooks, *The Road to Character* (New York: Random House, 2015), xi.

2. Author's analysis of data made available through American Family Survey (2022), public dataset, 2018.

3. Rachel Minkin and Juliana Menasce Horowitz, "Parenting in America Today," Pew Research Center, January 24, 2023, https://tinyurl.com/Wilcox GMz.

4. Orit Taubman-Ben-Ari, "Well-Being and Personal Growth in Emerging Motherhood: And What about Meaning?," in *Meaning in Positive and Existential Psychology* (New York: Springer, 2014), 415–434; Brad Wilcox and Wendy Wang, "The Group That's Happiest in the Pandemic May Surprise You," *Deseret News*, September 28, 2021, https://tinyurl.com/WilcoxGMa1; Robin W. Simon, "The Joys of Parenthood, Reconsidered," *Contexts* 7, no. 2 (May 1, 2008): 40–45, https://doi.org/10.1525/ctx.2008.7.2.40.

5. Julie M. Zissimopoulos, Benjamin R. Karney, and Amy J. Rauer, "Marriage and Economic Well Being at Older Ages," *Review of Economics of the Household* 13, no. 1 (2013): 1–35, https://doi.org/10.1007/s11150-013-9205-x; Teresa A. Mauldin et al., "Barriers and Facilitators to Saving Behavior in Low- to Moderate-Income Households," *Journal of Financial Counseling and Planning* 27, no. 2 (2016): 231–251, https://doi.org/10.1891/1052-3073.27.2.231; Robin W. Simon, "Revisiting the Relationships among Gender, Marital Status, and Mental Health," *American Journal of Sociology* 107, no. 4 (2002): 1065–1096, https://doi.org/10.1086/339225; Robert G. Wood, Brian Goslin, and Sarah Avellar, "The Effects of Marriage on Health: A Synthesis of Recent Research Evidence," Mathematica Policy Research, June 19, 2007, https://tinyurl.com/WilcoxGM1; Hasida Ben-Zur, "Loneliness, Optimism, and Well-Being among Married, Divorced, and Widowed Individuals," *Journal of Psychology* 146, no. 1–2 (2012): 23–36, https://doi.org/10.1080/00223980.2010.548414; and Waite and Gallagher, *The Case for Marriage*.

6. Analyses of the 2014–2018 GSS indicate that marital status was a stronger predictor of the odds of self-reported happiness for men and women ages 18 to 55 than education level, employment status, family income, age, race, and gender. Analyses also indicated that marital quality was a stronger predictor of the odds of self-reported happiness than education level, family income, job satisfaction, self-rated health, sexual frequency, and religious attendance. Here, marital quality was measured by analyzing married respondents who were "very happy" in their marriage compared to those who were "pretty happy" or "not too happy" and those who were not married. The GSS data indicate that 58 percent of those ages 18 to 55 who are "very happy" in their marriages are "very happy" with life, compared to 12 percent of those who are less than "very happy" in their marriages, and 21 percent of those who are not married. Likewise, job satisfaction was measured by analyzing employed respondents who were "very happy" in their jobs compared to those who were less than "very happy" in their jobs and those who were not employed. See also Norval Glenn and Charles Weaver, "The Contribution of Marital Happiness to Global Happiness," *Journal of Marriage and Family* 43, no. 1 (February 1981): 161–168, https://www.jstor.org/stable/351426; Eli J. Finkel, *The All-or-Nothing Marriage: How the Best Marriages Work* (New York: Dutton, 2017), 24.

7. Robert Waldinger and Marc Schulz, *The Good Life: Lessons from the World's Longest Scientific Study of Happiness* (New York: Simon & Schuster, 2023).

8. George E. Vaillant and Kenneth Mukamal, "Successful Aging," *Journal of American Psychiatry* 158, no. 6 (2001): 839–847.

9. Robert Waldinger, "The Good Life," TEDx Talks, YouTube video, November 30, 2015, https://youtu.be/q-7zAkwAOYg.

10. Philip Cohen, "How to Live in a World Where Marriage Is in Decline," *Atlantic*, June 4, 2013, https://tinyurl.com/WilcoxGM2.

11. John Gottman, *Why Marriages Succeed or Fail* (London: Bloomsbury, 1994), 16.

12. Wendy Wang, W. Bradford Wilcox, and Lyman Stone, "New Census Data: Key Takeaways on Divorce, Marriage, and Fertility in the U.S.," *Institute for Family Studies Blog*, September 22, 2022, https://tinyurl.com/Wilcox GM3.

13. Michelle J. K. Osterman et al., "Births: Final Data for 2020," *National Vital Statistics Reports* 70, no. 17 (February 2022).

14. "The American Family Today," Pew Research Center, December 17, 2015, https://tinyurl.com/WilcoxGM4.

15. Nicholas Zill, "Growing Up with Mom and Dad: New Data Confirm the Tide Is Turning," *Institute for Family Studies Blog*, June 18, 2021, https://tinyurl.com/WilcoxGM5.

16. Author's analysis of data from US Census (1960), made available through Steven Ruggles et al., IPUMS (2020), https://doi.org/10.18128/D010.V10.0; Christopher A. Julian, "A Decade of Changes in Shares of Single, Cohabiting, and Married Individuals, 2012–2022," National Center for Family & Marriage Research, 2023, https://doi.org/10.25035/ncfmr/fp-23-07.

17. Author's analysis of data from US Census (1960) and American Community Survey (2021), made available through Ruggles et al., IPUMS.

18. Richard Fry and Kim Parker, "Rising Share of U.S. Adults Are Living without a Spouse or Partner," Pew Research Center, October 5, 2021, https://tinyurl.com/WilcoxGM6.

19. Fry and Parker.

20. Steven Martin, Nan Marie Astone, and H. Elizabeth Peters, "Fewer Marriages, More Divergence: Marriage Projections for Millennials to Age 40," Urban Institute, April 29, 2014, https://tinyurl.com/WilcoxGM7.

21. Wendy Wang, "Record Share of Americans Have Never Married," Pew Research Center, September 24, 2014, https://tinyurl.com/WilcoxGM8.

22. General Social Survey (2014–2018).

23. Author's analysis of the 2021 American Community Survey, in Ruggles et al., IPUMS; Philip N. Cohen, "The Coming Divorce Decline," *Socius* 5 (2019): 1–6.

24. US Census Bureau, *Current Population Survey, June Fertility Supplement*, 1976 and 2020.

25. W. Bradford Wilcox and Lyman Stone, "Empty Cradles Mean a Bleaker Future," *Newsweek*, June 24, 2020, https://tinyurl.com/WilcoxGM9.

26. Lyman Stone, "How Many Kids Do Women Want?" *Institute for Family Studies Blog*, June 1, 2018, https://tinyurl.com/WilcoxGM10.

27. Valerie M. Hudson and Andrea M. den Boer, "Bare Branches: The Security Implications of Asia's Surplus Male Population," *Belfer Center Studies in International Security* (Cambridge, MA: MIT Press, 2004).

28. US Congress Joint Economic Committee, "An Invisible Tsunami: 'Aging Alone' and Its Effect on Older Americans, Families, and Taxpayers," Social Capital Project, January 24, 2019.

29. US Census and American Community Survey, in Ruggles et al., IPUMS.

30. Wilcox and Stone, "Empty Cradles."

31. John Yoon, "South Korea Breaks Record for World's Lowest Fertility Rate, Again," *New York Times*, August 24, 2022, https://tinyurl.com/WilcoxGM11.

32. Ben Dooley, "Japan Shrinks by 500,000 People as Births Fall to Lowest Number since 1874," *New York Times*, December 24, 2019, https://www.nytimes.com/2019/12/24/world/asia/japan-birthrate-shrink.html.

33. W. Bradford Wilcox and Samuel Sturgeon, "Too Much Netflix, Not Enough Chill: Why Young Americans Are Having Less Sex," *Politico*, June 20, 2022, http://politi.co/2EPna6g.

34. Wilcox and Sturgeon, "Too Much Netflix"; University of Tokyo, "Japan Increasingly Single, Disinterested in Dating: Study," Phys.org, Science X Network, November 9, 2020, https://tinyurl.com/WilcoxGM12; National Institute of Population and Social Security Research, *Fifteenth Japanese National Fertility Survey in 2015: Marriage Process and Fertility of Married Couples' Attitudes Toward Marriage and Family among Japanese Singles*, March 2017, https://tinyurl.com/WilcoxGM13; University of Tokyo, "First National Estimates of Virginity in Japan," *EurekAlert!* American Association for the Advancement of Science, April 7, 2019, https://www.eurekalert.org/news-releases/494759.

35. "Seniors Living Alone in Japan Topped 6 Million for First Time in 2015," *Japan Times*, July 13, 2016, https://tinyurl.com/WilcoxGM14.

36. Norimitsu Onishi, "A Generation in Japan Faces a Lonely Death," *New York Times*, November 30, 2017, https://tinyurl.com/WilcoxGM15.

37. Wilcox and Stone, "Empty Cradles."

Chapter 2: The Masters of Marriage

1. John Gottman, *Why Marriages Succeed or Fail* (New York: Bloomsbury, 1994), 24.

2. John Gottman, "Making Marriage Work," Gottman Institute, YouTube video, January 30, 2018, https://youtu.be/AKTyPgwfPgg.

3. John Gottman, *What Predicts Divorce? The Relationship between Marital Processes and Marital Outcomes* (New York: Psychology Press, 1993).

4. Anna North, "Our Love Affair with Predicting Divorce," *New York Times*, July 11, 2014, https://tinyurl.com/WilcoxGM16.

5. Gottman, *Why Marriages Succeed or Fail*. The original Four Horsemen in the New Testament represented the four plagues of war, famine, pestilence, and death.

6. Gottman, "Making Marriage Work."

7. Anderson, "Four Negative Patterns That Predict Divorce (Part 1)" YouTube video, April 18, 2012, https://youtu.be/FJDN3PKZ1KE.

8. North, "Our Love Affair with Predicting Divorce."

9. Statistics mapping out family structure in Seattle neighborhoods are derived from the US Census Bureau, Harvard University, and Brown University, "The Opportunity Atlas," undated, interactive infographic, https://www.opportunity atlas.org/. They apply to the share of children living in single-parent families from 2012 to 2016, by US Census tract.

10. Ian Rowe, *Agency: The Four Point Plan (F.R.E.E.) for All Children to Overcome the Victimhood Narrative and Discover Their Pathway to Power* (Conshohocken, PA: Templeton Press, 2022), 82.

11. Gary Buiso, "Mobile DNA-Testing Truck Gives New York City Fathers Paternity Proof," *New York Post*, June 16, 2013, https://tinyurl.com/Wilcox GM17.

12. "Opportunity Atlas."

13. "Opportunity Atlas."

14. "Opportunity Atlas."

15. Richard Fry and Paul Taylor, "The Rise of Residential Segregation by Income," Pew Research Center, August 1, 2012, https://tinyurl.com/WilcoxGM18.

16. Eli J. Finkel, "Educated Americans Paved the Way for Divorce—Then Embraced Marriage," *Atlantic*, January 8, 2019, https://tinyurl.com/Wilcox GM19.

17. Charles Murray, *Coming Apart: The State of White America, 1960–2010* (New York: Crown, 2013).

18. American Community Survey, 2021.

19. American Community Survey.

20. James Webb, *Born Fighting: How the Scots-Irish Shaped America* (New York: Crown, 2005).

21. W. Bradford Wilcox, "Who Said Red States Couldn't Foster Stable Families?" *National Review*, June 12, 2015, https://tinyurl.com/WilcoxGM20; Raymond D. Gastil, "Homicide and a Regional Culture of Violence," *American Sociological Review* 36, no. 3 (1971): 412–27, https://doi.org/10.2307/2093082; Pauline Grosjean, "A History of Violence: The Culture of Honor and Homicide in the U.S. South," *Journal of the European Economic Association* 12, no. 5 (October 1, 2014): 1285–1316, https://doi.org/10.1111/jeea.12096.

22. Deseret News and Center for the Study of Elections and Democracy at Brigham Young University, American Family Survey, 2022 (YouGov).

23. James Hunter, *Culture Wars: The Struggle to Control the Family, Art, Education, Law, and Politics In America* (New York: Basic, 1992); Brad Wilcox and Alysse ElHage, "Why Conservative Women Report Being the Happiest—and How You Can Be, Too," *Newsweek*, October 4, 2022, https://tinyurl.com/WilcoxGM21; Megan Brenan, "Americans Say Birth Control, Divorce Most 'Morally Acceptable,'" *Gallup*, June 9, 2022, https://tinyurl.com/Wilcox GM22.

24. Matthew Yglesias, "The Great Awokening," *Vox*, April 1, 2019, https://tinyurl.com/WilcoxGM23.

25. W. Bradford Wilcox and Vijay Menon, "No, Republicans Aren't Hypocrites on Family Values," *Politico*, November 28, 2017, https://tinyurl.com/Wilcox GM24; W. Bradford Wilcox and Nicholas H. Wolfinger, "Red Families vs. Blue Families: Which Are Happier?" *Institute for Family Studies Blog*, August 17, 2015, https://tinyurl.com/WilcoxGM25.

26. Chris Arnade, *Dignity: Seeking Respect in Back Row America* (New York: Sentinel, 2019), 44–45.

27. Wendy Wang and W. Bradford Wilcox, *State of Contradiction: Progressive Family Culture, Traditional Family Structure in California*, Institute for Family Studies, 2020, https://tinyurl.com/WilcoxGM26.

28. Abby Budiman and Neil G. Ruiz, "Key Facts about Asian Americans, a Diverse and Growing Population," Pew Research Center, April 29, 2021, https://tinyurl.com/WilcoxGM27.

29. Bruce Drake, "Asian-Americans Lead All Others in Household Income," Pew Research Center, April 16, 2013, https://tinyurl.com/WilcoxGM28.

30. W. Bradford Wilcox and Wendy Wang, "Strong Families Are Living the Dream," *American Mind*, Claremont Institute, February 24, 2020, https://tinyurl.com/WilcoxGM29.

31. Education and race/ethnicity data from American Community Survey (2021); ideology and religion data from General Social Survey (2014–2018).

32. W. Bradford Wilcox and Nicholas H. Wolfinger, *Soul Mates: Religion, Sex, Love, and Marriage among African Americans and Latinos*, illustrated ed. (New York: Oxford University Press, 2016); Tyler J. VanderWeele, "Religious Service Attendance, Marriage, and Health," *Institute for Family Studies Blog*, November 29, 2016, https://tinyurl.com/WilcoxGM30.

33. In the General Social Survey (2014–2018), ideology was a weaker predictor of divorce than education, ethnicity, and religion.

34. General Social Survey.

35. Yuanting Zhang and Jennifer Van Hook, "Marital Dissolution among Interracial Couples," *Journal of Marriage and Family* 71 (February 2009): 95–107.

36. General Social Survey. Based on adults ages 18 to 55 with children.

37. Controlling for age and gender, in the General Social Survey, religion is the most powerful predictor of marital quality, followed by education, a conservative identity, and race/ethnicity.

38. General Social Survey.

39. W. Bradford Wilcox, Jason S. Carroll, and Laurie DeRose, "Religious Men Can Be Devoted Dads, Too," *New York Times*, May 18, 2019, https://tinyurl.com/WilcoxGM31.

Chapter 3: The Flying Solo Myth

1. W. Bradford Wilcox, "Is Marriage Good for Men?" Prager University, May 9, 2016, https://youtu.be/EtvfHnZMcOY.

2. W. Bradford Wilcox and Nicholas H. Wolfinger, "Debunking the Ball and Chain Myth of Marriage for Men," *Institute for Family Studies Blog*, February 7, 2017, https://tinyurl.com/WilcoxGM32.

3. Amisha Padnani, "Is Marriage a Prize?" *New York Times*, May 15, 2020, https://tinyurl.com/WilcoxGM33.

4. Juliana Menasce Horowitz, Nikki Graf, and Gretchen Livingston, "Marriage and Cohabitation in the U.S.," Pew Research Center, November 9, 2019, https://tinyurl.com/WilcoxGM34.

5. Padnani, "Is Marriage a Prize?"

6. "State of YOUR Union: Don't Get Married," video, MSNBC, https://tinyurl.com/WilcoxGM35; Julie Bindel, Bruno Rinvolucri, and Leah Green, "Women, Face It: Marriage Can Never Be Feminist," video, *Guardian*, May 25, 2016, https://tinyurl.com/WilcoxGM36.

7. Horowitz, Graf, and Livingston, "Marriage and Cohabitation."

8. Matt Bruenig, "Marriage and Poverty," *American Prospect*, January 9, 2014, https://prospect.org/power/marriage-poverty/.

9. This story is adapted from W. Bradford Wilcox, "Don't Be a Bachelor: Why Married Men Work Harder, Smarter, and Make More Money," *Washington Post*, April 2, 2015, https://tinyurl.com/WilcoxGM37.

10. Elizabeth H. Gorman, "Marriage and Money: The Effect of Marital Status on Attitudes toward Pay and Finances," *Work and Occupations* 27, no. 1 (February 1, 2000): 64–88, https://doi.org/10.1177/0730888400027001004; W. Bradford Wilcox, "For Richer, for Poorer: How Family Structures Economic Success in America," American Enterprise Institute, October 28, 2014, https://tinyurl.com/WilcoxGM38; Steven L. Nock, *Marriage in Men's Lives* (New York: Oxford University Press, 1998).

11. Elizabeth H. Gorman, "Bringing Home the Bacon: Marital Allocation of Income-Earning Responsibility, Job Shifts, and Men's Wages," *Journal of Marriage and Family* 61, no. 1 (1999): 110–122, https://doi.org/10.2307/353887.

12. Kate Antonovics and Robert Town, "Are All the Good Men Married? Uncovering the Sources of the Marital Wage Premium," *American Economic Review* 94, no. 2 (2004): 317–321, https://doi.org/10.1257/0002828041301876.

13. John Iceland and Ilana Redstone, "The Declining Earnings Gap between Young Women and Men in the United States, 1979–2018," *Social Science Research* 92 (November 1, 2020): 102479, https://doi.org/10.1016/j.ssresearch.2020.102479.

14. Avner Ahituv and Robert I. Lerman, "How Do Marital Status, Work Effort, and Wage Rates Interact?" *Demography* 44, no. 3 (August 1, 2007): 623–647, https://doi.org/10.1353/dem.2007.0021.

15. Alexandra Killewald and Ian Lundberg, "New Evidence against a Causal Marriage Wage Premium," *Demography* 54, no. 3 (June 1, 2017): 1007–1028, https://doi.org/10.1007/s13524-017-0566-2.

16. Robert VerBruggen and Wendy Wang, *The Real Housewives of America: Dad's Income and Mom's Work*, Institute for Family Studies research brief, January 2019, https://tinyurl.com/WilcoxGM39.

17. US Bureau of Labor Statistics, National Longitudinal Survey of Youth, 1997 cohort (NLSY97). Amounts are in 2017 dollars.

18. NLSY97, second wave. Controls as described.

19. American Community Survey (2019). Controlling for work status, race/ethnicity, education, age, and presence of children.

20. NLSY97, second wave. Controlling for family structure, family income growing up, AFQT score, parents' education, and race/ethnicity.

21. National Association of Realtors, "2021 Profile of Home Buyers and Sellers," 2021, https://tinyurl.com/WilcoxGM40.

22. Jonathan Vespa and Matthew A. Painter, "Cohabitation History, Marriage, and Wealth Accumulation," *Demography* 48, no. 3 (2011): 983–1004, 984, https://doi.org/10.1007/s13524-011-0043-2.

23. NLSY79.

24. Based on NLSY79, surveyed in 2016, when respondents were ages 51 to 60. Controlling for family size, age, education, race/ethnicity, presence of children, and full-time/part-time work status.

25. Iceland and Redstone, "The Declining Earnings Gap between Young Women and Men in the United States, 1979–2018."

26. American Community Survey (2019). Controlling for work status, race/ethnicity, education, age, and presence of children.

27. American Community Survey (2019). Controlling for work status, race/ethnicity, education, age, and presence of children.

28. American Community Survey (2019). Controlling for work status, race/ethnicity, education, and age.

29. Based on NLSY79, surveyed in 2016, when respondents were ages 51 to 60. Controlling for family size, age, education, race/ethnicity, presence of children, and full-time/part-time work status.

30. "First Quarter of 2022 Brings Double-Digit Price Appreciation for 70 Percent of Metros," National Association of Realtors, May 3, 2022, https://tinyurl.com/WilcoxGM41; Francisco H. G. Ferreira, "Inequality and COVID-19," International Monetary Fund, June 2021, https://tinyurl.com/WilcoxGM42; Kate Whiting, "Cost of Living: This Chart Shows How the Price of Products Has Risen in the U.S.," World Economic Forum, May 25, 2022, https://tinyurl.com/WilcoxGM43; Briana Boyington, Emma Kerr, and Sara Wood, "A Look at College Tuition Growth Over 20 Years," *US News & World Report*, September 17, 2021, https://tinyurl.com/WilcoxGM44.

31. Emile Durkheim, *On Suicide*, ed. Richard Sennett, trans. Robin Buss, illustrated ed. (London: Penguin, 2006). But note that some contemporary scholars have challenged his conclusions. See, for instance, Frans Van Poppel and Lincoln H. Day, "A Test of Durkheim's Theory of Suicide: Without Committing the 'Ecological Fallacy,'" *American Sociological Review* (1996): 500–507.

32. Durkheim, *On Suicide*, 224–33.

33. Durkheim, 262–305.

34. Durkheim, 226.

35. For the role of norms in marriage, see Nock, *Marriage in Men's Lives*.

36. Clay Routledge, "Finding Meaning in Modern America," *Institute for Family Studies Blog*, May 21, 2018, https://tinyurl.com/WilcoxGM46.

37. Eric Klinenberg, *Going Solo: The Extraordinary Rise and Surprising Appeal of Living Alone* (New York: Penguin, 2013). Estimates for single adults derived from the US Census (1970) and American Community Survey (2020), IPUMS.

38. Eric Klinenberg, "One's a Crowd," *New York Times*, February 4, 2012, https://tinyurl.com/WilcoxGM47.

39. Mandy Len Catron, "The Case against Marriage," *Atlantic*, July 2, 2019, https://tinyurl.com/WilcoxGM48.

40. US Census Bureau, "Median Age at First Marriage: 1890 to Present," fig.e MS-2, https://tinyurl.com/WilcoxGM49.

41. Adapted from W. Bradford Wilcox, "Why Single Men May Not Be Having the Most Fun," *Washington Post*, February 13, 2016, https://tinyurl.com/WilcoxGM50.

42. Nicholas H. Wolfinger, "Marriage Means Community Engagement: A Response to Mandy Len Catron," *Institute for Family Studies Blog*, July 22, 2019, https://tinyurl.com/WilcoxGM51.

43. Institute for Family Studies/Wheatley Institute, State of Our Unions Survey, 2021 (YouGov).

44. Jack C. Smith, James A. Mercy, and Judith M. Conn, "Marital Status and the Risk of Suicide," *American Journal of Public Health* 78, no. 1 (January 1988): 78–80, https://doi.org/10.2105/AJPH.78.1.78.

45. Justin T. Denney, "Family and Household Formations and Suicide in the United States," *Journal of Marriage and Family* 72, no. 1 (2010): 202–13, https://doi.org/10.1111/j.1741-3737.2009.00692.x.

46. Justin T. Denney et al., "Adult Suicide Mortality in the United States: Marital Status, Family Size, Socioeconomic Status, and Differences by Sex," *Social Science Quarterly* 90, no. 5 (2009): 1167–1185, https://doi.org/10.1111/j.1540-6237.2009.00652; Caroline Uggla and Ruth Mace, "Someone to Live for: Effects of Partner and Dependent Children on Preventable Death in a Population Wide Sample from Northern Ireland," *Evolution and Human Behavior* 36, no. 1 (2015): 1–7, https://doi.org/10.1016/j.evolhumbehav.2014.07.008; Karri Silventoinen et al., "Changing Associations between Partnership History and Risk of Accidents, Violence and Suicides," *Journal of Epidemiological Community Health* 67, no. 3 (March 1, 2013): 265–70, https://doi.org/10.1136/jech-2012-201311.

47. Bruce Bower, "'Deaths of Despair' Are Rising. It's Time to Define Despair," *Science News*, November 2, 2020, https://tinyurl.com/WilcoxGM53.

48. Anne Case and Sir Angus Deaton, "Mortality and Morbidity in the 21st

Century," Brookings Institution, March 23, 2017, https://tinyurl.com/Wilcox
GM52.

49. Philip N. Cohen, "The Rising Marriage Mortality Gap among Whites,"
SocArXiv, November 1, 2019, https://doi.org/10.31235/osf.io/8374m. Also
see the corresponding supplement: Philip N. Cohen, "Marriage and Mortality," November 1, 2019, https://osf.io/gtez7/.

50. IFS/Wheatley Institute Family Survey, 2021. For 18-to-55-year-olds, the
loneliness gap between college-educated unmarried and married persons was
14 percentage points. For those who were less educated, the gap was 23 percentage points.

51. Klinenberg, "One's a Crowd."

52. "How To Be Single – Official Trailer 1," Warner Bros. Pictures, YouTube video,
November 18, 2015, 1:23 of 2:32, https://youtu.be/akwGjUeU6YA.

53. Deseret News and Center for the Study of Elections and Democracy at
Brigham Young University, American Family Survey, 2022 (YouGov).

54. See chapter 1.

55. Based on General Social Survey (2014–2018). Controlling for income, education, gender, race, and age.

56. General Social Survey (2014–2018), ages 18 to 55. Controlling for education,
race, gender, and age.

57. David G. Blanchflower and Andrew J. Oswald, "Well-Being over Time in
Britain and the USA," *Journal of Public Economics* 88, no. 7 (2004): 1359–86,
https://doi.org/10.1016/S0047-2727(02)00168-8.

58. Jean M. Twenge and A. Bell Cooper, "The Expanding Class Divide in Happiness in the United States, 1972–2016," *Emotion* 22, no. 4 (2022): 701–713,
https://doi.org/10.1037/emo0000774.

59. Jean Twenge, "Marriage and Money: How Much Does Marriage Explain the
Growing Class Divide in Happiness?" *Institute for Family Studies Blog*, July 20,
2020, https://tinyurl.com/WilcoxGM54.

60. Bella DePaulo, *Singled Out: How Singles Are Stereotyped, Stigmatized, and
Ignored, and Still Live Happily Ever After* (New York: St. Martin's Griffin,
2007).

61. Bella DePaulo, "What No One Ever Told You about People Who Are Single," TEDx Talks, YouTube video, May 11, 2017, https://youtu.be/lyZysfa
fOAs. Quote at 14:13.

62. DePaulo, "What No One Ever Told You." Quote at 12:45.

63. DePaulo, *Singled Out*.

64. See, for instance, Jason Schnittker, "Happiness and Success: Genes, Families,

and the Psychological Effects of Socioeconomic Position and Social Support," *American Journal of Sociology* 114, no. S1 (2008): S233–S259, https://doi.org/10.1086/592424.

65. Shawn Grover and John F. Helliwell, "How's Life at Home? New Evidence on Marriage and the Set Point for Happiness," *Journal of Happiness Studies* 20 (2019): 373–90, 373.

66. Grover and Helliwell, "How's Life at Home?" 373.

67. Tyler VanderWeele, "On the Promotion of Human Flourishing," PNAS, July 13, 2017, https://www.pnas.org/doi/abs/10.1073/pnas.1702996114.

68. M. F. Brinig and D. W. Allen, "'These Boots Are Made for Walking': Why Most Divorce Filers Are Women," *American Law and Economics Review* 2, no. 1 (January 1, 2000): 126–69, https://doi.org/10.1093/aler/2.1.126.

69. Janice K. Kiecolt-Glaser and Tamara L. Newton, "Marriage and Health: His and Hers," *Psychological Bulletin* 127, no. 4 (July 2001): 472–503.

70. Nock, *Marriage in Men's Lives*, 3.

71. Nock; Kiecolt-Glaser and Newton, "Marriage and Health."

72. American Family Survey (2022).

Chapter 4: The Family Diversity Myth

1. Wendy Wang and Brad Wilcox, *State of Contradiction: Progressive Family Culture, Traditional Family Structure in California*, Institute for Family Studies, 2020, https://tinyurl.com/WilcoxGM26.

2. Heineken, "Heineken TV Spot, 'Holiday' Song by Dean Martin," iSpot.tv video, November 30, 2018, https://www.ispot.tv/ad/d9Fh/heineken-holiday-song-by-dean-martin.

3. Wendy Chun-Hoon and Jared Make, "Embracing a More Realistic and Inclusive Definition of Family," *Huffington Post*, July 6, 2016, https://www.huffpost.com/entry/embracing-a-more-realisti_b_10842304.

4. Judith Stacey, "Good Riddance to 'The Family': A Response to David Popenoe," *Journal of Marriage and Family* 55, no. 3 (1993): 545–47, https://doi.org/10.2307/353335.

5. Angela Chen, "The Rise of the 3-Parent Family," *Atlantic*, September 22, 2020, https://www.theatlantic.com/family/archive/2020/09/how-build-three-parent-family-david-jay/616421/.

6. Philip N. Cohen, *The Family: Diversity, Inequality, and Social Change*, 3rd ed. (New York: W. W. Norton, 2020).

7. Philip N. Cohen, "Philip N. Cohen on *Fox and Friends*, 9/7/2014," YouTube video, May 26, 2016, https://www.youtube.com/watch?v=cALlMFO1jUw.

8. Matt O'Brien, "Poor Kids Who Do Everything Right Don't Do Better than Rich Kids Who Do Everything Wrong," *Washington Post*, October 18, 2014, https://tinyurl.com/WilcoxGM58.

9. Isabel V. Sawhill and Richard V. Reeves, "Modeling Equal Opportunity," *Russell Sage Foundation Journal of the Social Sciences* 2, no. 2 (May 2016): 60–97.

10. Jefferson Scholars Foundation website, https://www.jeffersonscholars.org.

11. W. Bradford Wilcox, "The Parent Trap," *Foreign Policy*, January 15, 2013, https://tinyurl.com/WilcoxGM55; David Leonhardt, "A One-Question Quiz on the Poverty Trap," *New York Times*, October 4, 2018, https://tinyurl.com /WilcoxGM56.

12. Diana Baumrind, "Effects of Authoritative Parental Control on Child Behavior," *Child Development* 37, no. 4 (1966): 887–907, https://doi.org/10.2307 /1126611.

13. In the 2002 Educational Longitudinal Study, "highly selective colleges" are those whose first-year students' test scores placed the school in the top fifth of baccalaureate-granting institutions. See US Department of Education, Educational Longitudinal Survey (2002).

14. Nicholas Zill and W. Bradford Wilcox, "What Unites Most Graduates of Selective Colleges? An Intact Family," *Institute for Family Studies Blog*, June 9, 2020, https://tinyurl.com/WilcoxGM57.

15. Zill and Wilcox.

16. Controls included family income, AFQT score, maternal education, race/ethnicity, and gender.

17. Children from intact, married families are 125 percent more likely to graduate from college than children from non-intact families, after controlling for family income, AFQT score, maternal education, race/ethnicity, and gender. Children from families with higher than median income are 73 percent more likely to graduate from college than children from families with lower than median income in the NLSY97. See also Melissa S. Kearney and Phillip B. Levine, "The Economics of Non-Marital Childbearing and the 'Marriage Premium for Children,'" Working Paper, National Bureau of Economic Research, March 2017, https://doi.org/10.3386/w23230.

18. C. McPhee et al., *National Household Education Surveys Program of 2016: Data File User's Manual* (NCES 2018-100), National Center for Education Statistics, Institute of Education Sciences (Washington, DC: US Department of Education, 2018); Nicholas Zill, "Family Still Matters for Key Indicators of Student Performance," *Institute for Family Studies Blog*, April 6, 2020, https:// tinyurl.com/WilcoxGM59.

19. Children from non-intact families are two times more likely to have their parents contacted for misbehavior than peers from intact families, whereas children from lower-income families are 25 percent more likely to end up in trouble than children from higher-income families, controlling for gender, maternal education, age, tested achievement, and race/ethnicity. US Department of Education, "Early Childhood Longitudinal Study, Kindergarten Class of 1998–1999," National Center for Education Statistics, 2007.

20. Melanie Wasserman, "The Disparate Effects of Family Structure," *Future of Children* 30, no. 1 (Spring 2020).

21. Young men from non-intact families are twice as likely to end up incarcerated as are peers from intact families, whereas young men from lower-income families are 54 percent more likely to end up incarcerated as are young men from higher-income families. Controlling for AFQT score, maternal education, and race/ethnicity, based on young men ages 28–34 in 2013–2014, NLSY97.

22. Robert Sampson, "Neighborhood and Crime: The Structural Determinants of Personal Victimization," *Journal of Research in Crime and Delinquency* 22 (1985): 7–40; Maria Tcherni, "Structural Determinants of Homicide: The Big Three," *Journal of Quantitative Criminology* 27 (2011): 475–96.

23. Claire Cain Miller, "A Disadvantaged Start Hurts Boys More Than Girls," *New York Times*, October 22, 2015, https://tinyurl.com/WilcoxGM60.

24. S. P. Hinshaw, "Externalizing Behavior Problems and Academic Underachievement in Childhood and Adolescence: Causal Relationships and Underlying Mechanisms," *Psychological Bulletin* 111, no. 1 (January 1992): 127–55, https://doi.org/10.1037/0033-2909.111.1.127; Herbert C. Quay, "Classification," in *Psychopathological Disorders of Childhood*, ed. Herbert C. Quay and John S. Werry (New York: Wiley, 1986), 1–34; and Sara McLanahan, Laura Tach, and Daniel Schneider, "The Causal Effects of Father Absence," *Annual Review of Sociology* 39, no. 1 (2013): 399–427, https://doi.org/10.1146/annurev-soc-071312-145704.

25. Herbert C. Quay and Donald R. Peterson, *Manual for the Revised Behavior Problem Checklist* (Coral Gables, FL: University of Miami, 1987), https://tinyurl.com/WilcoxGM61; Antonia N. Kaczkurkin, Armin Raznahan, and Theodore D. Satterthwaite, "Sex Differences in the Developing Brain: Insights from Multimodal Neuroimaging," *Neuropsychopharmacology* 44, no. 1 (January 2019): 71–85, https://doi.org/10.1038/s41386-018-0111-z; McLanahan, Tach, and Schneider, "Causal Effects of Father Absence."

26. Teens from non-intact families are 54 percent more likely to end up depressed than peers from intact families, whereas teens from lower-income families

are only 23 percent more likely to end up depressed than teens from higher-income families, and the income effect is not significant. Controlling for parental education, gender, composite achievement score, and race/ethnicity. US Department of Education, "Early Childhood Longitudinal Study, Kindergarten Class of 1998–1999," National Center for Education Statistics, 2007.

27. Sonya Negriff et al., "Characterizing the Sexual Abuse Experiences of Young Adolescents," *Child Abuse & Neglect* 38, no. 2 (2014): 261–70, https://doi.org/10.1016/j.chiabu.2013.08.021; William J. Oliver, Lawrence R. Kuhns, and Elaine S. Pomeranz, "Family Structure and Child Abuse," *Clinical Pediatrics* 45, no. 2 (2006): 111–118, https://doi.org/10.1177/000992280604500201; Patricia G. Schnitzer and Bernard G. Ewigman, "Child Deaths Resulting from Inflicted Injuries: Household Risk Factors and Perpetrator Characteristics," *Pediatrics* 116, no. 5 (November 2005): e687–e693, https://doi.org/10.1542/peds.2005-0296; Martin Daly and Margo Wilson, "Child Abuse and Other Risks of Not Living with Both Parents," *Ethology and Sociobiology* 6, no. 4 (January 1, 1985): 197–210, https://doi.org/10.1016/0162-3095(85)90012-3.

28. Aruna Radhakrishna et al., "Are Father Surrogates a Risk Factor for Child Maltreatment?" *Child Maltreatment* 6, no. 4 (2001): 281–89, https://doi.org/10.1177/1077559501006004001.

29. A. J. Sedlak et al., *Fourth National Incidence Study of Child Abuse and Neglect (NIS–4)*, Report to Congress (Washington, DC: US Department of Health and Human Services, Administration for Children and Families, 2010), https://tinyurl.com/WilcoxGM62.

30. Martin Daly and Margo Wilson, "Evolutionary Psychology and Marital Conflict: The Relevance of Stepchildren," in *Sex, Power, Conflict: Evolutionary and Feminist Perspectives* (New York: Oxford University Press, 1996), 9–28.

31. Daly and Wilson.

32. Gregory Acs and Sandy Nelson, "The Kids Are Alright? Children's Well-Being and the Rise in Cohabitation," *New Federalism: National Survey of America's Families*, B-48, Urban Institute, Washington, DC, July 2002, http://webarchive.urban.org/publications/310544.html; Susan L. Brown, Wendy D. Manning, and J. Bart Stykes, "Family Structure and Child Well-Being: Integrating Family Complexity," *Journal of Marriage and the Family* 77, no. 1 (February 2015): 177–90, https://doi.org/10.1111/jomf.12145; Sandi Nelson, Rebecca L. Clark, and Gregory Acs, "Beyond the Two-Parent Family: How Teenagers Fare in Cohabiting Couple and Blended Families," *New Federalism: National Survey of America's Families*, B-31, Urban Institute, Washington, DC, May 2001, http://webarchive.urban.org/publications/310339.html;

Negriff et al., "Characterizing Sexual Abuse Experiences"; Schnitzer and Ewigman, "Child Deaths"; Daly and Wilson, "Child Abuse and Other Risks"; and Sedlak et al., *Fourth National Incidence Study*.

33. Matthew Yglesias, "David Brooks' Scant Self-Awareness: Divorced Pundit Suddenly Not So Worried about Family Breakdown," *Slate*, December 17, 2013, https://tinyurl.com/WilcoxGM63.

34. This section is adapted from my article, W. Bradford Wilcox, "Even for Rich Kids, Marriage Matters," *Institute for Family Studies Blog*, December 19, 2013, https://tinyurl.com/WilcoxGM64.

35. Logistic regression for college graduation among young adults from the upper-third income bracket in cohort NLSY97. Controlling for gender, race/ethnicity, AFQT score, and maternal education.

36. Thomas Deleire and Leonard M. Lopoo, "Family Structure and the Economic Mobility of Children," Economic Mobility Project, Pew Charitable Trusts, April 2010, http://bit.ly/1yN12Do.

37. Nicholas H. Wolfinger, *Understanding the Divorce Cycle: The Children of Divorce in Their Own Marriages* (New York: Cambridge University Press, 2005); W. Bradford Wilcox and Samuel Sturgeon, "Three Reasons Not to Make This January Your Divorce Month," *Institute for Family Studies Blog*, January 11, 2017, https://tinyurl.com/WilcoxGM65; Julie Zissimopoulos, Benjamin Karney, and Amy Rauer, "Marital Histories and Economic Well-Being," Rand Corporation, December 16, 2008; Population Reference Bureau, "Older Women, Divorce, and Poverty," March 14, 2008, https://scorecard.prb.org/olderwomen/.

38. Carolyn J. Hill, Harry J. Holzer, and Henry Chen, *Against the Tide: Household Structure, Opportunities, and Outcomes among White and Minority Youth* (Kalamazoo, MI: W. E. Upjohn Institute, 2009), https://muse.jhu.edu/book/17385; Wilcox, "Even for Rich Kids, Marriage Matters."

39. US Census Bureau, "Income and Poverty in the United States: 2019," September 15, 2020, table B-2, https://tinyurl.com/WilcoxGM66; Ron Haskins, "The Family Is Here to Stay—or Not," *Future of Children* 25, no. 2 (2015): 129–53, https://eric.ed.gov/?id=EJ1079403.

40. Kelly Stamper Balistreri, "Family Structure and Child Food Insecurity: Evidence from the Current Population Survey," *Social Indicators Research* 138, no. 3 (August 2018): 1171–85, https://doi.org/10.1007/s11205-017-1700-7; Orestes P. Hastings and Daniel Schneider, "Family Structure and Inequalities in Parents' Financial Investments in Children," *Journal of Marriage and Family* 83, no. 3 (2021): 717–36, https://doi.org/10.1111/jomf.12741.

41. W. Bradford Wilcox, Joseph Price, and Robert I. Lerman, "Strong Families, Prosperous States: Do Healthy Families Affect the Wealth of States?" *American Enterprise Institute*, October 19, 2015, https://tinyurl.com/Wilcox GMu.

42. Hill, Holzer, and Chen, *Against the Tide*; Sara McLanahan and Gary D. Sandefur, *Growing Up with a Single Parent: What Hurts, What Helps* (Cambridge, MA: Harvard University Press, 1994); Robert I. Lerman and W. Bradford Wilcox, "For Richer, for Poorer: How Family Structures Economic Success in America," *American Enterprise Institute*, October 28, 2014, https://tinyurl .com/WilcoxGM38.

43. Based on a regression analysis that controls for family income in adolescence, maternal education, AFQT score, and race/ethnicity, using NLSY97. See also Raj Chetty et al., "Childhood Environment and Gender Gaps in Adulthood," *American Economic Review* 106, no. 5 (May 2016): 282–88, https://doi.org/10 .1257/aer.p20161073.

44. W. Bradford Wilcox, "Family Matters: What's the Most Important Factor Blocking Social Mobility? Single Parents, Suggests a New Study," *Slate*, January 22, 2014, https://tinyurl.com/WilcoxGM67.

45. Young adults from upper-income families are 40 percent more likely to end up in the middle class or higher, compared to their peers from lower-income families. Controlling for maternal education, AFQT score, race/ethnicity, and gender, using NLSY97.

46. Andrew J. Cherlin, *The Marriage-Go-Round: The State of Marriage and the Family in America Today* (New York: Random House, 2010).

47. Laurie DeRose and W. Bradford Wilcox, *The Cohabitation-Go-Round: Cohabitation and Family Instability across the Globe*, World Family Map series, Social Trends Institute and Institute for Family Studies, 2017, http://worldfamily map.ifstudies.org/2017/files/WFM-2017-FullReport.pdf; Wendy D. Manning, Pamela J. Smock, and Debarun Majumdar, "The Relative Stability of Cohabiting and Marital Unions for Children," *Population Research and Policy Review* 23, no. 2 (2004): 135–59, https://www.jstor.org/stable/40230853.

48. McLanahan and Sandefur, *Growing Up with a Single Parent*.

49. Peter Fallesen and Michael Gähler, "Family Type and Parents' Time with Children: Longitudinal Evidence for Denmark," *Acta Sociologica* 63, no. 4 (2020): 361–80, https://doi.org/10.1177/0001699319868522.

50. McLanahan and Sandefur, *Growing Up with a Single Parent*; Oliver, Kuhns, and Pomeranz, "Family Structure and Child Abuse"; Julia S. Goldberg and Marcia J. Carlson, "Parents' Relationship Quality and Children's Behavior in

Stable Married and Cohabiting Families," *Journal of Marriage and Family* 76, no. 4 (2014): 762–77, https://doi.org/10.1111/jomf.12120.

51. Laura Tach and Alicia Eads, "The Cost of Breaking Up," Institute for Research on Families (Fall-Winter 2013–2014), https://tinyurl.com/Wilcox GM68.

52. Julie M. Zissimopoulos, Benjamin R. Karney, and Amy J. Rauer, "Marriage and Economic Well Being at Older Ages," *Review of Economics of the Household* 13, no. 1 (2013): 1–35, https://doi.org/10.1007/s11150-013-9205-x.

53. See, for instance, Brian D'Onofrio and Robert Emery, "Parental Divorce or Separation and Children's Mental Health," *World Psychiatry* 18, no. 1 (February 2019): 100–101, https://doi.org/10.1002/wps.20590; Jonathan Gruber, "Is Making Divorce Easier Bad for Children? The Long-Run Implications of Unilateral Divorce," *Journal of Labor Economics* 22, no. 4 (2004): 799–833, https://doi.org/10.1086/423155.

54. McLanahan, Tach, and Schneider, "Causal Effects of Father Absence."

55. McLanahan and Sandefur, *Growing Up with a Single Parent*.

56. W. Bradford Wilcox, "The Evolution of Divorce," *National Affairs* (American Enterprise Institute), Fall 2009, https://tinyurl.com/WilcoxGM69.

57. According to the American Family Survey (Deseret News and Center for the Study of Elections and Democracy at Brigham Young University, 2022), Asian Americans ages 18 to 55 are more likely than others to agree with the statement, "Children are better off if they have two married parents" (61 percent vs. 51 percent), and conservatives are also more likely than liberals to agree with it (79 percent vs. 34 percent). So are religious vs. secular Americans (74 percent vs. 42 percent). In addition, college-educated adults 18 to 55 are more likely than those who have not graduated from college to believe children are better off if they have two married parents (59 percent vs. 48 percent).

Chapter 5: The Soulmate Myth

1. Elizabeth Gilbert, *Eat, Pray, Love: One Woman's Search for Everything across Italy, India, and Indonesia* (New York: Penguin, 2007), 12.

2. Gilbert, 10.

3. Gilbert, 16.

4. Gilbert, 287.

5. Carl Trueman, "How Expressive Individualism Threatens Civil Society," Heritage Foundation, May 27, 2021.

6. Gilbert, *Eat, Pray, Love*, 325.

7. Gilbert, 20.

8. Gilbert, 20.

9. Nick Craven, "After a String of Doomed Romances, the Author of 'Eat, Pray, Love' Is Still Looking for Love," *Independent Online*, April 6, 2020, https://tinyurl.com/WilcoxGM70.

10. Eli J. Finkel, *The All-or-Nothing Marriage: How the Best Marriages Work* (New York: Dutton, 2017).

11. Mary Kelleher, "Study: Americans Seek Soul-Mate Spouse," ABC News, June 13, 2001, https://tinyurl.com/WilcoxGM71.

12. Scott M. Stanley, *The Power of Commitment: A Guide to Active, Lifelong Love* (San Francisco: Jossey-Bass, 2005), 142.

13. W. Bradford Wilcox, "The Evolution of Divorce," *National Affairs* (American Enterprise Institute), Fall 2009, https://tinyurl.com/WilcoxGM72.

14. Richard Bach and Russell Munson, *Jonathan Livingston Seagull: The Complete Edition* (New York: Scribner, 2009).

15. Daniel Yankelovich, *New Rules: Searching for Self-Fulfillment in a World Turned Upside Down* (New York: Bantam, 1984).

16. Kelleher, "Americans Seek Soul-Mate."

17. Finkel, *All-or-Nothing Marriage*, 118.

18. Amber Lapp, "The Story We Tell about Love," *Institute for Family Studies Blog*, July 28, 2020, https://tinyurl.com/WilcoxGM73.

19. Based on California Family Survey, Institute for Family Studies, 2019, controlling for age, race/ethnicity, sex, education, family income, and presence of children (under age eighteen) at home.

20. Based on State of Our Unions Survey, Institute for Family Studies, 2022, controlling for age, race/ethnicity, sex, education, family income, and presence of children (under age 18) at home. The share who are currently going through a divorce or believe that their marriage is likely to end in the near future is 9 percent for married adults ages 18 to 60 who believe in the soulmate model, and 4 percent for those who believe in the family-first model.

21. Stephanie Coontz, *Marriage, a History: How Love Conquered Marriage* (New York: Penguin, 2006), 23.

22. Coontz, 306.

23. Jonathan Haidt, *The Happiness Hypothesis: Finding Modern Truth in Ancient Wisdom* (New York: Basic Books, 2005), 125; Louann Brizendine, *The Female Brain* (London: Transworld Digital, 2009).

24. Haidt, *Happiness Hypothesis*, 12.

25. Aristotle, *Aristotle's Nicomachean Ethics*, trans. Robert C. Bartlett and Susan D. Collins (Chicago: University of Chicago Press, 2012), 23.

26. Matthew 10:39.
27. As quoted in David Myers, *The Pursuit of Happiness: Discovering the Pathway to Fulfillment, Well-Being, and Enduring Personal Joy* (New York: William Morrow, 1993), 189–190.
28. Myers, 195.
29. W. Bradford Wilcox and Nicholas H. Wolfinger, *Soul Mates: Religion, Sex, Love, and Marriage among African Americans and Latinos*, illustrated ed. (New York: Oxford University Press, 2016), 124–25.
30. Model is based on California Family Survey, Institute for Family Studies, 2019, controlling for age, race/ethnicity, sex, education, family income, and number of children at home.
31. Dr. Tom Neal, "To Will the Good of the Other," Word on Fire, February 24, 2016, https://tinyurl.com/WilcoxGM74.
32. Jason Carroll, *The Marriage Compass* (Provo, UT: BYU Press), 43.
33. Michelle Obama, *Becoming* (New York: Crown, 2018), 111.
34. Obama, 204.
35. Obama, 172.
36. W. Bradford Wilcox and Elizabeth Marquardt, *When Marriage Disappears: The New Middle America*, State of Our Unions series, Institute for American Values and National Marriage Project, 2010, https://tinyurl.com/WilcoxGM75.
37. George Packer, "When the Culture War Comes for the Kids," *Atlantic*, September 13, 2019, https://tinyurl.com/WilcoxGM76.
38. W. Bradford Wilcox, "Marriage with Family at Its Center," *Wall Street Journal*, March 28, 2020, https://tinyurl.com/WilcoxGM77.

Chapter 6: We Before Me

1. Ricky O'Donnell, "College Basketball's Top 25 Teams in 2018–19, According to Us," SBNation, November 1, 2018, https://tinyurl.com/WilcoxGM78.
2. Dan Wolken, "Opinion: To Win Titles, Mike Krzyzewski and John Calipari May Need New Building-Roster Plan," *USA Today*, April 1, 2019, https://tinyurl.com/WilcoxGM79.
3. Gabe Fernandez, "Coach K's Trust in R. J. Barrett Ruins Duke's Final Four Dreams," *Deadspin*, April 1, 2019, https://tinyurl.com/WilcoxGM80.
4. Luke Mullin, "How RJ Barrett Ranks against Former NBA Top 5 Picks," *Sportsnaut*, May 10, 2019, https://tinyurl.com/WilcoxGM81.
5. Wolken, "Mike Krzyzewski and John Calipari."
6. "NCAA College Basketball AP All-America Teams," *Basketball Reference*, https://tinyurl.com/WilcoxGM82.

7. Jim Daly and Paul Batura, "Virginia Basketball Coach Tony Bennett's Five Pillars to Live By Is a Blueprint for Success," *Daly Focus* (blog by Jim Daly), April 10, 2019, https://tinyurl.com/WilcoxGM83; "Laying a Foundation: Coach Tony Bennett Discusses Philosophy and Goals," *University of Virginia Magazine*, Winter 2009, https://tinyurl.com/WilcoxGM84.

8. The Virginian-Pilot and Daily Press, *March to Redemption: Virginia's Historic 2019 Championship Season* (Chicago: Triumph, 2019), 8.

9. *March to Redemption*, 83.

10. Stephanie Sarkis, "Separate Accounts: It May Save Your Marriage," *HuffPost*, March 1, 2012, https://tinyurl.com/WilcoxGM85.

11. Casey Bond, "Eight Financial Rules You Should Break, According to Experts," *HuffPost*, June 6, 2018, https://tinyurl.com/WilcoxGM86.

12. Caroline Kitchener, "Why More Young Married Couples Are Keeping Separate Bank Accounts," *Atlantic*, April 20, 2018, https://tinyurl.com/WilcoxGM87.

13. Kitchener, "Separate Bank Accounts."

14. Joe J. Gladstone, Emily N. Garbinsky, and Cassie Mogilner, "Pooling Finances and Relationship Satisfaction," *Journal of Personality and Social Psychology* 123, no. 6 (2022): 1293–1314, https://doi.org/10.1037/pspi0000388, or PDF at https://tinyurl.com/WilcoxGM88.

15. Gladstone, Garbinsky, and Mogilner, "Pooling Finances."

16. Fenaba R. Addo and Sharon Sassler, "Financial Arrangements and Relationship Quality in Low-Income Couples," *Family Relations* 59, no. 4 (2010): 408–23, https://doi.org/10.1111/j.1741-3729.2010.00612.x.

17. Jenny Olson and Scott Rick, "Managing Debt and Managing Each Other: The Interpersonal Dynamics of Joint Financial Decisions," paper, Social Science Research Network, May 18, 2018, https://doi.org/10.2139/ssrn.2637637.

18. Laura Saslow et al., "Can You See How Happy We Are? Facebook Images and Relationship Satisfaction," *Social Psychological and Personality Science* 4 (July 2013): 411–18, https://doi.org/10.1177/1948550612460059.

19. Controlling for age, education, gender, household income, presence of children in the home, and race/ethnicity. See also Kara A. Laskowski, "Women's Post-Marital Name Retention and the Communication of Identity," *Names* 58, no. 2 (June 2010): 75–89, https://doi.org/10.1179/002777310X12682237915025.

20. State of Our Unions Survey (2022).

21. Teresa Newsome, "Little Self-Care Tips for a Happier Relationship," *Bustle*, May 17, 2016, https://tinyurl.com/WilcoxGM89.

22. Scott M. Stanley, "Me, You, and Us: We-Ness and Couple Identity," *Institute for Family Studies Blog*, June 14, 2021, https://tinyurl.com/WilcoxGM90.

23. See, for instance, Margaret S. Clark and Judson Mills, "The Difference between Communal and Exchange Relationships: What It Is and Is Not," *Personality and Social Psychology Bulletin* 19, no. 6 (1993): 684–91, https://doi.org/10.1177/0146167293196003.

24. The State of Our Unions Survey asked respondents, "How likely will your marriage end in divorce?" Responses included "not at all likely," "not likely," "somewhat likely in the distant future," "somewhat likely in the near future," and "We are currently going through a divorce." For most outcomes in this book, I compare respondents who said that it was "not at all likely" they would divorce to respondents who were less confident they would not divorce.

25. Controls include age, education, gender, household income, presence of children in the home, and race/ethnicity.

26. W. Bradford Wilcox and Elizabeth Marquardt, *When Baby Makes Three: How Parenthood Makes Life Meaningful and How Marriage Makes Parenthood Bearable*, State of Our Unions series, Institute for American Values and National Marriage Project, 2011, https://tinyurl.com/WilcoxGM91.

27. Scott M. Stanley et al., "Sacrifice as a Predictor of Marital Outcomes," *Family Process* 45, no. 3 (September 2006): 289–303, https://doi.org/10.1111/j.1545-5300.2006.00171.x.

28. In the American Family Survey (Deseret News and Center for the Study of Elections and Democracy at Brigham Young University, 2022), 90 percent of conservative husbands and wives ages 18 to 55 agreed that "Marriage is more about putting 'we before me'" (vs. "In a good marriage you have to look after your own needs first"), whereas that was true for 86 percent of liberal married men and women. The same survey found that 83 percent of married conservatives reported that they think about their spouse more in terms of "us" and "we" rather than "me and him/her," compared to 76 percent of liberal marrieds.

29. Controlling for race/ethnicity, education, age, income, presence of children, and gender.

30. W. Bradford Wilcox and Jeff Dew, *The Date Night Opportunity: What Does Couple Time Tell Us about the Potential Value of Date Nights?* National Marriage Project, 2012, https://tinyurl.com/WilcoxGM92.

31. After controlling for race/ethnicity, education, gender, presence of children, and income, the odds of being very happy with their sexual relationship were 2.46 times higher for those with frequent dates, compared to those with infrequent dates.

32. David G. Blanchflower and Andrew J. Oswald, "Money, Sex, and Happiness: An Empirical Study," *Scandinavian Journal of Economics* 106, no. 3 (September 2004): 393–415; Honor Whiteman, "Sex May Be Key to a Happy Marriage, Study Finds," *Medical News Today*, March 26, 2017, https://tinyurl.com /WilcoxGM93; Nancy Shute, "Is Sex Once a Week Enough for a Happy Relationship?" NPR.org, November 18, 2015, https://tinyurl.com/Wilcox GM94.

33. State of Our Unions Survey (2022).

34. Amy Shearn, "A 50/50 Custody Arrangement Could Save Your Marriage," *New York Times*, October 8, 2022, https://tinyurl.com/WilcoxGM95.

Chapter 7: The Parent Trap

1. Mark Mather, "The Decline in U.S. Fertility," Population Reference Bureau, July 18, 2012, https://tinyurl.com/WilcoxGM96.

2. Sylvia Maixner, "The 1979 *Alien* Movie Is All About Pregnancy and Early Parenthood," ScreenGeek, May 20, 2017, https://tinyurl.com/WilcoxGM97.

3. Brady E. Hamilton, Joyce A. Martin, and Michelle J. K. Osterman, "Births: Provisional Data for 2020," Vital Statistics Rapid Release report no. 012 (May 2021), National Center for Health Statistics, https://tinyurl.com/Wilcox GM98.

4. Kali Holloway, "American Parents Are Miserable: Moms and Dads Alike Face a Massive 'Happiness Gap,'" *Salon*, June 23, 2016, https://tinyurl.com /WilcoxGM99.

5. Matthew Johnson, "Why Having Children Is Bad for Your Marriage," *Washington Post*, May 6, 2016, https://tinyurl.com/WilcoxGM1a.

6. Travis Rieder, "Science Proves Kids Are Bad for Earth. Morality Suggests We Stop Having Them," NBC News, November 15, 2017, https://tinyurl .com/WilcoxGM1b.

7. Lauren Sandler, "Having It All without Having Children," *Time*, August 12, 2013, https://tinyurl.com/WilcoxGM1c.

8. A. Pawlowski, "'I Don't Think This Is for Me': 7 Reasons Why People Skip Parenthood," NBC Today, August 24, 2016, https://tinyurl.com/Wilcox GM1d.

9. Patricia Cohen and Tiffany Hsu, "Pandemic Could Scar a Generation of Working Mothers," *New York Times*, June 3, 2020, https://tinyurl.com/Wilcox GM1e; Amy Bernstein, "Covid-19 Dealt a Blow to Working Women. Can We Emerge Stronger?" *New York Times*, December 7, 2020, https://tinyurl .com/WilcoxGM1f; Amanda Taub, "Pandemic Will 'Take Our Women 10

Years Back' in the Workplace," *New York Times*, September 26, 2020, https://tinyurl.com/WilcoxGM1g.

10. Doug Mainwaring, "Moms Slam Biden for Tweet Suggesting It's Better for Them to Work Rather than Raise Their Kids," LifeSite News, November 23, 2021, https://tinyurl.com/WilcoxGM1h.

11. Juliana Menasce Horowitz, Nikki Graf, and Gretchen Livingston, "Public Views of Marriage and Cohabitation," Pew Research Center, November 6, 2019, https://tinyurl.com/WilcoxGM1j.

12. Chad Day, "Americans Have Shifted Dramatically on What Values Matter Most," *Wall Street Journal*, August 25, 2019, https://tinyurl.com/WilcoxGM1k.

13. Lyman Stone, "The Rise of Childless America," *Institute for Family Studies Blog*, June 4, 2020, https://tinyurl.com/WilcoxGM1m; Lyman Stone, "1 in 4: Projecting Childlessness among Today's Young Women," *Institute for Family Studies Blog*, December 7, 2022, https://tinyurl.com/WilcoxGM1n.

14. Louis Baragona, "12 Celebrities Who Have Opened Up about Their Choice to Not Have Kids," *Insider*, May 18, 2021, https://tinyurl.com/WilcoxGM1p.

15. Sandler, "Having It All."

16. Alex Williams, "To Breed or Not to Breed?" *New York Times*, November 20, 2021, https://tinyurl.com/WilcoxGM1q.

17. Williams.

18. Williams.

19. Lili Roquelin, "Childfree" (lyrics), https://www.liliroquelin.com/lyrics.

20. Holloway, "American Parents Are Miserable."

21. Holloway.

22. "How Having Children Robs Parents of Their Happiness," *South China Morning Post*, September 16, 2015, https://tinyurl.com/WilcoxGM1r.

23. Lisa Belkin, "Does Having Children Make You Unhappy?" *Motherlode* (blog), April 1, 2009, https://tinyurl.com/WilcoxGM1s; Chris M. Herbst and John Ifcher, "The Increasing Happiness of U.S. Parents," *Review of Economics of the Household* 14 (2016): 529–51, https://tinyurl.com/WilcoxGM1t.

24. Chris Herbst, "Are U.S. Parents Becoming Happier?" *Institute for Family Studies Blog*, April 20, 2017, https://tinyurl.com/WilcoxGM1u.

25. Brad Wilcox and Wendy Wang, "The Group That's Happiest in the Pandemic May Surprise You," *Deseret News*, September 28, 2021, https://tinyurl.com/WilcoxGM1v.

26. "Where Americans Find Meaning in Life," Pew Research Center, November 20, 2018, https://tinyurl.com/WilcoxGM1w.

27. Wilcox and Wang, "Group That's Happiest."

28. For example, Jennifer Glass, Robin W. Simon, and Matthew A. Andersson, "Parenthood and Happiness: Effects of Work-Family Reconciliation Policies in 22 OECD Countries," *American Journal of Sociology* 122, no. 3 (November 2016): 886–929, https://doi.org/10.1086/688892.

29. Institute for Family Studies/Wheatley Institute, State of Our Unions Survey, 2021 (YouGov). Controls include education, race, age, and income.

30. Paul Bloom, *The Sweet Spot: The Pleasures of Suffering and the Search for Meaning* (New York: HarperCollins, 2021); Anna Lembke, *Dopamine Nation: Finding Balance in the Age of Indulgence* (London: Headline, 2021).

31. Bloom, *Sweet Spot*, 192.

32. Bloom, 190.

33. Jennifer Senior, *All Joy and No Fun: The Paradox of Modern Parenthood* (New York: HarperCollins, 2014), 253.

34. Senior.

35. Johnson, "Why Having Children Is Bad."

36. Johnson.

37. Susan M. McHale and Ted L. Huston, "Men and Women as Parents: Sex Role Orientations, Employment, and Parental Roles with Infants," *Child Development* 55, no. 4 (1984): 1349–61, https://doi.org/10.2307/1130005.

38. Johnson, "Why Having Children Is Bad."

39. Jessica Grogan, "The Rocky Transition to Parenthood," *Psychology Today*, June 23, 2015, https://tinyurl.com/WilcoxGM1x.

40. Sara M. Gorchoff, Oliver P. John, and Ravenna Helson, "Contexualizing Change in Marital Satisfaction during Middle Age: An 18-Year Longitudinal Study," *Psychological Science* 19, no. 11 (November 2008): 1194–200, https://tinyurl.com/WilcoxGM1y; Jeffrey Dew and W. Bradford Wilcox, "If Momma Ain't Happy: Explaining Declines in Marital Satisfaction among New Mothers," *Journal of Marriage and Family* 73, no. 1 (February 2011): 1–12, https://tinyurl.com/WilcoxGM1z; B. D. Doss et al., "The Effect of the Transition to Parenthood on Relationship Quality: An 8-Year Prospective Study," *Journal of Personality and Social Psychology* 96, no. 3 (March 2009): 601–19, https://tinyurl.com/WilcoxGM2a.

41. Regina Kuersten-Hogan and James P. McHale, eds., "The Transition to Parenthood: A Theoretical and Empirical Overview," in *Prenatal Family Dynamics: Couple and Coparenting Relationships during and Postpregnancy* (New York: Springer, 2021), 3–21, https://tinyurl.com/WilcoxGM2b.

42. Controlling for age, education, race, income, and gender.

43. Wendy Wang, "Shrinking American Motherhood: 1-in-6 Women in Their 40s Have Never Given Birth," *Institute for Family Studies Blog*, November 29, 2022, https://tinyurl.com/WilcoxGM2c.

44. IFS/Wheatley Institute Family Survey, 2021.

45. Gabrielle Chung, "Why Kristin Cavallari Says Divorcing Jay Cutler Was the 'Best Thing I've Ever Done,'" E!News, June 30, 2022, https://tinyurl.com/WilcoxGM2d.

46. Arland Thornton, "Changing Attitudes toward Separation and Divorce: Causes and Consequences," *American Journal of Sociology* 90, no. 4 (1985): 856–72, https://www.jstor.org/stable/2779521; W. Bradford Wilcox, "The Evolution of Divorce," *National Affairs*, American Enterprise Institute, Fall 2009, https://tinyurl.com/WilcoxGMde.

47. Paul Taylor, Cary Funk, and April Clark, "As Marriage and Parenthood Drift Apart, Public Is Concerned about Social Impact," Pew Research Center, July 1, 2007, https://tinyurl.com/WilcoxGM2f.

48. State of Our Unions Survey (2022).

49. Controlling for age, education, race, income, gender, and presence of children.

50. State of Our Unions Survey (2022).

51. The relationships between family fun time, family chores, and marital quality are statistically significant, net of controls for age, education, gender, race, and income.

52. Based on adults ages 18 to 64 with children under age 18, American Community Survey (2019).

53. Zaid Jilani, W. Bradford Wilcox, and Wendy Wang, "Is the American Dream Dead? Not for This Group of Americans," *Deseret News*, December 16, 2021, https://tinyurl.com/WilcoxGM2g.

54. This is adapted from Jilani, Wilcox, and Wang, "Is the American Dream Dead?"

55. State of Our Unions Survey (2022).

Chapter 8: The "Maybe I Do" Mentality

1. Homer, "The Odyssey," XII, trans. A. S. Kline, Poetry in Translation (2004), https://tinyurl.com/WilcoxGM2h.

2. Homer.

3. Homer.

4. Scott Alexander, "There's a Time for Everyone," *Astral Codex Ten* (blog), January 12, 2022, https://tinyurl.com/WilcoxGM2j.

5. Philip Galanes, "My Daughter's Married Boyfriend Shouldn't Join Us on

Vacation, Right?" *New York Times*, January 13, 2022, https://tinyurl.com /WilcoxGM2k.

6. Jones: "Who could I be if I wasn't his wife? Maybe I would microdose. Maybe I would have sex with women. Maybe I would write a book." Honor Jones, "How I Demolished My Life: A Home-Improvement Story," *Atlantic*, December 28, 2021, https://tinyurl.com/WilcoxGM2m.

7. W. Bradford Wilcox and Elizabeth Marquardt, *When Marriage Disappears: The New Middle America*, State of Our Unions series, Institute for American Values and National Marriage Project, 2010, https://tinyurl.com/Wilcox GM75.

8. NORC at the University of Chicago, General Social Survey (2018).

9. W. Bradford Wilcox, Jeffrey P. Dew, and Betsy VanDenBerghe, "Flirting Online and Relationship Troubles Go Hand-in-Hand, Even If No One Finds Out, New Research Shows," *Washington Post*, August 6, 2019, https://tiny url.com/WilcoxGM2n.

10. W. Bradford Wilcox, Jeffrey P. Dew, and Betsy VanDenBerghe, *iFidelity: Interactive Technology and Relationship Faithfulness*, State of Our Unions series, National Marriage Project, Wheatley Institution, and School of Family Life, 2019, https://nationalmarriageproject.org/wp-content/uploads/2019 /07/SOU2019.pdf; Alfred DeMaris, "Burning the Candle at Both Ends: Extramarital Sex as a Precursor of Marital Disruption," *Journal of Family Issues* 34, no. 11 (November 1, 2013): 1474–99, https://doi.org/10.1177/0192 513X12470833.

11. Wendy Wang, "Who Cheats More? The Demographics of Infidelity in America," *Institute for Family Studies Blog*, January 10, 2018, https://tinyurl.com /WilcoxGM2p.

12. Wilcox, Dew, and VanDenBerghe, *iFidelity*.

13. iFidelity Survey (2019) conducted for Wilcox, Dew, and VanDenBerghe.

14. DeMaris, "Burning the Candle at Both Ends"; Elizabeth S. Allen and David C. Atkins, "The Association of Divorce and Extramarital Sex in a Representative U.S. Sample," *Journal of Family Issues* 33, no. 11 (November 1, 2012): 1477–93, https://doi.org/10.1177/0192513X12439692.

15. Wang, "Who Cheats More?"

16. Denise Previti and Paul R. Amato, "Is Infidelity a Cause or a Consequence of Poor Marital Quality?" *Journal of Social and Personal Relationships* 21, no. 2 (April 1, 2004): 217–30, https://doi.org/10.1177/0265407504041384.

17. Controlling for race, age, gender, education, income, and presence of children.

18. Ashlyn Brady, Levi R. Baker, and Rowland S. Miller, "Look but Don't

Touch? Self-Regulation Determines Whether Noticing Attractive Alternatives Increases Infidelity," *Journal of Family Psychology* 34, no. 2 (2020): 135–44, https://doi.org/10.1037/fam0000578.

19. Scott M. Stanley, *The Power of Commitment: A Guide to Active, Lifelong Love* (San Francisco: Jossey-Bass, 2005), 92.

20. Stanley, 105.

21. iFidelity Survey (2019).

22. General Social Survey (2014-2018).

23. Stanley, *Power of Commitment*, 44, 20.

24. Wilcox, Dew, and VanDenBerghe, *iFidelity*.

25. Eli J. Finkel, *The All-or-Nothing Marriage: How the Best Marriages Work* (New York: Dutton, 2017), 10.

26. Transcript from *Marriage Story*, Heyday Films, 2019.

27. Stephanie Coontz, "The Future of Marriage," *Cato Unbound*, January 14, 2008, https://tinyurl.com/WilcoxGM2q.

28. General Social Survey.

29. Rich Morin, "Is Divorce Contagious?" Pew Research Center, October 21, 2013, https://tinyurl.com/WilcoxGM2r.

30. Analysis of State of Our Unions Survey (2022), controlling for education, race, age, gender, income, and presence of children.

31. According to the State of Our Unions Survey (2022), conservative and religious spouses are about 20 percentage points more likely to endorse the idea that "marriage is for life (unless there is abuse or adultery)" compared, respectively, to liberal and secular spouses, who are about 20 percentage points more likely to endorse the competing view that "marriage is for as long as you feel fulfilled in the relationship."

32. Paul R. Amato and Stacy J. Rogers, "Do Attitudes toward Divorce Affect Marital Quality?" *Journal of Family Issues* 20, no. 1 (1999): 69–86, https://doi.org/10.1177/019251399020001004.

33. Coontz, "Future of Marriage."

34. Steven L. Nock, *Marriage in Men's Lives* (New York: Oxford University Press, 1998).

35. Megan Leonhardt, "Here's Why Suze Orman Says You Should Always Get a Prenup," CNBC, March 11, 2020, https://tinyurl.com/WilcoxGM2s.

36. Colleen Sullivan, "Considering a Prenup? Here's Everything You Need to Know," *Brides*, November 5, 2021, https://tinyurl.com/WilcoxGM2t.

37. Lynsey K. Romo and Noah Czajkowski, "An Examination of Redditors' Metaphorical Sensemaking of Prenuptial Agreements," *Journal of Family and*

Economic Issues 43, no. 1 (March 1, 2022): 1–14, https://doi.org/10.1007/s10834 -021-09765-5.

38. All Redditor comments are as quoted in Romo and Czajkowski, "Examination of Redditors' Metaphorical Sensemaking."

39. Laurie Israel, "Prenups Can Be Bad for Marital Health," *New York Times*, March 21, 2013, https://tinyurl.com/WilcoxGM2u.

40. Analysis of the State of Our Unions Survey (2022), controlling for race, education, gender, age, income, and presence of children.

41. Samantha Joel et al., "Machine Learning Uncovers the Most Robust Self-Report Predictors of Relationship Quality across 43 Longitudinal Couples Studies," *Proceedings of the National Academy of Sciences* 117, no. 32 (August 11, 2020): 19061–71, 19067, https://doi.org/10.1073/pnas.1917036117.

42. Analysis controlled for education, age, gender, race, income, and presence of children.

43. Stephanie Coontz, *Marriage: A History* (New York: Penguin, 2006).

44. W. Bradford Wilcox, "For as Long as Our Love Shall Last: No Recipe for Happily Ever After," American Enterprise Institute, May 20, 2020, https:// tinyurl.com/WilcoxGM2v.

Chapter 9: To Provide, Protect, *and* Pay Attention

1. Mary A. Fischer, "Why Women Are Leaving Men for Other Women," *O, the Oprah Magazine*, April 2009, https://tinyurl.com/WilcoxGM2w.

2. Macarena Gomez-Barris, "Anarchisms Otherwise: Pedagogies of Anarco-Indigenous Feminist Critique," *Anarchist Developments in Cultural Studies* 2021, no. 1 (2021): 119–31.

3. Steven Pinker, *The Blank Slate: The Modern Denial of Human Nature* (New York: Penguin, 2002).

4. Stephanie Coontz, *The Way We Really Are: Coming to Terms with America's Changing Families* (New York: Basic Books, 1997), 116.

5. Paul Kita, "The Chore War Is Real—and Your Marriage Is Losing," *Men's Health*, October 1, 2019, https://tinyurl.com/WilcoxGM2x.

6. Jill Filipovic, "It's a Bad Idea to Pay Women to Stay Home," blog post, April 12, 2022, https://tinyurl.com/WilcoxGM2y.

7. Elissa Strauss, "Husbands Who Have Wives Who Outearn Them Are Happier than Those Who Don't," *Slate*, August 22, 2016, https://tinyurl.com/Wil coxGM2z.

8. Strauss, "Husbands."

9. Gabrielle Jackson, "Force Men to Take Paternity Leave: It Will Make the

World a Better Place," *Guardian*, April 9, 2015, https://tinyurl.com/Wilcox GM3a.

10. Sheryl Sandberg and Adam Grant, "How Men Can Succeed in the Boardroom and the Bedroom," *New York Times*, March 5, 2015, https://tinyurl.com /WilcoxGM3b.

11. #ToxicMasculinity, TikTok hashtag page, https://www.tiktok.com/tag /toxicmasculinity.

12. Shawn Meghan Burn and A. Zachary Ward, "Men's Conformity to Traditional Masculinity and Relationship Satisfaction," *Psychology of Men & Masculinity* 6, no. 4 (2005): 254–63.

13. Matt Wilstein, "Former Fox News Host Abby Huntsman Shocked by Tucker Carlson's Anti-Women Rant," *Daily Beast*, January 3, 2019, https://tinyurl .com/WilcoxGM3c.

14. Aaron Renn, "Newsletter #23: Marrying Up," *Masculinist: Monthly Newsletter about the Intersection of Masculinity and Christianity*, July 18, 2018, https:// tinyurl.com/WilcoxGM3d.

15. David Buss, *The Evolution of Desire* (New York: Basic Books, 2003), 44.

16. Yue Qian, "Gender Asymmetry in Educational and Income Assortative Marriage," *Journal of Marriage and Family* 79, no. 2 (April 2017): 318–36, 318.

17. Qian, "Gender Asymmetry."

18. Aaron Sell, Aaron W. Lukaszewski, and Michael Townsley, "Cues of Upper Body Strength Account for Most of the Variance in Men's Bodily Attractiveness," *Proceedings of the Royal Society B: Biological Sciences* 284 (2017), https:// tinyurl.com/WilcoxGM3e; Linda H. Lidborg, Catharine Penelope Cross, and Lynda G. Boothroyd, "A Meta-Analysis of the Association between Male Dimorphism and Fitness Outcomes in Humans," eLife 11:e65031, February 18, 2022, https://elifesciences.org/articles/65031.

19. Buss, *Evolution of Desire*; David Buss, "Sex Differences in Human Mate Preferences: Evolutionary Hypotheses Tested in 37 Cultures," *Behavioral and Brain Sciences* 12 (1989): 1–49; Pelin Gul and Tom R. Kupfer, "Benevolent Sexism and Mate Preferences: Why Do Women Prefer Benevolent Men Despite Recognizing They Can Be Undermining?" *Personality and Social Psychology Bulletin* 45, no. 1 (2019): 146–61.

20. The results in this paragraph are all statistically significant, controlling for age, race, education, income, and presence of children.

21. In the State of Our Unions Survey (2022), the first result is statistically significant after controlling for age, race, education, income, and presence of children,

but the second result, his share of family income, is not statistically significant. See also Wendy Wang, "The Happiness Penalty for Breadwinning Moms," *Institute for Family Studies Blog*, June 4, 2019, https://ifstudies.org/blog/the-happiness-penalty-for-breadwinning-moms.

22. Results in this paragraph are statistically significant after controlling for age, race, education, and income in the State of Our Unions Survey (2022).

23. Gul and Kupfer, "Benevolent Sexism," 154.

24. W. Bradford Wilcox and Steven Nock, "What's Love Got to Do with It? Equality, Equity, Commitment and Women's Marital Quality," *Social Forces* 84, no. 3 (March 2006).

25. "Good providers" was based upon her report that it was "definitely true" that her husband was a good provider. "Very attentive" was based upon her report that her husband was "very attentive" to her.

26. The difference between the top two categories is not statistically significant, net of controls for education, race, age, and the presence of children.

27. The difference between the top two categories *is* statistically significant, net of controls for education, race, age, and the presence of children.

28. W. Bradford Wilcox and Elizabeth Marquardt, *When Baby Makes Three: How Parenthood Makes Life Meaningful and How Marriage Makes Parenthood Bearable*, State of Our Unions series, Institute for American Values and National Marriage Project 2011, https://tinyurl.com/WilcoxGM91.

29. Controlling for age, race, education, income, and presence of children.

30. State of Our Unions Survey (2022).

31. Gul and Kupfer, "Benevolent Sexism," 146.

32. Wendy Wang and Kim Parker, "Public Views on Marriage," ch. 1 of *Record Share of Americans Have Never Married*, web-published booklet, Pew Research Center, September 24, 2014, https://tinyurl.com/WilcoxGM3f.

33. Alexandra Killewald, "Money, Work, and Marital Stability: Assessing Change in the Gendered Determinants of Divorce," *American Sociological Review* 81, no. 4 (August 2016): 696–719, 716.

34. Rosemary L. Hopcroft, "The Ideal Husband? A Man in Possession of a Good Income," *Institute for Family Studies Blog*, October 5, 2021, https://tinyurl.com/WilcoxGM3g.

35. Rosemary Hopcroft, "The More Things Change: Husband's Income, Wife's Income, and Number of Biological Children in the U.S." *Institute for Family Studies Blog*, March 17, 2022, https://tinyurl.com/WilcoxGM3h.

36. Killewald, "Money, Work, and Marital Stability," 710.

37. "Economics and Female Sexual Freedom | Marina Adshade | TEDxVancouver,"

TEDx Talks, YouTube video, December 7, 2015, https://youtu.be/b9WLZ 8YTgUE.

38. Julius Frankenbach et al., "Sex Drive: Theoretical Conceptualization and Meta-Analytic Review of Gender Differences," *Psychological Bulletin* 148, nos. 9–10 (2002): 621–61, doi: 10.1037/bul0000366.

39. Alvin Powell, "How a Hormone Affects Society," *Harvard Gazette*, September 17, 2021.

40. Carole Hooven, *T: The Story of Testosterone, the Hormone that Dominates and Divides Us* (New York: Henry Holt, 2021), 194.

41. Controlling for age, race, education, income, and presence of children.

42. A battery of questions in the State of Our Unions Survey (2022) on gendered traits included describing your spouse as "ambitious," "attractive," "confident," a "good provider," "loving," "physically strong," "protective," "respectful," and/ or "sexually responsive." The top three predictors of global marital quality for men (describing their wives) were "respectful," "sexually responsive," and "loving." For women, they were the descriptions of their husbands as "loving," "respectful," and "good provider."

43. Brigid Schulte, "Couples Who Share Housework Have the Most Sex and Best Sex Lives," *Washington Post*, August 14, 2014, https://tinyurl.com /WilcoxGM7z.

44. Corinne Purtill, "For a Better Marriage, Partners Should Share These Chores," *Quartz*, April 4, 2018, https://tinyurl.com/WilcoxGM3j.

45. Married parents who shared childcare reported significantly more marital happiness and sexual satisfaction, while married moms who shared childcare reported more frequent sex, controlling for age, race, education, income, and presence of children.

46. Richard V. Reeves, *Of Boys and Men: Why the Modern Male Is Struggling, Why It Matters, and What to Do about It* (Washington, DC: Brookings Institution, 2022).

47. David Autor and Melanie Wasserman, "Wayward Sons: The Emerging Gender Gap in Education and Labor Markets," discussion paper, Third Way and NEXT, 2013, https://tinyurl.com/WilcoxGM3k.

48. See also Katharine G. Abraham and Melissa S. Kearney, "Explaining the Decline in the U.S. Employment-to-population Ratio: A Review of the Evidence," NBER Working Paper 24333, National Bureau of Economic Research, February 2018; Christina Hoff Sommers, *The War against Boys: How Misguided Policies Are Harming Our Young Men* (New York: Simon & Schuster, 2015).

49. David T. Courtwright, *The Age of Addiction: How Bad Habits Became Big Business* (Cambridge, MA: Belknap, 2019), 6; Nicholas Eberstadt and Evan Abramsky, "What Do Prime-Age 'NILF' Men Do All Day? A Cautionary on Universal Basic Income," *Institute for Family Studies Blog*, February 8, 2021, https://tinyurl.com/WilcoxGM3m.

50. Brad Wilcox, Wendy Wang, and Alysse ElHage, "'Life Without Father': Less College, Less Work, and More Prison for Young Men Growing Up without Their Biological Father," *Institute for Family Studies Blog*, June 17, 2022, https://tinyurl.com/WilcoxGM3n; Jonathan Rothwell, "Scarred Boys, Idle Men: Family Adversity, Poor Health, and Male Labor Force Participation," January 17, 2023, https://tinyurl.com/WilcoxGM3p.

51. Michael Kimmel, *Guyland: The Perilous World Where Boys Become Men* (New York: Harper, 2009), 259.

52. Richard Fry et al., "In a Growing Share of U.S. Marriages, Husbands and Wives Earn About the Same," Pew Research Center, April 13, 2023, https://tinyurl.com/WilcoxGM3q.

53. Brigid Schulte, "Nearly 40 Percent of Mothers Are Now the Family Breadwinners, Report Says," *Washington Post*, May 29, 2013; Sarah Jane Glynn, "Breadwinning Mothers Continue to Be the U.S. Norm," Center for American Progress, May 10, 2019, https://tinyurl.com/WilcoxGM3r.

54. According to 2022 Current Population Survey, 71.5 percent of breadwinner moms (>60 percent family income) are not married.

55. Stephanie Coontz, "Dads Count Too: Family-Friendly Policies Must Include Fathers," Council on Contemporary Families, September 19, 2019.

56. Richard V. Reeves, "How to Save Marriage in America," *Atlantic*, February 13, 2014; Richard V. Reeves, "In a world . . . ," Twitter post, March 16, 2023.

57. Joe Pinsker, "Lessons from 40 Men in Egalitarian Relationships," *Atlantic*, June 28, 2022.

58. Glynn, "Breadwinning Mothers."

Chapter 10: In God We Trust

1. Samuel L. Perry, *Addicted to Lust: Pornography in the Lives of Conservative Protestants* (New York: Oxford, 2019).

2. Isaac Chotiner, "A Sociologist of Religion on Protestants, Porn, and the 'Purity Industrial Complex,'" *New Yorker*, May 3, 2019.

3. Chotiner, "Sociologist of Religion."

4. W. Bradford Wilcox, "The Latest Social Science Is Wrong: Religion Is Good

for Families and Kids," *Washington Post*, December 15, 2015, https://tinyurl
.com/WilcoxGM3s.

5. Wilcox.

6. This introduction is adapted from Wilcox.

7. W. Bradford Wilcox and Nicholas H. Wolfinger, *Soul Mates: Religion, Sex,
Love, and Marriage among African Americans and Latinos*, illustrated ed. (New
York: Oxford University Press, 2016).

8. The distinctively high levels of marital happiness associated with joint attendance for husbands and wives, as well as for churchgoing evangelical husbands,
are all statistically significant, net of controls for age, education, household
income, the presence of children, and race/ethnicity.

9. Shanshan Li, Laura D. Kubzansky, and Tyler VanderWeele, "Religious Service
Attendance, Divorce, and Remarriage among U.S. Nurses in Mid and Late
Life," *PLoS ONE* 13, no. 12 (2018): e0207778, https://tinyurl.com/Wilcox
GM3t.

10. Analysis of the National Longitudinal Survey (1997) indicates that NLSY97
respondents who married at some point before 2010 and attended religious
services two times a month or more as adolescents were 32 percent less likely to
divorce by 2019, compared to those who rarely or never attended, controlling
for education, race, ethnicity, gender, and age.

11. Net of controls for age, education, household income, the presence of children,
and race/ethnicity.

12. Taylor Newton and Daniel N. McIntosh, "Unique Contributions of Reli-
gion to Meaning," in *The Experience of Meaning in Life: Classical Perspectives,
Emerging Themes, and Controversies*, ed. Joshua A. Hicks and Clay Routledge
(New York: Springer, 2013), 257–69; Sunshine Rote, Terrence D. Hill, and
Christopher G. Ellison, "Religious Attendance and Loneliness in Later Life,"
Gerontologist 53, no. 1 (February 2013): 39–50; David G. Myers and Ed Die-
ner, "The Scientific Pursuit of Happiness," *Perspectives on Psychological Science*
13, no. 2 (March 2018): 218–225.

13. Joint attendees in the State of Our Unions Survey are significantly more
happy with their lives, net of controls for age, education, household income,
the presence of children, and race/ethnicity.

14. Megan Brenan, "U.S. Mental Health Rating Remains below Pre-Pandemic
Level," Gallup, December 3, 2021, https://tinyurl.com/WilcoxGM3u.

15. American Family Surveys, https://tinyurl.com/WilcoxGM3v; State of Our
Unions Survey.

16. W. Bradford Wilcox, "Conservative Protestant Childrearing: Authoritarian or Authoritative?" *American Sociological Review* 63, no. 6 (December 1998): 796–809.

17. "Updated with Retraction: Religious Upbringing Associated with Less Altruism, Study Finds," University of Chicago News, November 5, 2015; [Retracted] Jean Decety et al., "The Negative Association between Religiousness and Children's Altruism across the World," *Current Biology* 25 (November 16, 2015): 2951–55, https://tinyurl.com/WilcoxGM3w.

18. W. Bradford Wilcox and Elizabeth Marquardt, *When Marriage Disappears: The New Middle America*, State of Our Unions series, Institute for American Values and National Marriage Project, 2010, https://tinyurl.com/Wilcox GM75; Vassilis Saroglou, "Religiousness as a Cultural Adaptation of Basic Traits: A Five-Factor Model Perspective," *Personality and Social Psychology Review* 14, no. 1 (December 2009): 108–25.

19. W. Bradford Wilcox and Nicholas H. Wolfinger, "Living and Loving 'Decent': Religion and Relationship Quality among Urban Parents," *Social Science Research* 37, no. 3 (September 2008): 828–43.

20. Emile Durkheim, *The Elementary Forms of Religious Life*, trans. Karen Fields (New York: Free Press, 1995), 226–27.

21. Durkheim, *Elementary Forms of Religious Life*, 44.

22. Jordan W. Moon, "Why Are World Religions So Concerned with Sexual Behavior?" *Current Opinion in Psychology* 40 (August 2021): 15–19.

23. Peter Berger quoted in Kevin Christiano, "Religion and the Family in Modern American Culture," in *Family, Religion, and Social Change in Diverse Societies*, ed. Sharon K. Houseknecht and Jerry G. Pankhurst (New York: Oxford, 2000), 43–78, quote on 47.

24. W. Bradford Wilcox, "As the Family Goes," *First Things*, May 2007, https://tinyurl.com/WilcoxGM3x.

25. Brad Wilcox et al., *The Divided State of Our Unions: Family Formation in (Post) COVID-19 America*, State of Our Unions series, Institute for Family Studies, American Enterprise Institute, and Wheatley Institution, 2021, https://tinyurl.com/WilcoxGM3y.

26. Ross M. Stolzenberg, Mary Blair-Loy, and Linda J. Waite, "Religious Participation in Early Adulthood: Age and Family Life Cycle Effects on Church Membership," *American Sociological Review* 60, no. 1 (February 1995): 84–103, https://www.jstor.org/stable/2096347?seq=1.

27. Amy M. Burdette et al., "Are There Religious Variations in Marital Infidel-

ity?" *Journal of Family Issues* 28, no. 12 (December 2007): 1553–81; Wilcox and Wolfinger, "Living and Loving 'Decent.'"

28. Peter Berger, *The Sacred Canopy* (Garden City, NY: Doubleday, 1967), 22.

29. Karen D. Lincoln and David H. Chae, "Stress, Marital Satisfaction, and Psychological Distress among African Americans," *Journal of Family Issues* 31, no. 8 (August 2010): 1081–1105.

30. Christopher G. Ellison et al., "Sanctification, Stress, and Marital Quality," *Family Relations* 60, no. 4 (October 2011): 404–20.

31. Controlling for age, gender, education, race/ethnicity, and presence of children.

32. State of Our Unions Survey, controlling for age, gender, education, race/ethnicity, and presence of children; Wilcox, "Conservative Protestant Childrearing."

33. Evan Carter et al., "Religious People Discount the Future Less," *Evolution and Human Behavior* 33, no. 3 (May 2012): 224–31, https://tinyurl.com/Wilcox GM3z.

34. Wilcox and Wolfinger, *Soul Mates*.

35. Brian J. Grim and Melissa E. Grim, "Belief, Behavior, and Belonging: How Faith Is Indispensable in Preventing and Recovering from Substance Abuse," *Journal of Religion and Health* 58 (2019): 1713–50, https://tinyurl.com/Wil coxGM4a.

36. Stephanie Godleski and Kenneth E. Leonard, "Substance Use and Substance Problems in Families: How Families Impact and Are Impacted by Substance Use," in *APA Handbook of Contemporary Family Psychology: Applications and Broad Impact of Family Psychology*, ed. B. H. Fiese et al. (Washington, DC: American Psychological Association, 2019), 587–608, https://tinyurl.com/WilcoxGM4b; Ludwig F. Lowenstein, "Causes and Associated Features of Divorce as Seen by Recent Research," *Journal of Divorce & Remarriage* 42, no. 3–4 (2005): 153–71, https://tinyurl.com/WilcoxGM4c; Shelby B. Scott et al., "Reasons for Divorce and Recollections of Premarital Intervention: Implications for Improving Relationship Education," *Couple and Family Psychology: Research and Practice* 2, no. 2 (2013): 131–45, https://tinyurl.com/Wil coxGM4d.

37. Perry, *Addicted to Lust*, 58–61.

38. Perry, 62–63.

39. Perry, 62.

40. Perry, 64.

41. Lyman Stone, "The Truth about Conservative Protestant Men and Porn,"

Institute for Family Studies Blog, June 19, 2019, https://tinyurl.com/Wilcox GM4e.

42. Wendy Wang, "Who Cheats More? The Demographics of Infidelity in America," *Institute for Family Studies Blog*, January 10, 2018, https://tinyurl.com /WilcoxGM4f.

43. Wang, "Who Cheats More?"; Wilcox and Wolfinger, *Soul Mates*.

44. Krystal M. Hernandez, Annette Mahoney, and Kenneth I. Pargament, "Sanctification of Sexuality: Implications for Newlyweds' Marital and Sexual Quality," *Journal of Family Psychology* 25, no. 5 (2011): 775–80, https://tinyurl.com /WilcoxGM4g.

45. State of Our Unions Survey. Reported religious differences in sexual consideration and responsiveness are significant, controlling for age, education, household income, the presence of children, and race/ethnicity.

46. Krystal M. Hernandez-Kane and Annette Mahoney, "Sex through a Sacred Lens: Longitudinal Effects of Sanctification of Marital Sexuality," *Journal of Family Psychology* 32, no. 4 (2018): 425–34, https://tinyurl.com/WilcoxGM4h.

47. State of Our Unions Survey. Joint religious attendees have more frequent sex, net of controls for age, education, household income, the presence of children, and race/ethnicity.

48. Joint religious attendees are significantly more sexually satisfied, controlling for age, education, household income, the presence of children, and race/ ethnicity.

49. Margaret Brinig and Doug Allen, "These Boots Are Made for Walking: Why Most Divorce Filers Are Women," *American Law and Economics Review* 2, no. 1 (January 2000): 126–269.

50. W. Bradford Wilcox, "The Divorce Revolution Has Bred an Army of Woman Haters," *Federalist*, May 19, 2016, https://thefederalist.com/2016/05/19/the -divorce-revolution-has-bred-an-army-of-woman-haters/.

51. Joint religious attendees report more stable marriages even net of controls for age, education, household income, the presence of children, and race/ethnicity.

52. Jeffery Sobal and Albert J. Stunkard, "Socioeconomic Status and Obesity: A Review of the Literature," *Psychological Bulletin* 105, no. 2 (1989): 260–75.

53. Nicholas Christakis, "The Hidden Influence of Social Networks," transcript, TED2010, https://tinyurl.com/WilcoxGM4j.

54. Rich Morin, "Is Divorce Contagious?" Pew Research Center, October 21, 2013, https://tinyurl.com/WilcoxGM4k.

55. Brad Wilcox, "Perspective: The Surprising Case for Marrying Young," *Deseret News*, June 21, 2022, https://tinyurl.com/WilcoxGM4m.

56. State of Our Unions Survey. Ten percent of husbands and wives who regularly attend indicated they are "extremely," "fairly," or "a little" unhappy in the survey.

Chapter 11: Orphaned

1. Bill Clinton, "Full Text of Clinton's Speech on China Trade Bill," *New York Times*, March 9, 2000, https://tinyurl.com/WilcoxGM4n.

2. David H. Autor, David Dorn, and Gordon H. Hanson, "The China Shock: Learning from Labor Market Adjustment to Large Changes in Trade," Working Paper 21906, National Bureau of Economic Research, January 2016, https://doi.org/10.3386/w21906.

3. David Autor, David Dorn, and Gordon Hanson, "When Work Disappears: Manufacturing Decline and the Falling Marriage Market Value of Young Men," *American Economic Review: Insights* 1, no. 2 (September 2019): 161–78, https://doi.org/10.1257/aeri.20180010.

4. Justin R. Pierce and Peter K. Schott, "Trade Liberalization and Mortality: Evidence from U.S. Counties," *American Economic Review: Insights* 2, no. 1 (March 2020): 47–64, https://doi.org/10.1257/aeri.20180396.

5. Oren Cass, "Opinion: What American Workers Really Want Instead of a Union at Amazon," *Politico*, April 20, 2021, https://tinyurl.com/WilcoxGM4p.

6. W. Bradford Wilcox and Samuel Hammond, "What Tucker Carlson Gets Right," *Atlantic*, January 9, 2019, https://tinyurl.com/WilcoxGM4q.

7. Oren Cass, *The Once and Future Worker: A Vision for the Renewal of Work in America* (New York: Encounter, 2018).

8. Author's calculations of the 1970 and 2019 Current Population Survey, Annual Social and Economic Supplement, using Sarah Flood et al., Integrated Public Use Microdata Series, Current Population Survey: Version 8.0 [dataset], Minneapolis, MN (IPUMS), 2020, https://doi.org/10.18128/D030.V8.0.

9. Nicholas Eberstadt, "A Portrait of the Un-Working American Man," *Institute for Family Studies Blog*, October 5, 2016, https://tinyurl.com/WilcoxGM4r; Nicholas Eberstadt, *Men Without Work: America's Invisible Crisis* (Conshohocken, PA: Templeton Press, 2016).

10. Author's calculations of the 1970 and 2019 Current Population Survey.

11. Joe Dixon, "Men Without Work: Author Nicholas Eberstadt Highlights the Troubling Class of Men Who Have Removed Themselves from the Job Market," *American Experiment*, July 13, 2017, https://tinyurl.com/Wilcox GM4s.

12. "The Long-Term Decline in Prime-Age Male Labor Force Participation"

(Washington, DC: Executive Office of the President of the United States, June 2016), Obama White House, https://tinyurl.com/WilcoxGM4t.

13. Eberstadt, *Men Without Work*.

14. Sommers, *War against Boys*.

15. Leonard Sax, *Boys Adrift: The Five Factors Driving the Growing Epidemic of Unmotivated Boys and Underachieving Young Men* (New York: Basic Books, 2016), cover quotation; Reeves, *Of Boys and Men*.

16. Douglas Belkin, "A Generation of American Young Men Give Up on College: 'I Just Feel Lost,'" *Wall Street Journal*, September 6, 2021, https://tinyurl.com/WilcoxGM4u.

17. Reeves, *Of Boys and Men*, 7.

18. Institute of Educational Sciences, National Center for Education Statistics, *Digest of Education Statistics: 2019*, table 233.20, "Percentage of public school students in grades 6 through 12 who had ever been suspended or expelled, by sex and race/ethnicity: Selected years, 1993 through 2012," February 2021, https://tinyurl.com/WilcoxGM4v.

19. Sax, *Boys Adrift*.

20. Data Lab, USAspending.gov, "Federal Investment in Higher Education," accessed May 2, 2021, https://datalab.usaspending.gov/colleges-and-universities/; Institute of Educational Sciences, National Center for Education Statistics, *Digest of Education Statistics: 2019*, table 401.30, "Federal on-budget funds for education, by level/educational purpose, agency, and program: Selected fiscal years, 1970 through 2019," February 2021, https://tinyurl.com/WilcoxGM4w.

21. Institute of Educational Sciences, National Center for Education Statistics, "Educational Attainment of Young Adults," *The Condition of Education: 2020* (May 2020), https://tinyurl.com/WilcoxGM4x.

22. W. Bradford Wilcox, "Making Young Men Marriageable," *American Compass*, February 24, 2021, https://tinyurl.com/WilcoxGM4y; Oren Cass, "The Misguided Priorities of Our Educational System," *New York Times*, December 10, 2018, https://tinyurl.com/WilcoxGM4z; Tamar Jacoby, "The College-for-All Model Isn't Working," *Los Angeles Times*, December 3, 2013, https://tinyurl.com/WilcoxGM5a.

23. Heather Boushey and Kavya Vaghul, "Women Have Made the Difference for Family Economic Security," Washington Center for Equitable Growth, April 4, 2016, https://tinyurl.com/WilcoxGM5b.

24. Nicholas Eberstadt, "Education and Men without Work," *National Affairs*, Winter 2020, https://tinyurl.com/WilcoxGM5c.

25. Angela Rachidi, "Health and Poverty: The Case for Work," American En-

terprise Institute, April 29, 2020, https://tinyurl.com/WilcoxGM5d; David Neumark and Elizabeth Powers, "The Effect of the SSI Program on Labor Supply: Improved Evidence from Social Security Administrative Files," *Social Security Bulletin* 65 (December 1, 2002); Nicole Maestas, Kathleen J. Mullen, and Alexander Strand, "Does Disability Insurance Receipt Discourage Work? Using Examiner Assignment to Estimate Causal Effects of SSDI Receipt," *American Economic Review* 103, no. 5 (August 2013): 1797–1829, https://doi .org/10.1257/aer.103.5.1797.

26. Sax, *Boys Adrift*, 91.

27. Mark Aguiar et al., "Leisure Luxuries and the Labor Supply of Young Men," *Journal of Political Economy* 129, no. 2 (February 2021): 337–82, https://doi .org/10.1086/711916.

28. David Courtwright, "How 'Limbic Capitalism' Preys on Our Addicted Brains," *Quillette*, May 31, 2019, https://tinyurl.com/WilcoxGM5e; Naomi Schaefer Riley, "America's Real Digital Divide," *New York Times*, February 11, 2018, https://tinyurl.com/WilcoxGM5f.

29. Nellie Bowles, "A Dark Consensus about Screens and Kids Begins to Emerge in Silicon Valley," *New York Times*, October 26, 2018, https://tinyurl.com /WilcoxGM5g.

30. Nick Bilton, "Steve Jobs Was a Low-Tech Parent," *New York Times*, September 10, 2014, https://tinyurl.com/WilcoxGM5h.

31. Patrick T. Brown, *Working-Class Americans' Views on Family Policies*, Institute for Family Studies, September 2021, https://tinyurl.com/WilcoxGM5i.

32. Richard V. Reeves and Isabel V. Sawhill, "Money: A New Contract with the Middle Class," Brookings Institution, September 22, 2020, https://tinyurl .com/WilcoxGM5j.

33. Reeves and Sawhill, fig. 01, "Middle Class Income Falling Behind."

34. Brown, *Working-Class Americans' Views*.

35. Mark J. Perry, "Chart of the Day . . . or Century?" American Enterprise Institute, January 17, 2021, https://tinyurl.com/WilcoxGM5k.

36. US President and Council of Economic Advisers, "Economic Report of the President," February 2020, https://tinyurl.com/WilcoxGM5m.

37. Patrick T. Brown, "Are Marriage and Parenthood Only for the Wealthy?" *Public Discourse*, November 30, 2022, https://www.thepublicdiscourse.com /2022/11/85947/. Melissa Kearney and Lisa Dettling found that a 10 percent increase in home prices leads to a 1 percent decrease in births among non-homeowners in an average metropolitan area. Lisa J. Dettling and Melissa Schettini Kearney, "House Prices and Birth Rates: The Impact of the

Real Estate Market on the Decision to Have a Baby," NBER Working Paper 17485, National Bureau of Economic Research, October 2011 (rev. June 2016), https://www.nber.org/papers/w17485.

38. Douglas J. Besharov and Neil Gilbert, "Marriage Penalties in the Modern Social-Welfare State," R Street, policy study 40, September 2015, https://tinyurl.com/WilcoxGM5u.

39. Jeffrey Drew, "Revisiting Financial Issues and Marriage," in *Handbook of Consumer Finance Research*, ed. Jing Jian Xiao, 2nd ed. (Cham, Switzerland: Springer International, 2016), 281–90, https://tinyurl.com/WilcoxGM5p.

40. Brown, *Working-Class Americans' Views*.

41. W. Bradford Wilcox and Erik Randolph, "The Working-Class Welfare Trap: How Policy Penalizes Marriage," *National Review*, October 27, 2020, https://tinyurl.com/WilcoxGM5q.

42. Wendy Wang, "Money Is Not the Main Reason Why Americans Who Desire Marriage Remain Single," *Institute for Family Studies Blog*, November 9, 2021, https://tinyurl.com/WilcoxGM5r.

43. W. Bradford Wilcox, Angela Rachidi, and Joseph Price, "Marriage, Penalized: Does Social-Welfare Policy Affect Family Formation?" American Enterprise Institute, July 26, 2016, https://tinyurl.com/WilcoxGM5s; Elaine Maag and Gregory Acs, "The Financial Consequences of Marriage for Cohabiting Couples with Children," Urban Institute, September 7, 2015, https://tinyurl.com/WilcoxGM5t; Besharov and Gilbert, "Marriage Penalties in the Modern Social-Welfare State."

44. Besharov and Gilbert, "Marriage Penalties."

45. Hayley Fisher, "The Effect of Marriage Tax Penalties and Subsidies on Marital Status," *Fiscal Studies* 34, no. 4 (2013): 437–65, https://www.jstor.org/stable/24440312.

46. Katherine Michelmore, "The Earned Income Tax Credit and Union Formation: The Impact of Expected Spouse Earnings," *Review of Economics of the Household* 16, no. 2 (June 1, 2018): 377–406, https://doi.org/10.1007/s11150-016-9348-7.

47. Wilcox and Randolph, "Welfare Trap."

48. Richard V. Reeves and Christopher Puliam, "Middle Class Marriage Is Declining, and Likely Deepening Inequality," Brookings Institution, March 11, 2020, https://tinyurl.com/WilcoxGM5v.

49. Scott Winship, "A Half-Century Decline in Marriage . . . That Ended 30 Years Ago for Disadvantaged Kids," American Enterprise Institute, April 2022, https://tinyurl.com/WilcoxGM5w.

50. Anne Rathbone Bradley, "The Good News about Our Economy and Families," writings from symposium on Humane Economy, Intercollegiate Studies Institute, July 19, 2021, https://tinyurl.com/WilcoxGM5x.

51. Patrick T. Brown, "A 'Working-Class Party'? Child Tax Credit Debate Is a Test for the GOP," *Institute for Family Studies Blog*, January 25, 2021, https://tinyurl.com/WilcoxGM5y.

52. Sarah Westwood, "White House Opposes Rubio-Lee Tax Plan," *Washington Examiner*, November 29, 2017, https://tinyurl.com/WilcoxGM5z; Jasmine C. Lee, Rachel Shorey, and Sara Simon, "See How Every Senator Voted on the Republican Tax Bill," *New York Times*, December 1, 2017, https://tinyurl.com/WilcoxGM6a.

53. Nikki Haley, "This Is No Time to Go Wobbly on Capitalism," *Wall Street Journal*, February 26, 2020, https://tinyurl.com/WilcoxGM6b.

54. Nikki Haley, "Joe Biden's Welfare Plan Won't Help Families Rise," *National Review*, May 6, 2021, https://tinyurl.com/WilcoxGM6c.

55. Congress of the United States, Joint Committee on Taxation, "Estimated Budgetary Effects of the Revenue Provisions of the Budget Reconciliation Legislative Recommendations, Scheduled for Markup by the House Committee on Ways and Means on February 10, 2021," JCX-5-21, February 8, 2021, https://www.jct.gov/publications/2021/jcx-5-21/; Committee for a Responsible Federal Budget, "What's in President Biden's American Families Plan?" April 28, 2021, https://tinyurl.com/WilcoxGM6d.

56. C. Eugene Steuerle, "Biden's Expanded EITC Adds Significant Marriage Penalties," Tax Policy Center, August 3, 2021, https://tinyurl.com/WilcoxGM6e; Committee for a Responsible Federal Budget, "Biden's American Families Plan."

57. Erica L. Green and Dana Goldstein, "Reading Scores on National Exam Decline in Half the States," *New York Times*, October 30, 2019, https://tinyurl.com/WilcoxGM6f; Sarah Mervosh, "The Pandemic Hurt These Students the Most," *New York Times*, July 28, 2021, https://tinyurl.com/WilcoxGM6g.

58. Albert Cheng et al., "The Protestant Family Ethic: What Do Protestant, Catholic, Private, and Public Schooling Have to Do with Marriage, Divorce, and Non-marital Childbearing?" American Enterprise Institute, *Institute for Family Studies Blog*, September 16, 2020, https://tinyurl.com/WilcoxGM6h.

59. W. Bradford Wilcox and Margarita M. Suarez, "President Biden, Let Hispanic Parents Have What They Want—Family Care, Not Day Care," *Deseret News*, June 10, 2021, https://tinyurl.com/WilcoxGM6i.

60. David Brooks, "Give Power to the Parents!" *New York Times*, April 29, 2021, https://tinyurl.com/WilcoxGM6j.

61. Derek Thompson, "Workism Is Making Americans Miserable," *Atlantic*, February 24, 2019, https://tinyurl.com/WilcoxGM6k.

62. Wendy Wang, Margarita M. Suarez, and Patrick T. Brown, "Familia Sí, Guardería No: Hispanics Least Likely to Prefer and Use Paid Child Care," *Institute for Family Studies Blog*, May 26, 2021, https://tinyurl.com/Wilcox GM6m.

63. This section is adapted in part from Wilcox and Suarez, "Let Hispanic Parents Have What They Want."

64. Patrick T. Brown, "A Distinctly American Family Policy," *Public Discourse*, November 11, 2021, https://www.thepublicdiscourse.com/2021/11/78939/.

65. J. D. Vance, "A Civilizational Crisis: A Country That Has Children Is a Healthy Country That Is Worth Living In. It Takes Courage to Protect That Kind of Country," *American Conservative*, July 27, 2021, https://tinyurl.com /WilcoxGM6n.

66. Kristen Bialik and Richard Fry, "Millennial Life: How Young Adulthood Today Compares with Prior Generations," Pew Research Center, February 14, 2019, https://tinyurl.com/WilcoxGM6p.

67. Catherine Gewertz, "What Is Career and Technical Education, Anyway?" *Education Week*, July 31, 2018, https://tinyurl.com/WilcoxGM6q.

68. James J. Kemple, "Career Academies: Long-Term Impacts on Work, Education, and Transitions to Adulthood," MDRC, June 2008, https://tinyurl.com /WilcoxGM6r.

69. This child tax credit proposal is adapted from Brad Wilcox and Wells King, "Perspective: What Family Policy Should Look Like in Post-Roe America," *Deseret News*, May 12, 2022, https://tinyurl.com/WilcoxGM6s.

70. Cheng et al., "Protestant Family Ethic."

71. Patrick T. Brown, "Multiple Choice: Increasing Pluralism in the American Education System," Social Capital Project, December 10, 2019, https://tinyurl .com/WilcoxGM6t.

72. Ed Choice, "Arizona: Empowerment Scholarship Accounts," https://tinyurl .com/WilcoxGM6u.

73. EducationData.org, "U.S. Public Education Spending Statistics," https:// tinyurl.com/WilcoxGM6v.

74. Wendy Wang and Paul Taylor, "For Millennials, Parenthood Trumps Marriage," Pew Research Center, March 9, 2011, https://tinyurl.com/Wilcox GM6w.

75. Ron Haskins and Isabel V. Sawhill, *Creating an Opportunity Society* (Washington, DC: Brookings Institution, 2009); Wendy Wang and W. Bradford Wilcox, "The Millennial Success Sequence: Marriage, Kids, and the 'Success Sequence' among Young Adults," American Enterprise Institute, June 14, 2017, https://tinyurl.com/WilcoxGM6x.

76. Wang and Wilcox, "Millennial Success Sequence."

77. Nat Malkus, "Uncommonly Popular: Public Support for Teaching the Success Sequence in School," American Enterprise Institute, December 2021, https://tinyurl.com/WilcoxGM6y.

78. Anita P. Barbee et al., "Impact of Two Adolescent Pregnancy Prevention Interventions on Risky Sexual Behavior: A Three-Arm Cluster Randomized Control Trial," *American Journal of Public Health* 106, supp. 1 (September 2016): S85–S90, https://doi.org/10.2105/AJPH.2016.303429; Anita P. Barbee, interview, "Impact of Two Adolescent Pregnancy Prevention Interventions on Risky Sexual Behavior," October 14, 2016, MedicalResearch.com, https://tinyurl.com/WilcoxGM6z.

79. Melissa S. Kearney and Phillip B. Levine, "Media Influences on Social Outcomes: The Impact of MTV's *16 and Pregnant* on Teen Childbearing," *American Economic Review* 105, no. 12 (December 2015): 3597–632, https://doi.org/10.1257/aer.20140012; Centers for Disease Control and Prevention, National Vital Statistics Reports, "Births: Final Data for 2015," December 23, 2015; Centers for Disease Control and Prevention, National Vital Statistics Reports, "Births: Final Data for 2016," December 2016; Centers for Disease Control and Prevention, "Natality Public-Use Data 2007–2017 [data set]."

80. Wilcox and Marquardt, *When Marriage Disappears*.

Conclusion: In Pursuit of Happiness

1. Jade Scipioni, "The Business Lesson Reed Hastings Learned from His Marriage Counselor that Helped Shape Netflix," CNBC, September 9, 2020, https://tinyurl.com/WilcoxGM7a.

2. Stephen J. Dubner, "Extra: What If Your Company Had No Rules?" Freakonomics Radio, audio recording (prod. Mary Diduch), https://tinyurl.com/WilcoxGM7b.

3. Scipioni, "Business Lesson."

4. Charles Murray, *Coming Apart: The State of White America, 1960–2010* (New York: Crown Forum, 2013).

5. Jean Twenge, "Marriage and Money: How Much Does Marriage Explain the Growing Class Divide in Happiness?" *Institute for Family Studies Blog*,

July 20, 2020, https://tinyurl.com/WilcoxGM7c. Data from the 2014–21 General Social Survey also indicates that adding a control for being happily married reduces the association between education and happiness for those ages eighteen to fifty-five by almost half in a model that also controls for race, age, and gender.

6. Matthew Yglesias, "The Great Awokening: A Hidden Shift Is Revolutionizing American Racial Politics—and Could Transform the Future of the Democratic Party," *Vox*, April 1, 2019, https://tinyurl.com/WilcoxGM7d.

7. Daniel Cox, "From Swiping to Sexting: The Enduring Gender Divide in American Dating and Relationships," Survey Center on American Life, February 9, 2023, https://tinyurl.com/WilcoxGM7e; Daniel Cox, "The Despair of Young Liberal Women: New Research Shows Young People Are in Crisis, but How Much Is Due to Politics?" *American Storylines* (blog), March 23, 2023, https://tinyurl.com/WilcoxGM7f.

8. Brian Willoughby and Spencer James, *The Marriage Paradox: Why Emerging Adults Love Marriage Yet Push It Aside* (New York: Oxford University Press, 2017), 196.

9. Brad Wilcox et al., *The Divided State of Our Unions: Family Formation in (Post) COVID-19 America*, State of Our Unions series, Institute for Family Studies, American Enterprise Institute, and Wheatley Institution, 2021, https://tinyurl.com/WilcoxGM3y.

10. Heather M. Rackin and Christina M. Gibson-Davis, "The Increasing Importance of Political Identity on Fertility Desires for Youth from 1989–2019," paper given at the annual meeting of the Population Association of America, New Orleans, LA, 2023.

11. Data from the 2021 IFS/Wheatley Institute Family Survey.

12. Michelle Goldberg, "Don't Let Politics Cloud Your View of What's Going on With Teens and Depression," *New York Times*, February 24, 2023, https://tinyurl.com/WilcoxGM7h; Jon Haidt, "Why the Mental Health of Liberal Girls Sank First and Fastest," *After Babel* (blog), March 9, 2023, https://tinyurl.com/WilcoxGM7i; Brad Wilcox et al., "How Liberals Can Be Happier," *New York Times*, November 25, 2021, https://tinyurl.com/WilcoxGM7j; W. Bradford Wilcox, "Why Are Liberals Less Happy Than Conservatives?" *UnHerd*, The Post, October 10, 2022, https://tinyurl.com/WilcoxGM7k.

13. Models controlling for race, age, and gender in the General Social Survey, 2021, find that conservative and religious Americans ages 18 to 55 are significantly more likely to be "very happy" than, respectively, liberal and nonreligious Americans. Additional models adding binary variables tapping

marital status and marital quality—whether the respondent is in a "very happy" marriage versus being less than very happy in his/her marriage or unmarried—reduce these ideological and religious premiums by between approximately one-third and one-half. Marital status and marital quality mediate the effect of ideology and religious attendance more than do race, age, or gender.

14. Jean Twenge, *Generations: The Real Differences between Gen Z, Millennials, Gen X, Boomers, and Silents—and What They Mean for America's Future* (New York: Simon & Schuster, 2023), 487.

15. Lyman Stone and Brad Wilcox, "More Americans Want a Same-Politics Partner: Which Is Bad News for Marriage," *Atlantic*, June 10, 2023.

16. Wilcox et al., "How Liberals Can Be Happier."

17. Jonathan Haidt, *The Righteous Mind: Why Good People Are Divided by Politics and Religion* (New York: Vintage, 2012), 341.

18. Kay Hymowitz et al., *Knot Yet: The Benefits and Costs of Delayed Marriage in America*, National Campaign to Prevent Teen and Unplanned Pregnancy, Relate Institute, and National Marriage Project, 2013, https://tinyurl.com/WilcoxGM7s; Alan J. Hawkins et al., "Capstones vs. Cornerstones: Is Marrying Later Always Better?" State of Our Unions series, 2022, https://tinyurl.com/WilcoxGM7m; Lyman Stone and W. Bradford Wilcox, "The Religious Marriage Paradox: Younger Marriage, Less Divorce," *Institute for Family Studies Blog*, December 15, 2021, https://tinyurl.com/WilcoxGM7n; Nicholas H. Wolfinger, "Want to Avoid Divorce? Wait to Get Married, But Not Too Long," *Institute for Family Studies Blog*, July 16, 2015, https://tinyurl.com/WilcoxGM7p.

19. National Center for Education Statistics, "Fast Facts: Public and Private School Comparison," https://tinyurl.com/WilcoxGM7q; National Center for Education Statistics, "Homeschooled Children and Reasons for Homeschooling," May 2022, https://tinyurl.com/WilcoxGM7r.

20. Learn more about Communio at https://communio.org.

INDEX

Note: Page numbers followed by *f* or *t* indicate figure or tables.

flying solo myth *(continued)*
 impacts of lack of social and
  personal bonds, 44–51
 marital happiness contrasted to
  single life, 51–55, 51*f*
 men's doubts about value of
  marriage, ix–x, 36–42, 221–23
 men's financial and social benefits
  from marriage, 38–44, 40*t*, 42*f*
 women's doubts about benefits of
  marriage, 37
 women's financial and social benefits
  from marriage, xi–xii, 40*t*, 42–44,
  44*f*
Fox & Friends (television program), 61
Frailich, Ryan, 97
Franklin, Angela, 87
Free to Be . . . You and Me (recording),
 xvii
free-market ideologies, 195, 206, 216.
 See also capitalism
friendships, religion, and reduced risk
 of divorce, 192–93

Gallagher, Maggie, xix
General Social Survey (GSS), 3, 10,
 30, 48, 132, 135, 139, 142, 184,
 222
Gilbert, Elizabeth, 78–80, 84, 85, 86
Going Solo (Klinenberg), 47
"Gold Digger" (song), 144
Goldberg, Michelle, 221
Gomez-Barris, Macarena, 149–50
Good Life, The (Harvard study), 4–5
"Good Riddance to 'The Family'"
 (Stacey), 61
Gottman, Dr. Julie Schwartz, 17
Gottman, John, 6, 10, 16–19, 34
government. *See* public policy, impacts
 on marriage
Grant, Adam, 152
"Great Awokening, The," 28, 220
Great Recession, impacts of, 2, 7, 11,
 111, 119
Grover, Shawn, 54
Growing Up with a Single Parent
 (Sandefur), 76
Guardian, 152, 175
Gul, Pelin, 157

Haidt, Jonathan, 85–86, 223
Haley, Nikki, 206–7
Hammond, Samuel, 195–96
happiness, in marriage, 149–72
 "blank-slate feminism" and, 150–52
 childcare, chores, and sex, 152,
  165–66, 167
 liberal v. conservative cultural
  divide, 219–25, 224*f*, 225*f*
 marriage and paradox of, 84–88
 marriage as predictor of, xiv, 3–5, 4*f*
 men's income and marital stability,
  160–61
 neotraditional model of marriage
  and, 172
 religion and, 175–76, 176*f*, 177, 177*f*
 "revealed" versus "stated" preferences
  and, 149–50, 150–52, 223*f*
 single life contrasted, 51–55, 51*f*
 soulmate myth and happiness model
  of life, 78–84
 tasks ahead for encouraging of,
  228–29
 what men look for in women,
  161–65
 what women look for in men,
  152–60, 156*f*, 158*f*, 171–72
 women's income and male
  disengagement, 167–70, 169*f*
Harvard Study of Adult Development,
 4–5
Hasting, Reed, 217–18
Heineken advertisements, 59–60
Helliwell, John, 54
Henrich, Joseph, xix
Herbst, Chris, 115
Hillel, 3
Holloway, Kali, 114–15
home ownership, marital stability and,
 161
Hooven, Carole, 163
Hopcroft, Rosemary, 161
hormones, romantic feelings and, 85
"How Divorce Lost Its Groove" (Paul),
 xxi
How to Be Single (film), 51
"How to Live in a World Where
 Marriage Is in Decline"
 (*Atlantic*), 6

ABOUT THE AUTHOR

Brad Wilcox is a professor of sociology and the director of the National Marriage Project at the University of Virginia, the Future of Freedom Fellow at the Institute for Family Studies, and a nonresident senior fellow at the American Enterprise Institute. He studies marital quality, marital stability, and the impact of strong and stable marriages upon men, women, and children. The author and editor of six books, Wilcox has written for scientific journals such as the *American Sociological Review* and the *Journal of Marriage and Family*, and the *New York Times*, the *Wall Street Journal*, the *Atlantic*, and *National Review*. A Connecticut native, he now lives in Charlottesville, Virginia, with his wife and family.